WHITE SOCIETY IN THE ANTEBELLUM SOUTH

STUDIES IN MODERN HISTORY

General editors: *John Morrill and David Cannadine*

WHITE SOCIETY IN THE ANTEBELLUM SOUTH

Bruce Collins

LONGMAN
London and New York

LONGMAN GROUP LIMITED
Longman House, Burnt Mill, Harlow
Essex CM20 2JE, England
Associated companies throughout the world

*Published in the United States of America
by Longman Inc., New York*

© Longman Group Limited 1985

First published 1985

BRITISH LIBRARY CATALOGUING IN PUBLICATION DATA
Collins, Bruce
  White society in the antebellum South. – (Studies in
  modern history)
  1. Southern States – Social conditions
  I. Title II. Series
  305.8′13075   HN79.A163
  ISBN 0-582-49194-0

LIBRARY OF CONGRESS CATALOGING IN PUBLICATION DATA
Collins, Bruce.
  White society in the antebellum South.

  (Studies in modern history)
  Bibliography: p.
  Includex index.
  1. Southern States – Social conditions. 2. Southern
  States – Civilization – 1775–1865. I. Title. II. Series:
  Studies in modern history (Longman (Firm))
  HN79.A13C65 1985   975′03   84–19469
  ISBN 0-582-49194-0 (pbk.)

Set in 10/11pt AM Times
Printed in Hong Kong by
Wing Lee Printing Co Ltd

CONTENTS

PREFACE

This is a work of interpretation, not a textbook. Although it is written in, I hope, a straightforward style and does not go into the more recondite byways of scholarship or complexities of methodology, the following essay presents an argument addressed to scholars as well as a viewpoint and analysis aimed at use by students. The nature of the present work is partly governed by the existing historical literature on Southern white society. On one side, Clement Eaton's *The Growth of Southern Civilization, 1790–1860* provides an introductory text, and numerous later books elucidate specific topics treated inadequately in that volume. Yet, on the other side, a great deal of recent monographic literature on *white* society does not fit into any framework of interpretation or is ignored in such interpretative articles or survey texts that have proliferated since Eaton's synthesis was published in 1961. The present essay draws upon that corpus of recent books, articles and doctoral dissertations and owes a great deal to them. But it is also informed by a considerable amount of research, largely on Mississippi and Georgia, with some on North Carolina.

A number of difficulties should be stated at the outset. First, the approach adopted has of necessity to be a selective one. Very few good, modern community studies of the rural and small-town South have so far been published. This means that we lack completely rounded pictures of towns or counties, encompassing their religious, demographic, economic and social life. The reason for that lack lies partly in the nature of the surviving evidence. Although it is relatively easy to study the distribution of wealth and the population turn-over in individual counties between 1850 and 1860, when the census returns were ample enough for analytical purposes, it is extremely difficult to find private papers and even a full run of newspapers to flesh out that statistical outline for a single county or small town. Even local studies, therefore, tend to generalize across a number of counties. But it is also the case that historians, naturally, tend to investigate particular issues – the incidence of crime, the work of the churches, geographical mobility, for instance – in particular communities, so using local cases for the purposes of topical or thematic investigations. Given that fact, anyone examining Southern society more generally is bound to refer, as the present book does, to examples and case studies apparently somewhat randomly located in place and period. While I have tried to focus upon the Confederate South, and more specifically on the Deep South, I have occasionally looked beyond that area for evidence of what are believed to be more general tendencies.

Second, we still have very little direct testimony from the mass of ordinary whites. An examination of court records and of petitions sent to the state governors and legislatures offers some guide to 'popular' attitudes and grievances, but such records have to be used with restraint; they arose, after all, when things went wrong. There is a growing tendency for social historians to adopt anthropological methods and ideas in scrutinizing such incidents as have been recounted from the early and mid nineteenth centuries. This approach owes a great deal to writings on cultural analysis by the anthropologist Clifford Geertz. It has the temperamental and methodological benefits of rescuing historians from the advance of often mechanical or technically obtuse quantification. Yet it tends to produce 'a kind of old-fashioned ethnographic museum, in which text after text piles up, parts catalogued without a sense of the whole' (Walters 1980: 553). This stricture does not uniformly apply. Some social historians are quite prepared to extrapolate, from what Geertz calls 'thick descriptions' of particular episodes, quite wide-ranging arguments concerning the antebellum South. Professor Wyatt-Brown (1982) has argued at great length that a special code of honour and sense of family differentiated the South from other regions in the nineteenth century. Michael P. Johnson (1977; 1980) detects patriarchy at the root of a peculiar value system; patriarchal ideas fed upon the institution of slavery and reinforced planters' dominant position within their own, white, families. Looking at different elements of white society, Steven Hahn (1979; 1982) draws a coherent threat of increasing yeoman antagonism towards the planters from assorted rhetoric and from economic trends in the 1850s. Such overarching interpretations in themselves pose comparative and contextual difficulties. Wyatt-Brown certainly has a point when he emphasizes the role of personal honour in antebellum Southern social relations. But do the contexts he cites – largely made up of family disputes, legal controversies, feuds, duels and murders – yield a rounded value-system for Southern white society? Are not detailed and extensive comparisons with frontier violence and personal relationships required in order for us to decide how far codes of honour were specific to the South? So, too, it might be suggested that patriarchal values, while reinforced by the existence of slavery and by slaveowners' desire to portray themselves as heads of extended households including slaves, were typically Victorian rather than peculiarly Southern. Indeed, the absence of patriarchal values would have been more surprising than their articulate expression. Finally, the idea of incipient class struggle in the Deep South is an old one that makes periodic appearances in the historical literature (Shugg 1939). But it seems to be supported more by snippets of evidence than by any record of organized and continuous opposition from ordinary farmers to the prevailing political and social arrangements. It fits, in other words, uneasily within a more general context of social consensus.

Having said that some interpretations of the South fail fully to sustain their claims for Southern distinctiveness, one must concede that finding the correct comparative framework is frustratingly difficult. In 1980 the *American Historical Review* (Bowman 1980; McDonald and McWhiney 1980; Pessen 1980) offered a dazzling array of comparisons, taking the reader to, among other places, the Scottish Highlands and the Junker estates of Prussia to find true understanding of the American South. It was not immediately clear that an excursus into the finer points of Burkean conservatism, the labour problems of Prussian landowners and the herding instincts of Celts through the ages greatly aided comprehension of a region as peculiarly confected as the American South. Professor Pessen did rather better in re-roasting the old chestnut of North–South differences and similarities. But he ended up by saying that, while the South was a distinctive civilization, the contrast it posed to the North has been grossly exaggerated. This was because historians essentially swallowed the Republican myth of the mid nineteenth-century North as a section of manifest egalitarianism, liberalism and progressiveness; its unequal distribution of wealth, defects in corrupt and machine politics, illiberal aberrations and rural and small-town exceptions to progressive rule all made it less unlike the South than some writers suppose. Much of this makes immediate sense; Southerners, after all, were Americans who took a generation racked by political dispute and enlivened by persistent and fierce anti-Northern rhetoric before deciding, and then only under the pressure of events, to secede. But it still does not quite tell us why historians take such interest in the South itself; nor why sectional differences became more important than national similarities.

The present work looks in upon the South rather than outwards to grand but elusive historical forces. Some comparisons are made where they seem necessary to an understanding of Southern conditions. And it can be conceded that more might be said in detail of developments which were national rather than purely Southern in impact; family size, physical mobility, the distribution of wealth, openness of economic opportunity, respectability, prison reform, even Indian relations were all subjects upon which close North–South comparisons could be made. But the examination of how *different* the South was from the North is not the purpose of this essay. Rather, it takes as given what the present writer, as well as more eminent historians, has argued elsewhere (Collins

1981); the sectional conflict was sparked off by political and constitutional controversies over slavery extension which in turn raised questions and anxieties over the ultimate fate of slavery in the South. What is interesting, and worth exploring from the perspective of social history, is why ordinary Southern whites felt excited enough by the 'Southern' cause and exercised enough by sectional rivalry to support so vigorously and for so long the political and subsequently the military defence of slavery and the South. In saying that Southern whites were attached to their section by such factors as economic opportunity, political democracy, social mobility, family, rituals of life and so forth, one is not denying that such factors were also at work and vital in the North. One is simply saying that such phenomena which may have been national as well as Southern characteristics were *perceived* to be – and indeed were – part of the fabric of a society whose existence and dynamism were threatened, or appeared to be threatened, by attacks upon one of its peculiar elements. Southerners did not defend the South solely to preserve slavery; they did so because they endowed Southernism with a whole range of attributes and because they derived their sense of community or sectional loyalty from a variety of sources. It is with the discussion of those attributes and sources that this essay is concerned.

ACKNOWLEDGEMENTS

Much of the work for this book was made possible by a year's study leave granted to me by the University of Glasgow in 1981–82. I am beholden to Mr Geoffrey Finlayson, then head of the Department of Modern History, for his understanding and good offices in enabling me to secure that leave, and to the University Court for awarding it. A seven-week visit to the United States was made possible by research grants from the University and from the Carnegie Trust for the Universities of Scotland. During that visit, spent mostly at the University of North Carolina at Chapel Hill, I had the good fortune to study at the Southern Historical Collection, whose staff were assiduously helpful. I also benefited from conversations with Professors Harry Watson and William Barney, and a graduate student, Mr Cecil-Fronsman, at U.N.C. More substantial research was possible through the generosity of the British Academy, a grant from which institution enabled me to spend three months in Mississippi and Georgia. I owe a considerable debt of gratitude to the staff of the Mississippi Department of Archives and History, of the Georgia State Archives at Atlanta, of the special collections department at the Robert W. Woodruff Library, Emory University, and of the Rare Books and Manuscripts department and Georgia room at the University of Georgia Library, Athens. One of the pleasures of working on American sources is the sheer efficiency and helpfulness of the library and archive staff. At the University of Georgia I was shown much kindness by Professors Kenneth Coleman and Nash Boney. Professor Boney discussed a number of points with me and gave me a good deal of welcome encouragement. In Britain, Professor William Brock gave me important and much appreciated support. And at Glasgow, Miss Patricia Ferguson typed the manuscript with the efficiency and speed that members of the Department of Modern History have come to depend upon over the years.

On my recent visits to America, my friends Tom and Ellen Cole have given me hospitality, encouragement and a helpful perspective. At home my aunt and uncle, Kathleen and Robert Leeds, have, as usual, aided and stimulated my endeavours. I am most particularly grateful to my wife – Dr Linda Nash – for tolerating my long absences and vexatious preoccupations. I also thank her for casting a critical eye over what follows.

Dr David Cannadine most generously asked me to contribute to this series and has tried subsequently to keep me on time and up to the mark. He has proved to be an understanding as well as energetic general editor. Professor Peter Parish read the typescript with great acuity and helpfulness; not every one of his suggestions has been followed up, but all were given close consideration. While absolving him – and others named here – from responsibility for the final product, I would still like to thank Professor Parish for his written critique of this work and for the advice and warm encouragement he has given to its author.

BRUCE COLLINS
University of Glasgow
January 1984

ABBREVIATIONS

(Used in references and notes)

GDAH	Georgia Department of Archives and History
Ga. Govrs' Papers	Georgia Governors' Papers
J. of H. Ga.	Journal of House, Georgia
J. of Sen. Ga.	Journal of Senate, Georgia
MDAH	Mississippi Department of Archives and History
SHC	Southern Historical Collection, University of North Carolina, Chapel Hill
TCC	Telamon Cuyler Collection, Georgia Governors' Papers. University of Georgia Libraries.
U. Ga.	University of Georgia, Athens

INTRODUCTION

I

James Baldwin, I believe, commented that it was not difficult to be a marked man in the South; all you had to do was go there. Such a reaction, from a black, a novelist and an explicit bisexual, could well have been provoked by other places at other times than the South of the 1950s and 1960s. But in an important respect Baldwin's was a response typical of many Northern, and many non-American, observers' feelings of unease, disquiet, even threat, when they travelled far south of the Mason–Dixon line. Southerners themselves recognized the prevalence of this outsiders' image of their region. When the promoters of Atlanta's economic development during the 1960s sought to dispel that negative perception they boasted that their city was 'too busy to hate'. The implication was that the rest of the South was both entrepreneurially unenterprising and bogged down in its traditions of racial animosity. Rhetoric of such reassuring kind has become, by the 1980s, increasingly unnecessary. But the earlier conditions of racist conservatism and outsiders' distrust stretched back to the early nineteenth century.

Not the least of the paradoxes of the American South was its inability by the mid nineteenth century to live up to its Revolutionary and Enlightenment traditions. Precisely when Southern politicians and intellectuals ceased to be – as, for instance Thomas Jefferson and James Madison had been – at the forefront of reform is more difficult to say. But the sense of Southern distinctiveness and backwardness was very well developed by the 1840s, and it provided a bold contrast with the contributions made to American political Enlightenment in the 1770s and 1780s by Southern leaders. In 1842, the Northern Liberty party advanced what was to become a Northern generation's stock explanation for this distinctiveness and backwardness. The distortion of democratic promise, the denial of economic opportunity, the destruction of black men's hopes as well as liberties were all attributed to

1

the class structure of the white South. The Slave Power – the slaveowners in action – controlled the Southern economy and politics and fixed the pattern of social life and culture. They did so, as the argument unfolded among many Northerners in the 1840s and 1850s, increasingly to preserve their privileges, maintain slavery and prevent that economic diversification from the plantation norm which would offer better jobs and increased social mobility to ordinary, non-slaveowning whites. Their concern for securing their position within the South led to the slaveowners' aggressive assertions in national politics both of Southern rights and of the need for slavery's expansion into new territories. Such assertions in turn created a political sense of Southern distinctiveness. In cultural terms, also, the anachronistic existence of slavery led to a growing isolation for the South. Prominent Northern visitors, such as, most notably, the journalist Frederick Law Olmsted, were dismayed at much of what they witnessed. The autobiographies of runaway slaves, published in the North from the 1830s, created an image of Southern white brutality or, at best, indifference to blacks' plight that was to endure into and beyond the 1960s. Such narratives provided both inspiration and model for Harriet Beecher Stowe's classic indictment of the human consequences of slavery. The written word, the apparent lack of tangible opportunity for whites, and Southerners' distrust of outsiders' possible anti-slavery tendencies combined to deter Northerners and foreigners alike from settling in the South. To go South, except into the handful of big cities, was indeed to be a marked man by the 1850s.

The Slave Power image gained increasing credibility. Once the Confederacy was formed and Civil War erupted, the idea that the conflict had been brought on by the slaveowners' political machinations and selfishness became variously embellished. Two classic formulations of the Northern anti-slavery notion were written in 1862 and 1863 by the British liberal political economist, John E. Cairnes, and by Karl Marx. Both located the origins of the war in the South's class structure. Cairnes asserted: 'In the North we find a government broadly democratic alike in form and spirit; in the South one democratic in form, but in spirit and essence a close oligarchy' (Cairnes 1863: xvi). Marx further elaborated; the extension of slavery into the territories was deliberately pressed by the slaveowning oligarchy in order to placate the non-slaveowners, 'to square the interests of these "poor whites" with those of the slaveholders, to give their turbulent longings for deeds a harmless direction and to tame them with the prospect of one day becoming slaveholders themselves'. Moreover, the establishment of the Confederacy at Montgomery consolidated the slaveowners' special position (Marx 1961: 69, 79):

> the oligarchy of three hundred thousand slaveholders utilized the
> Congress of Montgomery not only to proclaim the separation of the

South from the North. It exploited it at the same time to revolutionize the internal constitutions of the slave states, to completely subjugate the section of the white population that had still maintained some independence under the protection and the democratic Constitution of the Union. Between 1856 and 1860 the political spokesmen, jurists, moralists and theologians of the slaveholders' party had already sought to prove, not so much that Negro slavery is justified, but rather that color is a matter of indifference and the working class is everywhere born to slavery.

At root, therefore, the Civil War was the outcome of a clash over slavery brought to a head by the slaveowners' insistence on slavery expansion. That insistence flowed, according to Cairnes, from the inefficiencies of plantation agriculture, from its requirement for new and freshly fertile lands, from its dependence on unskilled labour which was incapable of cultivating more intractable terrain, and from its tendency to deplete good soils. Marx more bluntly argued that expansionism simply seduced the non-slaveowners into believing that opportunities for social improvement would be available to them in new territories opened to slavery by the federal government in the West.

Cairnes and Marx were both foreigners and were both heavily dependent upon the writings of Northern anti-slavery publicists. They agreed upon the economic and class roots of the Civil War from, interestingly enough, very divergent intellectual presuppositions. Cairnes held up the free labour system of the North, with its small farmers, craftsmen and small businessmen as his ideal type of social organization and opportunity; Marx had no such warmth of feelings about Northern bourgeois society, but rather regarded the eventual disappearance of the Southern economic system as a natural step in the extending sweep of capitalist ideas, methods and institutions. Yet, despite these differences, they were at one in trying to persuade European readers that the Civil War was not about constitutional rights, was not a praiseworthy struggle for Southern political freedom from Northern majority tyranny, but was instead a contest between two divergent economic and class systems.

The interpretation offered by Cairnes and Marx, based as it was upon a reading of contemporary anti-slavery literature, is not merely of antiquarian interest; their essential argument has continued to enjoy wide endorsement and support, not least in an insistence that the origins of the Civil War are to be found in economic and social tensions between the sections and engendered by slavery. The argument principally holds that slavery gave rise to a very specific economic system which in turn maintained an oligarchy of slaveowners who engineered secession in the face of a Republican victory in 1860. The Slave Power acted thus because it realized that its future security depended upon slavery's continued expansion. Secondarily, the argument claimed that slavery was not merely inefficient but constricted the opportunities open to ordinary whites. These poorer whites were virtually debased in their social and cultural condition, partly because all manual labour was tainted with the supposed degradation of 'nigger' work. Cairnes took pains to prove his contention that the bulk of whites were in fact 'mean whites' (Cairnes 1863: 358–76). And, for Marx, secession held the additional advantage to the Slave Power of enabling it to curtail non-slaveowners' political rights.

Various aspects of this central interpretation continue to inspire historical research. Emory M. Thomas argues that 'planter interests prevailed in the South', and did so because the planter class secured the deference of other white social groups to their wills (Thomas 1979: 8–9). Professor Genovese has most eloquently adopted Marx's writings to modern purposes (1965; Fox-Genovese and Genovese 1983), asserting that the slave oligarchy differed utterly from the middle-class élites ruling the North. Bertrand Wyatt-Brown (1982) and Michael P. Johnson (1977; 1980) have detected a profound difference between Southern and Northern values, with Southerners displaying either an attachment to codes of honour or a deference to patriarchy of extraordinary and 'pre-modern' intensity. Such clinging to declining modes of belief and behaviour arose from the requirements and habits of slaveownership. Professor Johnson (1977) and Steven Hahn (1979; 1982) go further and see secession itself as the desperate reaction of a slaveowning class scared at the prospect of a Republican administration in Washington dangling political favours before the dull but increasingly dissatisfied non-slaveowning farmers. Secession was thus a pre-emptive strike enabling the Slave Power to secure its position at home. More generally, secession is widely seen by historians against Northerners' belief in the superiority – moral, social, economic and political – of their own special producerist, or bourgeois, section. Resistance to the Confederacy made sense to the North not solely for constitutional reasons (though those were important), but also because the South was regarded as a distinctive region, ruled by an obnoxious and rapacious master class (Foner 1970).

But does a class analysis indeed take us to the heart of Southern white society and truly explain the coming and fighting of the Civil War? Clearly, it was in the slaveowners' interests to defend slavery to their utmost. Yet the maintenance of race subjection appealed also to masses of non-slaveowners who despised blacks and feared competition for land or lowly jobs from free blacks. While there was a manifestly unequal distribution of wealth in the South, that inequality did not necessarily signify the blocking of opportunity or the denial of some hope for modest social improvement for the bulk of white farmers. More important, a strictly class explanation breaks down where *slave-ownership* is equated with an oligarchy. In most of the Deep South (where secession originated) about 40 per cent of white families owned slaves. No doubt these people and those less well off than themselves regarded the planters (or slaveowners with twenty or more slaves) as models for emulation, at least in terms of getting and spending. No doubt also the 'plain folk' elected slaveowners to public office. But such tendencies meant very little unless slaveownership was restrictive and privileged, and unless political power was exercised to promote definable 'planter class interests' (Thomas 1979: 8). The difficulty is to discover many occasions – apart from the basic safeguarding of slaveownership and, more patchily, the preservation of unequal representation for slaveholding areas – when detectable issues could be linked to the needs, desires and actions of any planter oligarchy as distinct from the needs, desires and actions of a much larger body of slaveowners and farmers on the margins of slaveownership. To say that power was monopolized by wealthier Southerners establishes nothing about the peculiarity of that section, since, quite obviously, the more affluent enjoyed a preponderant share of public office and a dominant voice in public affairs in the North as well as in the slave states. And the distribution of wealth was as unequal in the North as in the South. Southern wealth-holding and Southern office-holding did not of themselves mark the South off from some egalitarian or 'middle-class' norm. What made the South so odd was slavery. Yet the preservation of slavery enjoyed a remarkable breadth of support among Southern whites; no anti-slavery movement flourished within the South by the 1850s and no yeoman farmer protest against the Slave Power existed on any significant scale. Moreover, the notion of an oligarchy has severely misleading connotations; the South's distinctiveness arose more from the problems created by slavery than from any special class structure that grew out of that institution.

Yet, if one does not accept that the Slave Power controlled the South, how do we explain the formation and stern defence of the Confederacy? Southern patriotism, or at least a willingness to fight, was intense. An extraordinarily high proportion of all white males of military age served in the Confederate armies. Perhaps as many as one-third of those who served died. And, although desertions multiplied in the final phase of the war, Confederate resilience in the face of privation and destruction was remarkable. It could be claimed that it was only natural that the nearer war reached Southerners' homelands, the more resolute the imperative to resist 'Yankeedom' became. Yet not all mass armies have reacted thus; as the French revealed in 1940. So the power of the Southern ideal requires explanation. What follows is an attempt to explain Southernism and its popular appeal by reference to influences and factors other than the passivity of the white masses in the face of the Slave Power and its political requirements.

II

It would be facile to seek some single clue to the character of the South. The South, despite its reputation for economic torpor or primitiveness, was a complex region; elements of advanced economic organization were interspersed with communities dependent upon face-to-face exchange; romantic ideals of personal honour jostled with 'middle-class' evangelical notions of collective moral responsibility; the cult of the hero was modified by acclaim for democratic processes. Such 'contradictions' – or, preferably, contrasts – need not cause surprise. They were to be expected in any dynamic, fluid society in the nineteenth century. But, allowing for such tensions and contrasts, this essay argues that a range of social bonds fostered broad support for the Southern 'cause' in the face of Northern sectional claims or political demands. First, and unremarkably, cotton, plentiful land and the abundance of game and easily cultivable soil underpinned an economy that allowed most small farmers ready access to cash crops and provided the means of subsistence for all. Wide inequalities provoked little in the nature of class politics and were not incompatible with the steady democratization of institutions and politics in the two generations from 1790 to 1860. They were not so strident or iron-clad as to leave the poorest whites in intolerable poverty or without possibility of upward mobility for their most ambitious sons. One may not be saying much in emphasizing that the abundance of game, the ease of herding and the availability of public lands to farm without legal title all militated against savage want and actual starvation for the very poor. And Cairnes certainly objected that the numbers of marginal backwoodsmen were too large and their way of life was too different from anything in the North to allow them to be treated as a mild aberration from a Southern – and American – yeoman farmer norm (Cairnes 1863: 367–71). Yet the extent of this deviation from settled agricultural life should not be exaggerated; nor should the parallel case of a Northern, urban lower class suffering a very marginal existence be lightly dismissed. Moreover, safeguards against total deprivation were not readily secured to agricultural societies during the nineteenth century (witness Ireland in the 1840s) or, for the 'Third World', in this century either. The South's ability, through natural abundance, to accommodate the very poor contributed to social bonding and was not quite so much a matter to be shrugged off as many observers believed.

Secondly, and more distinctively, the creation of 'the South' spawned a self-image of whites as a chosen people. Large areas of the slave states were closer to the experience of Indian war and Indian displacement than were comparable areas of the mid-West in the 1840s and 1850s. A sense of a shared and quite rugged past blended with white discrimination against and disparagement of the blacks to sustain potent race pride. Such racism was fanned by intellectuals and coincided with slaveowners' interests. But it flourished long before it was systematically defended. And it continued long after the intellectual establishment condemned it in the mid-twentieth century. Nor were slaveowners as a 'class' necessarily responsible for generating or fomenting the most blatant forms of white racism. Planters often, and perhaps condescendingly and unfairly, blamed maltreatment of slaves on their lower caste overseers (Scarborough 1966). State legislatures tried – notably unsuccessfully – to bridle some of the excessive punishments meted out by patrols or vigilantes upon slaves. None of this went as far as a clash of policy or approach between planters and ordinary whites. But the most blatant form of racism did not always coincide with planters' self-interest or conscience. Indeed, an important sub-theme of antebellum Southern history was the competition between 'respectables' and 'roughs' for the spirit of the section. There were planters, and non-slaveowners too, who wanted, in answer to the inner calls of religious sentiment or of humane feelings towards slaves, to regulate, rationalize and even liberalize owners' treatment of their chattels. Opposing such paternalistic impulses to stewardship were slaveowners and ordinary whites who never thought about, let alone agonized over, their proper relationship with the slaves, and who resorted without reflection, rationalization, or restraint to the most brutal, as well as casual, use of force. Similar conflicts occurred in other spheres; over temperance legislation, for instance. But it was most pronounced over the treatment of slaves. Racial lines were frequently crossed. Planters sometimes developed close and important relationships with individual slaves. Larger cities witnessed a certain amount of racial intermingling. Rural cross-roads stores and bars were the scenes of some inter-racial fraternizings and friendships. Whites sometimes entered into illicit traffic with slaves in stolen goods and alcoholic drink. Yet, just as the effective reach of planter paternalism should not be exaggerated, so the affective embrace of poorer whites' fraternity with blacks should not be over-played. Race pride, inflated by the historical record of successful Indian wars, subsumed such colour-blind contrary tendencies.

Reinforcing this feeling of racial distinctiveness was the enjoyment of freedom of space. The spatial differentiation of the most strongly contrasted ranks in white society perhaps explains the paucity of any organized and articulate pressure for improved state government services. Political representatives from poorer areas who were themselves non-slaveowners made little effort in this direction. And the records of state government reveal no reservoir of social discontent. While it is wrong to suppose that the economically less developed counties – usually in the hills or mountains where extensive plantation agriculture was physically impossible – lacked wealthy and indigenous slaveowners, those counties tended to consist predominantly of poorer and non-slaveowning whites. Local slaveowners were powerful in these county communities, but they were not obtrusive and did not supply the most affluent or self-conscious planters. The latter were to be found instead in areas of highly concentrated plantation agriculture where whites formed only 30 per cent or so of the total population and where large slaveholdings were common. Such areas were widely separated from each other; those in Virginia and South Carolina had been long settled and supported planter families who aped gentry manners; those in Alabama's black belt and Mississippi's rich delta were scarcely more than a generation old in 1860. In between, the bulk of the 'South' consisted of prosperous agricultural lands where small and medium-sized plantations (defined as units with twenty or more slaves) were intermingled with farms; and where the white population, especially the landless part of it, was extremely mobile. The spatial separation of the extremes of wealth and poverty helped preserve different types of social life, a landed gentry in one social context living apart from, and thus leaving intact, the more primitive culture of backwoods herders and poor farmers. This fact, together with the restless movement of labourers and small farmers across the great expanse of the Cotton Kingdom, accounted, in part, for the absence of protest politics.

Finally, Southern whites were drawn together in other ways than by facts of race and a Nietzschean conquest of adversity. Their rural society allowed a great deal of psychological as well as physical space. Old superstitions and the cultural assumptions of a pre-literate society co-existed in places with creeping commercialism and increasing ties to a money economy. In many respects, white society was loosely textured. Government seemed scarcely to intrude. A visiting Englishwoman noted in 1858 from New Orleans: 'It is curious to see everywhere the want of officials. In Europe there are too many, in America every man is his own official' (Bodichon 1972: 97). Taxes stayed low; citizens' obligations to government were few. Weakened state power trimmed the possibilities for state and county governments to lavish privilege and profitable office upon the few. No *noblesse de robe* battened on to the public coffers. The conduct of government was informal. Governors were readily petitioned by individual citizens. State legislatures met in state capitals that were typically modest in size and in social accoutrements. Law courts were accessible. County government was limited and amenable to public pressure. Militias were ramshackle organizations. Much of this struck some politicians as regrettable, perhaps worse; but their efforts to energize state governments were generally unavailing, except in prising lands from the Indians and yielding public financial guarantees to railway companies. If government helped to fuel social harmony by, in effect if not intentionally, declining to take actions that jeopardized it, so a variety of social rituals and aspirations provided additional social bonds. The rhythm of agricultural life, more especially of cotton cultivation (which affected even non-slaveowning small farmers), served as a common focus of attention. Shared rituals of hunting, horseracing, chasing runaways and electioneering drew whites of all ranks together. Religious activity and the quest for a 'respectable' secular order were more divisive; but the division was often, though not axiomatically, across lines of affluence or status. If slaves expressed a yearning for escape from worldly oppression, then many evangelical whites, poor and planter alike, viewed their present existence as the merest prelude and preparation for eternal life hereafter. As one white spiritual intoned, 'A few more struggles here … And we shall weep no more'. If religiosity naturally set the people of faith and prayer against their neighbours, backsliders and the non-religious alike, it also directed much of the most robust and potentially reformist white energies away from 'social' and race issues towards matters of individual conscience and conduct.

The lack of government restraint was complemented by numerous social rituals, by tight ties of family and by the search for respectability to shape individuals' sense of identity with their section. These various phenomena were not necessarily Southern; economic opportunity, unobtrusive government, social mobility, family, a quest for self-improvement (spiritual and material) and so forth were American – indeed, many contemporaries argued, more distinctly Northern – rather than Southern characteristics. Yet they were *perceived* to be, and were, part of the fabric of a society whose existence and dynamism were threatened, or appeared to be threatened, by attacks upon one of its peculiar elements. Southerners did not celebrate and defend the South solely to preserve slavery; they did so because they endowed Southernism with a whole range of attributes and because they derived their sense of community or sectional loyalty from a variety of sources.

To argue – as this book endeavours to do – that social bonds helped to create a sectional identity in a region whose formal institutional framework was weak and loose is not to claim that a full and all-encompassing consensus prevailed. Differences in moral and religious outlook, in partisan affiliation, in cultural aspiration and in vision for the South's future infused Southern life and thought. These differences vitiated a simple class analysis of Southern politics. But they also make it important for us to define the ligaments that enabled the section to co-ordinate its actions and to move to its own self-defence. In many ways and for most outsiders the South was not an appealing region to visit or to settle for the 140 years from the early 1830s. Yet the Confederacy elicited from the majority of its white inhabitants a determined patriotism, loyalty and vast blood sacrifice. It is that fact that this essay seeks to explain, through an analysis of the social bonds that gave white Southerners their sense of shared identity.

The following work thus explores the white Southerners' point of view, as manifested in an effusive but typical comment about Southerners' westward migration (and more generally American ideals) written by a South Carolinian and published at Nashville, Tennessee, in 1860:

> Hills and plains, lake and river, field and forest, have welcomed the strangers, and the invitation yet is, COME. Come one, come all. Come to freedom, come to abounding plenty. Come from the dominion of the despot's power. Come from the heavy burdens of exacting hierarchies ... from tithes, indulgences, and inquisitorial cruelty. Come and help to build up the People's Empire, where subjects are sovereigns, and rulers are servants, and under his own 'vine and fig tree' each may sing the song of his Zion, and none may hinder his worship. (A Southern Country Minister 1860: 166)

We may not always agree that such pride was warranted by Southern circumstances; but our task as historians is to understand, not to deplore, or condone, it.

Chapter one

A SOUTH OF MANY SOUTHS

I

When six slave states of the Deep South founded the rebellious Confederacy in February 1861, they invoked an ideal, the 'South', which had only taken shape since the 1790s. As one historian has recently noted, 'Before the American Revolution few English settlers south of Pennsylvania thought of themselves as "Southerners". Indeed, beyond a tenuous allegiance to Great Britain, they articulated no meaningful sense of common identity. They shared no cultural symbols, no myths about a common past' (Breen 1976: 8). By the 1820s sectionalism had developed not merely in politics but also in popular thought. Such sectionalism strengthened in the three decades to 1860 as arguments and ideas about Southern identity were widely canvassed and took deep root. The Civil War itself then created a sense of grievance and loss which cast its shadow upon white Southerners for about a century after 1865. During most of that century, the South embarrassed most of America's intellectual establishment, either by its economic backwardness or by its violent racism, or by both. Even when the economic changes of the 1960s and thereafter, and the Civil Rights movement of the same years, heralded the emergence of a genuinely new South, the credit for that transformation tended to go to black protesters, to Northern activists, and to the federal authorities; those, that is, who were not part of the mainstream of Southern society. Southern white opinion appeared generally to be conservative and racist. As W. J. Cash (1954: 12) wrote:

> ... if it can be said there are many Souths, the fact remains that there is also one South. That is to say, it is easy to trace throughout the region ... a fairly definite mental pattern, associated with a fairly definite social pattern ... which, if it is not common strictly to every group of white people in the South, is still common in one appreciable measure or another, and in some part or another, to all but relatively negligible ones.

If Cash advanced an essentially consensus view of Southern ideology, he did not advance an entirely conservative one. Indeed, he punctured romantic notions of a Southern aristocracy, emphasizing instead the fluid, frontier-like character of Southern development.

The South as first defined comprised those states condoning slavery after the spate of gradual emancipation measures in the 1790s. Southerners totalled 1,961,174 out of America's population of 3,929,000 in 1790. Of all Southerners more than one in three was black. (Figures in this and subsequent paragraphs are from Potter 1965: 684–87; and Bureau of the Census 1960: 7–13.) And 1,461,000 of them lived in Virginia, North Carolina and Maryland, in that order of size of population. By 1860 Southern settlement westwards had distended the section almost as far as the North had projected itself into the continental heartland. The population had expanded to 12.3 millions, of whom about a third were blacks. Such physical expansion created new or larger-scale contrasts within the section. Some Southern states, while perpetuating slavery, held a modest stake in that institution; only 13 per cent of Maryland's population, 10 per cent of Missouri's, and 1.5 per cent of Delaware's were slaves. At the opposite extreme, over half the inhabitants of Mississippi and South Carolina in 1860, and from 40 to 50 per cent of those in Alabama, Florida, Georgia and Louisiana were slaves. Not surprisingly, these were the six states which first established the Confederacy, to be joined shortly by Texas and later, when fighting began, by the more hesitant and northerly slave states of Virginia, North Carolina, Tennessee and Arkansas. In very broad terms, therefore, it would be misleading to depict the South as uniform in its racial mix and pattern of agricultural effort. Even within the contrasting states, a full range of agricultural activity was pursued; plantation belts existed in all Southern states, as did hill regions of few slaves and limited cash-crop cultivation. Yet, clearly, if geographical regions did not coincide with state boundaries, political decisions were affected by the racial composition of states' populations; Missouri's political leaders were under very different pressures from Mississippi's.

During the period of territorial expansion from the creation of the USA in 1789 to the founding of the Confederacy in 1861, the 'South' acquired other basic and very general characteristics than its commitment to slavery. It was very little touched by urbanization. In 1860 one in five Americans lived in a 'town' of 2,500 people or more. Rhode Island (with 63 per cent of its people in towns), Massachusetts (60%), and New York (39%) were the most urban states. Although Maryland, due largely to the major port of Baltimore, had a high level of town-dwelling, 34 per cent, and Louisiana, again owing to the presence of the flourishing and cosmopolitan port of New Orleans, was above the national level, at 26 per cent, most Southern states were very markedly rural. Of the nine states (out of thirty-three in 1861) which had 5 per cent or fewer of their people living in towns, seven were slave states: Alabama

(5%), Florida, Tennessee and Texas (4%), North Carolina and Mississippi (3%), and Arkansas (1%). It would be wrong to draw an over-sharp contrast between an 'urban' North and a rustic South. In the great region from Ohio to Iowa, including seven states by 1861, the proportion of urban inhabitants ranged consistently from 9 to 14 per cent, with only Ohio at 17 per cent. But if other regions were also scantily urbanized, the South was most particularly notorious for its lack of a vibrant urban culture. Such great or middling cities as it possessed hugged the coasts or were river ports – like Louisville or Memphis – and appeared to be peripheral to Southern whites' typical life-style.

By 1860 also the South was less ethnically variegated than other parts of the country. No fewer than 13 per cent of Americans were foreign-born. Yet in nine of the fifteen slave states, 2 per cent or fewer of the people were not native Americans; and the native-born were very largely Southerners in provenance. Only Maryland, Missouri and Louisiana, with their booming ports of Baltimore, St Louis and New Orleans, hovered around the national norm for people born overseas. This lack of significant foreign immigration into the South profoundly affected the region's potential for urban growth, since foreigners flocked to the towns. It also distorted the South's demographic weight in the nation. In 1790, 40 per cent of *white* Americans lived in the South; in 1860, only 30 per cent did so. The enormous influx of foreign immigrants into America during the years 1845–54 swelled the North's – and the West's – cities and labour force; and it pushed the proportion of seats allocated to those sections in the federal House of Representatives ever upwards (McCardell 1979: 339). Politically and psychologically, as well as in population, the South was rapidly becoming more of a minority section even as it expanded westwards into new farming areas and increased its output of cash crops vital to the national economy. Such consciousness of minority status was compounded by the very lack of white ethnic variety that denied big additions to the mid nineteenth-century South's population.

If the South was somewhat insulated from the rest of the United States by its increasing white ethnic homogeneity and by its lack of significant urban development, much internal variety co-existed with these basic social facts. Although the South was receiving no fresh immigrants en masse in the mid nineteenth century, it was not entirely uniform in background and customs. No 'typical' state can be cited as a model for the South. Virginia had a reputation for 'gentry' politics even as late as the 1850s; and its planters at least claimed descent from the seventeenth-century founders. Maryland was given a special character by Baltimore and by the decline of tobacco growing in the early nineteenth century. Coastal South Carolina supported a planter class that yielded no ground in point of self-esteem or pretensions to culture and political ambition to that of Virginia. But the hill country of the interior, though fertile enough to support plantations and their sometimes overbearing owners, was not distinguishable from other stretches of the South. Georgia's planters were, at least in general popular perception, less grand than those of neighbouring South Carolina. Moreover, about half the state had been Indian country until the 1820s and 1830s; so that, although Georgia was the last colony to be founded by the British before the Revolution (in 1732), it was still in part a frontier region only twenty-five years before secession. Even fresher from its pristine wilderness was Florida. Added to the USA in 1819, the former Spanish colony (which retained strong traces of Spanish culture and settlement on its Atlantic edge) did not become a state until 1845, at the conclusion of a long, bloody and costly war against the Seminole Indians. Obviously, even the Atlantic seaboard South displayed wide contrasts; the gentrified plantations of the Chesapeake Bay, whose creation dated from the seventeenth century, were graphically set off from the Indian frontier in Georgia of the mid 1830s and central Florida in the early 1840s.

To the West as well the slave states provided contrasts in cultures and origins. If Florida had come from the Spanish, Texas was prised, by indirection in truth, from the Mexicans in the 1830s and 1840s, becoming an American state in 1845. Texas already possessed on the eve of the Civil War something of its later reputation for violence, frontier-style politics and casual materialism. But it was big enough – an empire of agricultural opportunity in itself – to support quite divergent types of settlement. Slaveowning small farmers from the lower South moved into eastern and south-east Texas while non-slaveowners from Tennessee, Kentucky, Missouri and Arkansas made northern and north-central Texas their home. The state's southern corner even attracted Mexican immigrants (Jordan 1979: 211–14). More enduring foreign influence was felt in Louisiana, a French crown colony from 1731 to 1762, a Spanish possession in 1762–1801 and, briefly, French again before being sold to the USA in 1803. Louisiana became a state in 1812, but retained a legal code, a Creole culture and a cosmopolitan society in New Orleans that reflected French influences decades after the voluntary termination of French rule. Economically, Louisiana shared with Mississippi to the East and Arkansas to the North a common stake in the fabulously rich alluvial soils of the Mississippi valley. Like them, Louisiana by 1860 supported a very highly developed plantation order (though in its case the cash crop was sugar rather than cotton) within its boundaries. But like them too Louisiana possessed large tracts of infertile lands whose occupants were much poorer farmers.

Parts of the trans-Mississippi west were thoroughly locked into the Southern system; but the most northerly slave state in that region, Missouri, was one of the most tentative adherents to the Southern cause. Only 10 per cent of its appreciable population (1,182,000 in 1860; more than that of any other slave state except for Virginia) was enslaved. And, although Missouri's leadership was dominated by the Democrats and was dedicated to the constitutional defence of slavery, it was not immune from very considerable criticism of its pro-slavery stance in the late 1850s. A locally vigorous anti-slavery movement flourished in St Louis; and Missouri was entirely unable to cope coherently with secession in 1861; a civil war within the Civil War was its subsequent fate. Even so, and although Missouri and the border South will not be treated in the following analysis, the commitment to slavery endured in antebellum Missouri, and the opposition to the Slave Power there remained weak in numbers and local in influence.

Different soil types within the South and differing degrees of access to river transport affected the development of agricultural enterprise. That in turn produced contrasting styles of slavery. About half the slaves did not live on plantations; and only about one-quarter lived on larger plantations, defined rather arbitrarily in the twentieth century as units of fifty or more slaves. Not only did many slaves live on middling farms; some slaves and a larger number of free blacks even lived in towns and cities where their tasks were not the stereotyped ones of attending to King Cotton. Despite such differences in work, however, slavery naturally produced a common phenomenon of race subordination and white determination to uphold slaveownership. The struggling farmer in south-west Missouri who possessed a single slave had a stake in the prevailing order equal to that of the South Carolinian planter with 200 bondsmen, women and children, under his thrall; or so he believed and felt. This shared, vital and glaring interest lay behind outsiders' and historians' efforts to understand the South in terms of the Slave Power. For it was the slaveholders as a body, according to Genovese, who 'slowly if largely unconsciously forged themselves into a ruling class of a distinct type and with a special character' (Genovese 1969: 118).

The South became, therefore, distinctive not simply for its legal retention of slavery after the 1790s, not just for its rather insulated white ethnic mix, not only for its general lack of urbanization, but also for its allegedly peculiar class system growing out of slavery and corroding politics both in Washington and south of the Mason-Dixon line.

II

Quite self-evidently, being a planter carried with it high and enviable status. The number of antebellum planters was small; of nearly 400,000 slaveholders in 1860, only 12 per cent qualified as planters by meeting the later and artificial quota of twenty or more slaves. About 10,000 slaveowners held title to fifty slaves or more, and only about 3,000 owned over 100. The overwhelming mass of slaveowners lived lives far removed from the plantation idyll. This fact provides the first reason for scepticism about such assertions as Genovese's that *slaveowners* developed 'class cohesion and consciousness' (Genovese 1969: 122–3); or Marx's, and many other writers', portrayal of the slaveowners as an oligarchy wielding influence and power in a fairly self-aware and certainly exclusive fashion. In fact, slaveownership was widespread in parts of the South; 35 to 50 per cent of white families in 1860 held slaves in South Carolina, Mississippi, Alabama and Georgia, in that order of importance (Olsen 1972: 101–16). Those states were the forcing-houses of secession. Over a wider area, the South as a whole, about one white family in four held a slave. These people hardly formed an 'oligarchy'. Nor was entry to the slaveowners' ranks difficult. During the period 1830–60, at least 170,000 individuals became slaveowners. The vast majority of this 'class' in 1850, three-quarters of them, possessed fewer than ten slaves; and tens of thousands of these owners were skilled artisans, tradesmen, merchants, teachers, lawyers, doctors or so on, not solely farmers or planters (Oakes 1982: 37–41, 59–62, 67).

It was not entirely clear what was meant by being a planter. We use the conveniently statistical definition of a planter as someone who held at least twenty slaves. Yet, from an extremely large sample of that group as recorded by the federal census-takers in 1860, about half described themselves, or were marked down by the enumerators, as farmers (Menn 1964: 172). This verbal blurring may have had some social significance. For it was true also that men holding very few slaves occasionally accounted themselves to be planters. The term was probably used and invoked – not always, of course – to denote breeding, birth or aspiration to high respectability. Its social use did not, therefore, necessarily connote economic power. Such a conclusion follows from Daniel R. Hundley's lengthy treatise on Southern society published in 1860. Hundley tried to dispel the image of a cohesive Slave Power by bringing to his readers' attention the various archetypes of planter, not all of whom were to be admired for their delicacy of refinement, honourableness of motive and conduct, and attention to plain good manners. In fact, many planters were gross, rapacious, boastful and idle. Hundley's archetypes – differentiating as he did between the Southern Gentleman and the Southern Yankee, and showing suitably acute embarrassment at the behaviour of the region's plentiful Cotton Snobs – revealed that, while there was a model available for proper emulation in the shape of the Southern Gentleman, there were considerable differences of opinion and behaviour within the planter elite (Hundley 1979). Indeed, the planter ideal served as much to expose important divisions within that group as it did to provide a comprehensive description of the planters' manners and world-view. Some at least of the South's intellectual defenders were simply willing the section's disparate top 10,000 to act in a fashion consonant with their wealth and power.

Even if it were possible, however, to define a planter 'class' – and no one has done so in prosaic but important terms of names and numbers – it would be difficult to determine the scope of that class's power and privileges. Some historians look to analogies with British society, naturally enough seeking a point of reference that corresponded both with Southern whites' own ethnic background, and with the social parallels and comparisons that were available to Southerners themselves from the late eighteenth century to the mid nineteenth. One historian has written of Chesapeake Bay's most affluent landowners of the 1770s and 1780s: 'The style and manners of the planter aristocrats, their books, and many of their ideas were those of the English aristocracy of fifty years earlier' (May 1976: 133). A leading textbook echoes British upper-class usage of the eighteenth and nineteenth centuries in sketching out the gentry ethos adhered to by the antebellum planters: 'The eighteenth-century social contempt for trade persisted. Agriculture, the army, the church, and the law were the only proper careers for a planter's son' (Morison, Commager and Leuchtenburg 1977: 204). Such an image of the South's ruling elite has been fostered by observers and scholars as dissimilar as the Republicans of the 1850s, Marx and the latter-day Marxians and historians gratefully deploying a terminology that offers to make some sense of the confusing tendencies of the 1850s. Yet it distorts our perception of Southern white society.

The plantation order would have failed to secure the legitimacy it needed and enjoyed if the planters had so despised trade and so monopolized exclusive office as we are led to believe. Indeed, as Professor Genovese has sketched out in hypothetical form, one critical means by which planters won the loyalty and friendship of their poorer and humbler neighbours was by taking the part of commercial factotums. Planters provided ordinary farmers with informal banking services, legal advice, information on the condition of distant commodities prices, facilities for marketing cash crops and assistance in heavier agricultural operations. By these means, they made their expertise available and gained the friendship, trust, or at least dependence of the humbler farmers in their communities (Fox-Genovese and Genovese 1983: 258–60. For the eighteenth century, see Land 1965). They did not achieve such ends by rejecting the calls of trade.

Moreover, the openness and pluralism of leading institutions in the South and in the nation prevented any particular oligarchy from enjoying protected access to preferment. The federal army of the 1850s was very small (15,000 to 18,000 men in total strength) and very unsmart. Officers entered principally through West Point, where cadetships were partly under congressmen's patronage. But officers' training had a practical as well as a gentlemanly bent. No less than 70 per cent of all time-tabled formal study at West Point concerned engineering, mathematics and physics (Williams 1981: 192). One attraction of such a training, certainly from the 1830s, was that a young officer could leave the army for a lucrative career as a civil engineer,

17

especially with a railway company. When the Western Military Institute at Georgetown, Kentucky, advertised in one of Mississippi's small-town newspapers, it boasted of the thorough training it offered in civil engineering and, to rub the point home, listed the salaries being received by its graduates as railway engineers (Aberdeen, *Monroe Democrat*, 26 June 1850). Such an advertisement was directed at families wealthy enough to pay for a young man's college education. Not all those who obtained a military training sought other careers; but the drabness and slowness of army life encouraged many to do so. When Jefferson Davis gained promotion to a first lieutenancy, he had been transferred from the infantry to the impressive-sounding First Dragoons. Yet his posting at that time was to Fort Gibson, in present-day eastern Oklahoma, a place not notable for a stylish or diverting career (Eaton 1977: 18). Perhaps it is not altogether surprising to learn, therefore, that the number of Southerners who held US Army commissions was broadly in line with the South's share of the total population rather than largely in excess of it (Cunliffe 1969: 360–70). Military service was not a peculiarly Southern career.

State militias offered a more ready access to status. But being a militia officer hardly amounted to a career. And the place had to be worked for. In Virginia in 1860, for example, the state legislature elected the five major-generals of division and the twenty-eight brigadier-generals. But the men themselves chose their company lieutenants and captains (Code of Virginia 1860: ch. XXIV, sec. 1, 7). In Mississippi in the 1850s, even general officers were obliged to run for election within their brigade or divisional areas; though one assumes that many elections were not contested. With war, however, the stakes of high command seem to have been raised to competitive heights. In 1846, Jefferson Davis was elected colonel of the First Mississippi Rifles (volunteers) only in a second ballot, after he trailed behind a militia general in a first ballot in which five candidates wooed 900 votes (Eaton 1977: 58). The peacetime militia was not nearly so glamorous; lack of state financial backing was a perennial grievance, and training was merely casual when it did not degenerate into farce.

Careers in 'the church, and the law' were similarly rather more humdrum than the words, harking back as they do to British social exclusivity, imply. 'The church' in an English sense did not exist by the mid nineteenth century, as it had existed in Virginia, though on a modest scale, a hundred years earlier. There was no established church to serve as a largely docile and dutiful adjunct to the secular authorities, no church in which landowners or the Crown, through its political servants, appointed to comfortable livings or leading ecclesiastical office. Some congregations, especially among Presbyterians, selected scholarly and gentlemanly ministers. But no denomination enjoyed the wealth, political influence and state support which made the Church of England so central a part of the Victorian social establishment. Similarly, perhaps, with the law; although wealthy planters and their sons practised law, lawyers were not a well-regulated and closely screened profession. Entry was still very informal in the antebellum period; and in the Western slave states at least 'the law' probably offered a career open to the talents of the humble by birth, if not also to humble talents.

There is no compelling reason for drawing comparisons between the Southern planters and the British aristocracy and gentry (two different, though interlocking entities, by the way) except that Americans in the 1850s and long since have frequently employed that measure of comparison. Such contrasts as can be made are instructive in revealing the 'looseness' and lack of tight interconnectedness of the planter elite, and in emphasizing how far the South was an aggregation of autonomous foci of power.

One crucial characteristic of the British landed establishment was its territoriality. The aristocracy and gentry were landowners whose estates were retained in families across the generations. In the seventeenth and eighteenth centuries the manor house and the deer park, suitably distant from the village, became the symbol of British gentry status (Mingay 1976: 148–9). This enviable model found eager imitators in eighteenth-century Virginia. By 1787, the 100 wealthiest men in Virginia were gathered from a narrow circle of interrelated families; nine were Cockes, eight each belonged to the Fitzhugh, Lee and Washington families, and seven each were Carters, Harrisons and Randolphs. The richest were the seven Carters, whose aggregate land holdings amounted to 170,000 acres (Main 1954). Over time, however, this concentrated wealth tended to be dispersed. The dismantling of laws of primogeniture and entail in the late eighteenth century, the practice of partible inheritance and the steady migratory drift of planter families westwards removed vital props to the maintenance of local planter elites. Wealth soon became dissipated among a number of heirs. Individual plantations were rarely larger than 2,000–5,000 acres, and some of the greatest landholdings were secured for speculative purposes rather than for direct development by managerial owners. The very richest planters often owned a number of modest-sized plantations, to enable them to pass land, and slaves, on to a number of children. By the mid nineteenth century, such holdings might be scattered among not only a number of counties but also a number of states. For slaveowners with just one plantation and say thirty to sixty slaves, inheritance laws and customs had a devastating effect on the accumulation of wealth in the hands of an elite. Such holdings of land and slaves were very likely to be subdivided on their owner's death, and a planter's children could thus readily find themselves reduced to modest slaveowners. For example, when Nathaniel Francis of Southampton county, Virginia, died in 1849, he left his widow and each of his four sons about 600 acres of land. His widow received one-third of his slaves, and the rest were distributed among his children. In this way, an estate of nearly 3,500 acres and 37 slaves, built up from a farm of 137 acres and 7 slaves over twelve years old in 1827, was completely broken down. And the young sons of this deceased planter, aged 43, were individually worse off than their grandfather had been on his death in 1815 as the owner of over 1,000 acres and 16 slaves (Boney 1974: 450, 456).

Geographical movement, the availability of inexpensive land and the comparative ease of entry into the planters' ranks constantly weighed against the influence of the old-established estates. By 1830, for example, the largest concentration of Virginia's slaves was no longer in the tidewater of seventeenth-century settlement; it was in the piedmont, opened up only two generations earlier (Freehling 1982: 19–20). Families who had established continuous settlement and influence in one tidewater county from the early eighteenth century became, by the mid nineteenth century, households of extremely local importance, as the centres of dynamic wealth multiplied and moved elsewhere. The immobile remnant might even see their relative local significance diminish. In one long-established Maryland county on Virginia's border, the share of assessed property held by the wealthiest 5 per cent of households – those with twenty or more slaves and land – declined from 32 per cent in 1790 to 20 per cent in 1841 (Marks 1979: 358–9, 366). Nor was this social fluidity confined to eastern areas of relative economic decline. Those who moved on to found plantations in more inviting lands to the West and South-west often continued to be highly mobile. Among the richest planters of sample counties in south-west Georgia and western Alabama, for instance, only about 30 per cent in the former and 50 per cent in the latter persisted within the elite of wealthy planters in the same county between 1850 and 1860 (Formwalt 1981: 410–13). There is no reason to believe the 1850s to have been atypical in that respect.

This fluidity, even impermanence, was important to the antebellum South. It very much modified the power of the planter elite, by making such power as planters held difficult to transmit across the generations. To say that the planters did not form an elite closely resembling the British aristocracy and gentry – because they exerted no comparable continuous territorial authority, and because they failed to control key sources of influence, and employment for their offspring, in church and army – does not deny that Southern planters enjoyed considerable social status and political weight. Instead, it emphasizes the distinctive and essentially moderated role of the principal landowners in Southern life.

At the higher reaches, planters were prominent in Southern politics. But the practice of politics was not an illustrious activity, nor was participation in politics limited to an elite. The governing habit was learned in dreary circumstances. State capitals offered no opportunities for planter cliques to entertain or to conduct business on the grand scale while also legislating for their states. Although Richmond, Virginia, was both a political centre and an important city, state capitals such as Columbia, South Carolina, Milledgeville, Georgia, Montgomery, Alabama, Jackson, Mississippi, and Little Rock, Arkansas were one-dimensional towns. When James H. Hammond acquired a house at Columbia in 1841 he found that visitors looked upon his European paintings 'with the apathy of Indians'; the townspeople possessed neither 'intellect nor information' (Faust 1982: 228–9). Southern states' elites, in other words, found few physical environments in which to develop their personal relationships and promote their group identity. Admittedly, Charleston, South Carolina, served both as a key commercial city in its state and as a fashionable place of summer residence and social resort. But its wealthy clientele was drawn largely from within the state; it did not function as a national planters' social centre, or as a model for other Southern cities. Savannah had something of Charleston's role in neighbouring Georgia; but it had internal commercial rivals in Augusta and Columbus. Mobile, Alabama, was simply a thriving port, while Mississippi's Natchez – which certainly combined commerce with very elegant living – did not fulfil a state-wide social role. Arkansas, like Texas, was virtually without towns.

In a physical sense, a planter elite could not readily be forged. The foci of pleasure as well as power were widely distributed across the South. Similarly, political power was spread wide and far. Property qualifications for office-holding had disappeared from virtually all Southern states by the 1840s. Sinecure offices were few and, by the mid nineteenth century, had to be 'earned' by political usefulness rather than acquired by personal connections. By the 1850s even the office of justice of the peace was usually open; blacksmiths and innkeepers served as JPs in Georgia in that decade, an invasion of gentlemanly privilege which would have been unthinkable in contemporary Britain. After the 1830s, few Southern families – if any – controlled congressional districts in the manner in which British county families exerted great, even blatant, 'influence' at the polls until 1884 (Nossiter 1975: 69). It was possible in Victorian Britain for prominent county families to dominate a constituency from generation to generation; some MPs scarcely bothered to visit their constituencies, let alone canvass them. Against that yardstick, planters' political power was circumscribed by the operation of democratic procedures. Local *political* elites were capable of shaping party choices in their communities. In North Carolina in 1844, at a high point in the two-party system, the Whig and Democratic parties ran each other close in the presidential election. But in over two-thirds of the state's counties the two candidates were at least 20 percentage points apart in their popular support. A general pattern of close-run partisanship thus co-existed with a local mosaic of one-party dominance, dominance brought about through the decisions and determination of county leaders (Watson, Harry L. 1981: 310–12). That sort of pattern probably prevailed widely in the South. But it flowed

21

from the activities and exertions of local party organizers and leaders, who may or may not have been mostly drawn from the planter group.

Even at the local level, political office-holding was opened up by the early nineteenth century. In a rare case-study of county officials, Professor Ridgway has discovered who held office in three sharply contrasting contexts in Maryland during the period 1790–1840. In two plantation counties, with fairly stagnant economies in those decades, influential public posts were held by planters as frequently in the 1830s as in the 1790s. Even so, about 45–56 per cent of influential posts in the 1830s were in the hands of men with assessed wealth of under $3,000; such men could well have been younger sons of planters, but, unfortunately, we have no information on their family background, or on the extent to which the rulers of the 1830s belonged to the same families as their predecessors forty years earlier. Some oligarchic families, such as the Lloyds of Wye and the Goldsboroughs of Talbot county, became landowners in the seventeenth century and continued to enjoy power into the nineteenth century. Few families, it seems, were equally fortunate. In contrast, a piedmont county's elite was never as oligarchic in character as were the planters in the coastal counties of seventeenth-century origin. Only 6 per cent of influential offices in Frederick county of the 1790s were filled by planters; a mere 3 per cent were in the 1830s. Baltimore county, with its distinctive urban conditions and social fluidity, offered yet another pattern; its political system was far more open and offices went largely to men of little wealth (Ridgway 1979: 29, 129–44, 162–70).

A good deal more information is generally available on office-holding at a higher level. Among seven Deep South states in the 1860s, the overwhelming majority of state legislators were slaveowners, but only in South Carolina were a majority of them planters; in four of the seven states planters constituted under 30 per cent of all legislators; and among seven Upper South states (excluding Delaware) planters constituted under 20 per cent of legislators in five. While, therefore, legislative power was in slaveowners' hands, it was not concentrated in the hands of the plantation owners. Moreover, the rate of turnover in legislative seats was high. In the decade 1849–59, only 10 per cent of Kentucky's legislators served more than one term; in Arkansas only 6 per cent of the members of the state house of representatives did so during the period 1835–61; among those in Virginia's House of Delegates in 1849–61, a more substantial number, but still merely 18.3 per cent of the total membership, was elected for more than two terms. State by state, the overwhelming majority of legislators never held public office again, and most had held no office before entering their state legislatures (Wooster 1969: 39–41; Wooster 1965: 42–44).

It is a highly debatable point among political scientists whether the holding of public office is necessarily equated with the exercise of public power. Planters' special interests could easily have been defended and advanced in the state legislatures by lawyers or by minor slaveowners subscribing to the planters' ideology. Yet this is not quite how the Southern scene has always been described. Professor Genovese (1965: 28) once wrote:

> The planters commanded Southern politics and set the tone of social life ... In the planters' community, paternalism provided the standard of human relationships, and politics and statecraft were the duties and responsibilities of gentlemen. The gentlemen lived for politics not, like the bourgeois politician, off politics.

And, if one were to note how the British upper classes viewed politics, Genovese's comment makes sense; British aristocrats and gentry did not regard public office as something to be handed over, like the management of the family's legal affairs, to subservient lawyers. Yet, as we have seen, the planters failed to monopolize local and state posts to the extent which Genovese's description suggests. Explaining why this was so leads us back to the texture of Southern society.

One reason for a relative lack of planter participation in politics was that the demands of the electoral system were too heavy and the rewards of public office too light to attract generations of planters to the hustings. James H. Hammond of South Carolina was a very rich, if also exceedingly petulant, planter who tired of pandering to the 'despotism of the monster multitude ... ruled ... by the basest appetites, prejudices and vanities' (Faust 1982: 331). Another was that planters simply did not have sufficient leisure to flock in large numbers into party politics; politics was not a higher calling for planters on a par with running an estate. A third was that state governments did not do enough to stimulate planters' interest or to provoke their self-defence against encroachments upon their rights and possessions. (More on this is contained in Ch. 7.) A fourth was that the tone and pace of Southern political discourse and action were set by events, debates and decisions in Washington. As long as planters were prominent among the South's congressmen and senators, as they continued to be, then it did not much matter who held places in the state legislatures; if, that is, those state legislatures posed no challenge to planters' economic and ideological interests. This consideration leads to a final point. Planters and slaveowners together held a preponderant share in the distribution of local and state offices. Yet no opposition arose in the antebellum South to object to that political dispensation. The slaveowners as a group were too large in the Deep South to be socially exclusive and thus to provoke 'class' opposition; they were too committed to governmental *laissez-faire* to oppress the non-slaveowners. State and local governments did not extract onerous taxes or disagreeable services from their citizens.

It was precisely because slaveowners, as a large, fluid, ill-defined group, failed to form a closed, self-conscious, rich and distinctly cultured oligarchy that they were able to hold on to power so effectively.

Their sole unifying political demand, the defence of slavery, easily won non-slaveowners' general endorsement, if for no better reason than that slavery kept blacks in a fixed and inferior role.

III

Even so experienced a cynic as Senator Hammond was surprised, pleasantly, by the popular Southern response to secession; it was, he wrote in early 1861, 'a movement of the *People* of the South', not a 'bullying movement of the politicians' (Faust 1982: 360. Original emphasis). Part of this public enthusiasm for the Confederate cause and for the war it brought on was simple bravado. The very names of the first batch of volunteer companies suggest the spirit of 1861; Southern Avengers, Bartow Yankee Killers, Southern Rejectors of Old Abe, Cherokee Lincoln Killers, Dixie Heroes, Tallapoosa Thrashers did not have the air of sober Presbyterian church elders about them (Wiley 1943: 20). Part of the enthusiasm may also have been sheer relief at the apparent escape from an eleven-year-old crisis over slavery expansion which secession and a brief war promised to bring. Once the shock of battle and the accumulation of suffering began, then more sober views surfaced.

The war itself raised many ambiguities about Southern white society. On one side there was much grumbling, foot-dragging and desertion. Yet it has been calculated that virtually every man and teenage boy of military age must have served in the Confederate army, and that about one in three such men and teenage boys died in the Confederate cause (Livermore 1900: 21, 29, 63). Again: there is ample evidence of class resentment among the soldiery. Some privates bitterly complained of officers' privileges. Others groaned at serving under their social inferiors. As one soldier said of General Nathan B. Forrest, 'I must express my distaste to being commanded by a man having no pretension to gentility – a negro trader, a gambler ... Forrest may be and no doubt is, the best Cav[alry] officer in the West, but I object to a tyrannical, hotheaded vulgarian's commanding me.' Looking downwards rather than upwards in rank, one junior officer recorded his amazement at having 'found literary taste among mechanics and tradesmen' in his company. Another educated young man of affluent background interpreted his duty in a different way and became a private; 'all men that own property to any extent and especially negro property should take a part in this war as it has a tendency to encourage the poorer classes' (Wiley 1943: 235–41, 337–9, 149).

Responses to war varied so widely, according to the competence or failings of officers and the morale of the men, that generalization is naturally difficult and dangerous. But what the Confederate army created bore some resemblance to the topsy-turvy society from which it so hastily sprang. Social niceties existed and yet could be abruptly flouted. The ideal of a 'gentleman' was powerful; but gentlemen might find themselves privates serving under officers selected by the men for their popular manners rather than for their proper bearing. Privileges were frequently sought by the officer caste, yet they were resented and protested against – sometimes forcibly – by the privates. A 'democratic' approach was appreciated, even expected. An unusually popular general was described in characteristically rustic terms: 'he put me very much in mind of some old farmer, rideing [*sic*] around hunting up some stray cattle and couldnt [*sic*] find them. He is ... very attentive to any request a private may make of him' (Wiley 1943: 241). If the ordinary Confederate believed implicitly, indeed powerfully, in his cause, his willingness to fight and endure was conditional upon the maintenance of his self-respect. Social deference and officious discipline drew vigorous, sometimes direct, criticism and abuse. But such a response suggested also that the 'plain folk' refused to tolerate upper-class pretensions, either because such behaviour was alien to their everyday civilian experience, or because it was inconsistent with the sacrifices they were making in military service.

Wars – and especially great patriotic wars – generate their own momentum. The Confederates' determination to struggle through a conflict of world historical importance for four years and against overwhelming odds grew partly at least from the very march of events; blood-sacrifice begot blood-sacrifice. Yet the experience of war reflected also upon the Southern whites' experiences of peace. The section was indeed a South of many Souths. It contained counties which boasted the highest per capita wealth in America; but it was a by-word for rural backwardness, illiteracy, economic blight and persistent brutality employed against the slaves. It was a section devoted to agriculture, yet dependent upon world capitalist markets. Its country people were evangelical Protestants; yet its cities derived much of their religion and culture from Catholic forebears. Its political leaders declared their devotion to conservative constitutional and social principles, while pressing for ever more territorial expansion as a requirement of social mobility and while representing one of the world's few democracies. Some planters privately deplored the passing of an eighteenth-century gentry order at the very time that Northerners condemned the South for its subservience to an anachronistic Slave Power. And so the catalogue could continue. But, paying all due regard to these internal contrasts and tensions – contrasts and tensions indicating dynamism and potential rather than imminent collapse – the Confederate cause evoked a response of such bloody magnitude as requires some exploration of the social bonds that held whites together; and made the 'South' a potent rallying point in the face of numerous centrifugal and particularist loyalties and interests pulling Southerners apart.

Chapter two

COTTON

I

Cotton in the nineteenth century was almost a code-word, a short-hand for Southern economic endeavour. When Senator James H. Hammond boasted of the South's special place in the world and of Britain's dependence on the South, he encapsulated his argument in the simple boast, 'Cotton is King!' The Cotton Kingdom was a commonplace soubriquet for the Lower South. And the cotton field in blossoming crop, dotted with bending black slaves, and set in the foreground of a columned planter mansion has become a familiar and supposedly representative image of the antebellum South. Yet cotton was not the be-all and end-all of the section. Most cotton farms and perhaps virtually all cotton plantations were self-sufficient in food, the leading food-crops being corn, beans and sweet potatoes, and the corn being used to fatten pigs as well as sustain people. Moreover, large areas of the slave South grew very little cotton; this was peculiarly the case in the upper slave states of Missouri, Kentucky, North Carolina, Virginia, Maryland and Delaware. Alternative cash crops – notably hemp and tobacco – were raised there with slave labour; and much attention was devoted to wheat, general farming and herding (Lee and Passell 1979: 154–61). Even so, for large areas of the South, cotton was the prime source of income and the talisman of prosperity. Strong British demand for raw cotton stimulated the quest for a technique by which upland cotton could be processed speedily; Whitney's cotton gin of 1793 was the product of that quest and enabled upland cotton to be grown readily throughout most of the Lower South. Fast expanding world demand in the period 1830–60 underlay the further geographical spread of cotton cultivation, while the capacious availability of suitable lands brought that spread about. By the 1850s, raising cotton was widespread. At one end of the scale, cotton plantations were profitable, perhaps quite handsomely so; at the other end, non-slaveholding farmers from the most fertile soils of Georgia to the hill and valley country of Arkansas grew some cotton as a cash crop. Cotton was a ubiquitous symbol of the South.

It was, of course, more than just a symbol. Raw cotton dominated US exporting. After the War of 1812, it accounted for about one-third, varying from year to year, of the total value of American exports. By the mid-1830s that proportion had risen to about half, and remained there, again allowing for occasional variations, throughout the 1840s and 1850s. In 1850, for instance, cotton exports were worth $72 million while total exports earned $144.4 million; in 1860 these totals were $191.8 million and $333.6 million respectively. Tobacco was the next leading export commodity in the 1820s and 1830s, though it trailed a long way behind cotton in value. During the 1840s and 1850s raw tobacco exports rose substantially in actual value, but they were pushed into third place in the pecking order of principal exports by wheat flour (North 1966: 233). Southern claims, and notably the claims of market-orientated cotton and tobacco planters, to furnish the key staples for America's overseas commerce, and the wherewithal allowing America to import manufactured goods and, for example, iron rails, tallied with the statistics displayed in the commercial record. Moreover, cotton loomed as large in the national economy as it did in Southern consciousness. The country's gross national product in 1860 may have been about $4,000 millions; if that is a true estimate, then cotton exports alone accounted for about 5 per cent of total economic output. Another comparison is perhaps even more instructive. In 1859, total taxes raised in all the slave states, except for tiny and marginal Delaware, were $24.4 million; this was the total gleaned by state, county, municipal, school and other taxing authorities. For the whole nation such state and local taxes brought in $93.7 millions (*Statistics* 1866: 511). Raw cotton exports alone in 1859 fetched $161.4 million, so dwarfing the business of all state and local government operations combined. Perhaps not surprisingly, cotton, important only from the 1790s, was the wonder crop of America, the pride of Southerners, and, according to those who raised and marketed it, the key to their country's commercial place in the world.

If the Cotton Kingdom looked across the Atlantic for its source of growing income, it reached across the Appalachians for its source of continuing supply. The flow of settlers to the Western lands showed the general trend. Total white population of the slave states increased from 1,271,488 in 1790 to 6,222,418 in 1850. In 1790 there were scarcely any whites in Alabama, Arkansas, Florida and Tennessee; by 1850 there were 789,940 of them. In 1810 Mississippi territory and Louisiana contained 57,335 whites; by 1850, 551,209 whites inhabited the states of Mississippi and Louisiana. Steadily the Southern population was distributed westwards. If Virginia remained the most populous slave state, it was being hard-pressed in the 1850s by Kentucky, which held only 61,133 whites in 1790 to Virginia's 442,115. Already in 1810, well-established South Carolina was overtaken in white population by frontier Tennessee. The lure of the West was not invariably the lure of cotton lands; sugar in Louisiana and tobacco in Kentucky were other leading crops; and Missouri's white population grew from 17,227 in 1810 to 592,004 in 1850 without the state specializing heavily in cotton (De Bow 1854: 45). But in Tennessee and to the South-west, settlers were attracted principally by fresh lands that could be quickly put under cotton and which would yield large cotton returns. Soil exhaustion in the East was less of a cause of the shift westwards than a consequence of the speedy abandonment of those eastern lands in favour of fresher soils to the West (Wright 1978: 17).

One result of this quest for cotton lands was to attenuate the lines of national communication ever further. Such communications remained important because the South failed to generate a great financial and commercial centre of its own. New York remained essential to the South: as America's main importing point, as the banking hub for the whole country, as the store-house for a host of financial and commercial intelligence, and as the command-post of merchandizing. Yet, in the early 1850s, the most direct mail-route from New York to Charleston was 790 miles long, rather farther than the distance from London to Vienna; from New York to Mobile, Alabama, was 1,476 miles, a few miles short of that from London to Constantinople; and from New York to New Orleans, the principal alternative to the Yankee metropolis in the Deep South, was all of 1,640 miles, longer than the route separating Paris from St Petersburg. And transport routes were sometimes even more daunting. To get goods from Pittsburgh, a major trans-shipment point for the entire western trade, to New Orleans by river transport involved a journey of 2,175 miles, comparable in Europe to the land route from St Petersburg to Madrid (De Bow 1854: 35). While, therefore, the cotton growers of the South-west remained heavily dependent upon the commercial and financial services of New York city, they became, as the Cotton Kingdom spread, increasingly distant from that bloated exchange and mart.

The Cotton Kingdom failed to spawn commercial cities. New Orleans was a major exporting city, through which vast quantities of cotton and wheat from the free states of the northern Mississippi valley poured on their way to Europe. And the city's merchants, factors and bankers offered a host of commercial services to an area extending far beyond the city's hinterland and the state of Louisiana. But, in the Deep South at least, no ports approached New Orleans in size or range of services. The slave states other than Delaware, Maryland (which boasted Baltimore), and Missouri (which contained St Louis), had in 1860 only twenty towns of over 5,000 people. Mississippi, Texas, Arkansas and Florida were devoid of such towns; North Carolina had but one; Alabama, Tennessee and South Carolina had two each. This was an extraordinary dearth, for most of those states were, in land area, on a par with European countries and yet they made do with extremely rudimentary urban services. The typical urban community in much of the South was no more than a village. And even such towns as existed had low sky-lines, spacious lay-outs and styles of housing and architecture that suggested their rural roots and, often, the rural occupations and interests of their inhabitants (Goldfield 1982: 28–36). This feeble urban development resulted largely from the peculiar characteristics of cotton and, less extensively, tobacco. Cotton especially was so bulky as to require river transport and since Southern rivers offered easy lines of access to coastal ports, major internal entrepôts were not generally necessary; interior river ports such as Columbus and Augusta in Georgia were exceptional in their size. As cotton and tobacco were both exported raw, they created fewer domestic processing needs than did Northern wheat; while ginning and baling could be accomplished on plantations without recourse to urban facilities. Moreover, although Southern consumer demand for manufactured goods was not insignificant, the scale of that demand was modified by the fact that one in three Southerners were slaves. Admittedly, slaves had to be clothed, shod, housed, treated medically and fed; but the quality of goods and services provided for them was low. And rural slaves enjoyed very limited, if any, disposable income of their own to stimulate domestic consumer output. Yet, if cotton and slavery in that sense restricted the Southern economy, there was sufficiently strong consumer demand among whites to sustain the cross-roads stores and small village consumer centres, as well as the larger, if rare, towns.

The South was but little involved in manufacturing. It accounted for about 10 per cent of national manufacturing output in both 1850 and 1860. And Southern manufacturing firms were particularly weak in their levels of capitalization and output. The average capital invested in each Southern firm in 1860 was slightly lower than the average invested in equivalent Western firms and much lower than the average in similar establishments in New England. And Southern manufacturing's output per employee was left far behind by even the West's performance in 1850 and 1860; while New England and the middle Atlantic seaboard states attained even higher levels of productivity. The record was not, however, all grim. Western manufacturing was not in character peculiarly more 'advanced' than the South's; for basic food processing played a large role in both sections, and the average number of employees per manufacturing establishment was the same in the two sections in 1860. So, too, there were pockets of Southern manufacturing activity which rivalled those of the mid-West. In 1860, Richmond's per capita manufacturing production was only slightly less than that of Cincinnati, and Richmond and Louisville both surpassed Pittsburgh, Indianapolis and Chicago in per capita industrial output. New Orleans was a large and bustling manufacturing centre in the 1850s (Bateman and Weiss 1981: 16–19, 21–3). But these *were* pockets, not pace-setters. Why this was so has been much discussed.

Suggestions that income was insufficient to generate demand, or was so badly distributed as to skew demand towards luxury goods for a small minority, are not very compelling. Southern income appears to have been adequate to sustain consumer markets; and our knowledge of the distribution of wealth – though less is known of income – shows that while wealth was unequally shared, its apportionment was not markedly more unequal than the wealth distribution in the country at large. Whether or not slavery in itself impeded industrialization is still a matter of very considerable controversy among economic historians. On one side, it can clearly be said that slavery discouraged technical innovation in agriculture and limited 'entrepreneurship'. It also, for social and economic reasons, deterred white immigration from overseas into the South, and so lessened the potential labour supply for factory growth. Productivity gains in cotton cultivation were brought about by physical movement from the 1810s into very fertile lands in the South-east and by increasing concentration on cotton within the overall crop mix (Wright 1978: 102–27). On the other side, it has been urged that some slaves were used in manufacturing. Urban slavery's failure to grow, in relative not absolute numbers, during the 1840s and 1850s owed more to potent demands from the agricultural sector rather than to the inherent incompatibility of slavery with an urban environment. The failure of industrial development did not mean that manufacturing in the South was of necessity unprofitable. It may even have been more profitable than cotton planting, though such comparisons are statistically perilous to draw. Certainly the environment smiled upon manufacturing initiative; capital was available; consumer markets existed; and firms could be set up without fears, generally speaking, of being kept out or elbowed out by large monopolistic enterprises exploiting the special advantages of big economies of scale. What, therefore, ultimately drove Southern entrepreneurs away from further industrial development was not their section's factor endowment or market possibilities, but rather a conscious preference for cotton production. This choice was presumably influenced by the status that was attached to being a planter. But the differences in the rewards accruing to industry and to planters were so modest and unpredictable that social values probably yielded only a marginally 'irrational' effect (Bateman and Weiss 1981: 46–8, 157–63).

The lack of industry and towns attracted contemporary criticism. Many Northerners asserted that this deficiency showed how primitive the cotton economy remained. Some Southern patriots groaned that the Cotton Kingdom depended excessively – even slavishly, a true mark of abject inferiority – upon Northern finance and British markets, and needed to diversify into industry and commerce and thereby acquire greater self-sufficiency. To add to these mid nineteenth-century arguments, twentieth-century economists have asserted that, however profitable plantation slavery may have been to the planters themselves, cotton monoculture or something approaching monoculture retarded the Southern economy in the long term. Such criticisms, old and new alike, tend, however, to be ahistorical: in treating sectional economies in aggregate terms, in erecting excessively clear-cut notions of rational choice, and in portraying present-day ideas of productivity as being applicable to the 1850s and as being separable from contemporary images of industrial society that were far from favourable to the factory order.

Northern critics of the South sought to buttress a case that slavery in itself, being a moral wrong, brought also economic devastation in its wake. At the opposite extreme, Southern separatists were preparing their section for economic as well as political independence rather than disinterestedly describing the prevailing order. And late twentieth-century economists have conceded that, in the period 1830–60, Southern economic choices were rational, although they hasten to add that cotton culture made no economic sense by the 1880s.

More generally, though, the national and international division of labour which maintained the South as a mass producer of cotton was premised upon assumptions about American national integrity and the persistence of British free trade which were logical and historically valid in the 1850s. Although hindsight may make us look at the 1850s in terms of impending disaster and sectional fissure, few people at the time consistently believed the country would be torn apart. Even the argument over Southern political rights in the territories was conducted in a context where Southern victory seemed probable until 1858–60. It was not really until Senator Stephen A. Douglas's rebellion against the Buchanan Administration in 1858 and the further confirmation of his dissent in 1859–60 that a sectional disruption appeared likely. A national division of labour was far from being illogical in the 1850s. So, too, international economics vindicated Southern monoculture. British free trade was much extended in the early and middle 1840s, and in 1854 inspired an agreement concerning reciprocal free trade in raw materials between British North America and the USA. The latter continued to impose duties on imported (including British) manufactured goods and on raw materials other than the products of British North America. But the British themselves showed no signs of wavering in their commitment to international free trade, which, in turn, offered easy and expanding markets for American raw produce.

In addition, modern economists regard the rush to industrialize and urbanize as the obvious road to sustained economic growth and prosperity. This, again, may in the long view be the case. But primary producing countries have historically enjoyed considerable and quite long-sustained economic success, and the building of cities and industries has not always appeared as the most socially attractive option. In the 1850s industrialization's side effects were commonly described as unpleasant and unacceptable. Some Southern writers eagerly recounted such attendant horrors of industrial cities as burgeoning crime, overcrowded housing, heavy pauperism, high prostitution and corrupt, boss-ridden politics. Any outbreak of crowd violence or minor riot, any occurrence of political jobbery, any egregious example of distress or debauchery in New York or Philadelphia was swiftly enlisted by Southern newspapers in an implicit but persistent war of images upon industrial, urban culture. New York and Philadelphia may have been grossly unrepresentative, and the incidents and images chosen may have been crudely exaggerated, but the effect was to reduce the apparent wisdom of encouraging industrial or major urban growth. The social costs of British and Northern industrial specialization made the British path to 'modernity' look a rough and inhumane one.

The establishment of an industrial order even in Britain and certainly in the North was both more recent in the 1850s and more precarious than hindsight makes it seem. Prominent industrial areas existed in late eighteenth-century Britain, but an industrial economy did not prevail until the 1810s or even later. Northern industrialization chugged on at a low level until the 1830s, and did not stretch much beyond eastern Pennsylvania, New York city's conurbation and Rhode Island and eastern Massachusetts in the 1850s. And the international financial and industrial system of the early and mid nineteenth century was often described by contemporary economic theorists as highly unstable, liable to periodic panics and crashes; for Marx, it was vulnerable to sudden and complete collapse. One irony of the 1850s was that Marx argued that industrial capitalism would be hastened to its doom by such self-inflicted traumas as the panic of 1857 (Merrington 1975: 91–2); whereas Marxist historians write of the impending triumph of capitalism and the conservative folly of Southerners' commitment to a dated and increasingly inefficient mode of agrarianism. The general point is that economic life and the contrasts and apparent choices it offered were less simple than they are sometimes made out to have been. Strong regional economic specialization both within the USA and in trans-Atlantic exchanges made good sense. And the inevitability and social desirability of Southern industrialization and urbanization were not as clear then as they have since become.

Southerners' affair with cotton in the two generations before 1860 had both conservative and innovative repercussions. It locked the section into an agricultural life that was familiar and familial. It reduced some of the risks that might have accompanied diversification into industry. Industrial work-forces' dependence upon wages alone and city-dwellers' vulnerability to the cycle of boom and bust were deeply impressed upon Southerners by the financial crashes of 1837, 1839 and 1857. Banking came to be viewed virtually as the Devil's work in the South-west during the 1840s; and that distrust of banks and finance capital lingered into the 1850s. Rural folk, while not immune to such swings in international trade, were at least able, if they retained their farms in periods of rising indebtedness, to fall back upon their land for sustenance.

Yet if cotton culture severely limited technological innovation and economic diversity, that culture was not equated with risk-avoidance and peasant traditionalism. The search for cotton lands from the 1790s settled Southerners in places their parents had scarcely dreamed of; it threw them into a ferment of land evaluation, trading and speculation which was very far from being risk-free. Cotton-growing itself demanded hard labour and marketing involved close attention to ever shifting prices. Small farmers had further to judge the 'right' mix of crops for their family farms. Communities had to be built from scratch. Sometimes, in the early days, Indians had to be combatted and removed, or at least closely watched. Transport routes had to be selected and made good and small forwarding river ports and marketing centres – scarcely worthy of being designated towns – laid down. The sheer volume of the increase in cotton output down to 1860 – from 10,000 bales in 1793 to 5,387,000 in 1859 – and the demands it made upon factors, carriers, merchants and shippers further intensified the sense of dynamism and fluidity in the South as a whole, and especially in the South beyond the eastern seaboard, throughout the first sixty years of the nineteenth century. What from the James River manor-houses or Charleston Battery's drawing-rooms looked like stale replication of established farming ways; what from the Beacon Hill library looked like frontier shiftlessness and money-making without a thought for morality or to-morrow; what from the stern equations and bleak graphs of the modern development economist looked like socially conditioned agricultural inertia; was at the time something of an odyssey and an adventure, and one far from being devoid of risk, responsiveness to market conditions, and carefully anticipated reward.

II

Cotton made the South a far more concentratedly agricultural section than any other part of the country. When one takes into account the occupations of blacks and whites together, the labour force was overwhelmingly devoted to agriculture and to such support functions as transport. Yet if one considers the free population alone and regards the slaves as property held by whites rather than as autonomous actors in Southern society, then the distorting effect of cotton upon the Southern economy is less obvious. Overall distribution of wealth North and South was broadly similar; although *agricultural* wealth alone was more heavily placed in the top wealth-holders' hands in the South than it was in the North, total wealth has to be considered because the Northern rich were urban financiers, real-estate dealers, lawyers and businessmen. Furthermore, the Southern occupational profile was not strikingly dissimilar from that of the mid-West.

A convenient way of comparing employment is to take the leading occupational categories and note what proportion of the labour force belonged to them. The principal callings were farmers, labourers, farm labourers and servants. For the South, a few groups are added to give a full picture of the weight of these basic occupations. Planters are added to farmers, not least because the distinction was not consistently adhered to in the census returns. Domestics are added, where they infrequently appear, to servants. And overseers are included among the South's basic occupations definition since they fell somewhere between farmers and farm labourers in the agrarian order. Not all these occupations are necessarily rural; labourers and servants in the free population could work in villages and towns. But lumping these principal jobs together gives a good measure of the agricultural and unskilled (these terms are not meant to be synonymous) occupations as part of the total pattern of employment. (*Population* 1864: passim)

As shown in Table 1, the census-takers in 1860 were told that from 62 to 79 per cent of respondents in twelve of the fifteen slave states were engaged in agricultural or basic occupations. Only in Louisiana (48.2%), Maryland (49.5%) and Delaware (56.8%) was the occupational structure more diverse; this resulted, in Louisiana and Maryland, from the urban occupations of New Orleans and Baltimore; while Delaware was a very marginal slave state. Elsewhere, other skilled and 'urban' jobs were related to the preoccupations of cotton culture. In Alabama, for instance, the main occupations after the basic ones already listed were clerks, merchants, carpenters, teachers, mechanics, physicians and blacksmiths. In Georgia, the next leading jobs were clerks, carpenters, merchants and, unusually, factory hands and seamstresses; the last two categories commanded modest numbers. Clerks and merchants, the employees and operators of small stores as well as offices, obviously served the cotton economy as they plied their trade in cross-roads villages and market towns.

There are a number of considerations raised by this employment profile. How peculiarly Southern was it? How far was it distorted by plantation specialization? And does it not disguise an important functional interplay between farmers and planters by lumping the two together?

A simple comparison may help answer the first query. The fact that 62–79 per cent of those employed were in agricultural and basic callings was not distinctively Southern. The seven states of the lower South – excluding Louisiana – displayed the full range of variation in their occupational profiles, from Florida's 62.6 per cent to Arkansas's

78.5 per cent. In size and 'representativeness', Texas's 69.3 per cent, Georgia's 71.3 per cent, Alabama's 73.5 per cent and Mississippi's 73.8 per cent probably offer the best guides to the occupational specialization of the Cotton Kingdom. To assess the typicality of this profile, let us take six selected free states. Together these free states had 1,740,371 people listed as employed, to the lower South's 681,336. Of the free state sample, Iowa, Wisconsin and Michigan were in the upper tier of Northern states, not much settled by migrants of Southern birth. In 1860, 73.4 per cent of Iowa's work-force, 71 per cent of Wisconsin's and 69.5 per cent of Michigan's were in the four agricultural and 'basic' categories of farmers, labourers, farm labourers and servants; obviously, planters and overseers did not appear in the returns for those states. Rather more mixed in their people's regional provenance, indeed just across the Ohio river from border slave states, were Indiana and Ohio. These two states contained people of Southern origins, and neither was militantly anti-Southern in politics in the late 1850s. But

TABLE 1. Employment in the Southern States, 1860

	Total number of those in occupations	Percentage in basic farming and labouring categories	Percentage farmers and planters
More 'urbanized'			
Maryland	177,691	49.5	16.3
Louisiana	107,498	48.2	20.0
Upper South			
Missouri	299,701	68.3	41.7
Kentucky	257,218	70.5	43.1
Tennessee	215,887	74.6	48.1
North Carolina	192,674	75.6	44.2
Virginia	297,354	67.3	36.7
Delaware	36,104	56.8	20.2
Lower South			
Arkansas	85,001	78.5	57.5
Texas	105,491	69.3	49.1
Mississippi	93,298	73.8	53.0
Alabama	137,419	73.5	49.3
Florida	21,982	62.6	39.6
Georgia	156,514	71.3	45.1
South Carolina	81,631	65.7	46.1

Note: The basic farming and labouring categories are: farmers, farm labourers, labourers, overseers, planters and servants (domestics also sometimes separately entered).

both were self-evidently free states and Ohio boasted a number of cities and some industry. Yet 73.6 per cent of Indiana's working population and 63.9 per cent of Ohio's were in the agricultural and 'basic' sectors. Finally, just to show that even in New England, where Massachusetts, Rhode Island and Connecticut were markedly urbanized, there were some significantly rural areas, one might note that 70.9 per cent of Vermont's 100,318 people at work in 1860 were in agriculture and 'basic' jobs. These six free states thus displayed an occupational profile similar to that for the free population of most of the Deep South. Obviously, there were heavily populated Northern states – the three New England states just mentioned, New York, New Jersey and Pennsylvania – where the distribution of jobs was very different. But the point here is that the agricultural West generated a profile similar to the Deep South's; cotton did not peculiarly distort the pattern of free employment.

Grouping the leading occupations together might, however, create two further imbalances. It does not differentiate between those who were farmers (and planters) and those who were mere labourers and servants. Nor does it help define the socio-economic relationship between ordinary farmers and the more wealthy planters. Only in Iowa and Indiana did the proportion of farmers among those at work fall within the range, from 45 to 53 per cent, most common in the Deep South. Farmers constituted a much lower 34.6 per cent of Ohio's work force, 37.4 per cent of Michigan's, 38.8 per cent of Vermont's and 40.2 per cent of Wisconsin's. Such proportions were similar to that obtaining in Virginia, but not elsewhere, in the non-urbanized states of the cotton or plantation South. This fact can be interpreted in various ways. It could mean, simply, that a higher proportion of labourers and servants in the mid-West indicated a bigger urban population. It could mean that Southerners were more conscious of status than were Northerners, with farm labourers tending to promote themselves into farmers in the census returns; but we know that this sort of thing happened North *and* South. It could also suggest that there was *some* basis (though not an especially broad one) for the distinction drawn between Southern whites and Northern whites on the grounds that the latter laboured at menial and manual tasks deemed unfit for white people to tackle in the South. But what it also indicates is that cotton culture did not pinch white opportunities or reduce ordinary whites to dependency upon planters.

Approximately 45 per cent of the free working population of the lower South were farmers; from other sources it seems that about 70 per cent of farmers owned their own land (Clark 1971: 27–9). Roughly one-third of the work-force, then, were owner-occupier farmers. Such a figure becomes especially impressive when it is further emphasized that in the twelve slave states excluding Louisiana, Maryland and Delaware, only 5 per cent (Arkansas) to 9.6 per cent (Virginia) of whites were aged fifty years or more, while from 53.8 per cent (Virginia) to 60 per cent (Arkansas) of whites were under twenty years old (De Bow 1854: 51).

Thus the proportion of those well into middle age, when wealth-holding was likely to be most common, was low, whereas the proportion of young people, who entered the work-force in their mid or late teens, was very high. Since the age of marriage for men tended to be in their mid-twenties, there is good reason to suppose that many white farm labourers were sons of farmers, young, unmarried and working their way gradually to farm ownership. In this way, the occupation figures, though crude and aggregated, do not supply any prima-facie case for arguing that cotton deprived whites of opportunities.

It is possible, however, that planters were in very real economic functions and responsibilities distinguished from plain farmers. From the eighteenth century large plantations became, in function if not in fact, virtual villages in themselves. Wealthy planters acted as informal local bankers providing credits to their poorer neighbours; they acted as collecting agents for small farmers sending small quantities of cotton to market; they furnished cotton ginning, flour milling and other processing facilities to the rural community; and those qualified to do so probably offered legal advice as well. It was not uncommon for a planter to engage a tutor whose 'classes' would then be attended by neighbouring families' offspring, so that the costs would be widely shared. For these reasons, a wealthy planter was not simply an agrarian; nor would farmers and planters necessarily sit comfortably together as co-equals.

Yet, despite the obvious influence which a multiplicity of economic roles gave rich planters, the extent of planter control should not be exaggerated. For one thing, there were not that many big plantations. And wealthy planters customarily spread their assets around, holding substantial plantations in various counties and even in various states; in so dispersing their potential economic risks, they also diluted their potential social power. Moreover, there were practical limits to the interdependence of plantation and small farm. It was at one time argued by historians that plantations specialized so thoroughly in cotton growing as to rely on smaller farms or the mid-West for their food supplies. It seems, however, that plantations as a rule aimed at, and very largely achieved, self-sufficiency in food-stuffs, partly because the fullest utilization of slave labour throughout the agricultural year encouraged the cultivation of more crops than just cotton. On their side, small farmers, when they wanted to raise cash, turned to cotton for distant markets rather than to food for nearby planters. While some economies of scale made large plantations more efficient in cotton output, those economies were not so great or so glaring as to create a patchwork agricultural order of cotton factories of the field jumbled together with mixed small farms. Professor Wright has estimated that in the Cotton South – an area defined, broadly, as that south of Virginia, Kentucky and Missouri – some 48 per cent of the population were slaves, some 50 per cent of farms were without slaves, yet only 28 per cent of farms grew no cotton. Slaveless farmers and planters, with some variations for the quality of the soils and soil types, lived together in such fashion that 'It is some exaggeration, but not much, to say that the Cotton South was like a stick of Brighton Rock – bite it off anywhere and the character of the economic cross-section was much the same' (Wright 1978: 18–9, 23–4).

The facts that even the richest planters did not concentrate their land and slave holdings into huge estates; that land-ownership among farmers was the norm and that farmers formed easily the biggest occupational group in the South; that plantations and farms both strove to be self-sufficient in food and were not bound together in cloying interdependence; that cotton production was widespread and access to markets open; and that physical mobility militated against the creation of very fixed social ties subordinating farmers to planters all show that it would be misleadingly simplistic to equate cotton cultivation solely with plantation society or with a planter-dominated white order.

III

So far we have assumed that cotton culture affected whites in generally similar ways even if not in precisely similar degrees. There were in fact areas very largely untouched or but lightly touched by the mania for cotton. Herding remained a mainstay of life in considerable, if sparsely populated, areas of the upland and less fertile country. When J. F. H. Claiborne visited the piney woods of southern Mississippi in the early 1840s he found communities which had minimal contacts with the outside world; they failed even to elect officials to operate the skeletal frame of county government (Claiborne 1906: 487–538). More elaborately, Professor Hahn has argued that yeomen farmers of Georgia's upper piedmont country consciously eschewed market transactions, adopted 'habits of mutuality' – by co-operating together in log-rollings, house-raisings and corn-shuckings – and refused to be drawn into 'the economic and cultural orbit of the planter class'. Unlike yeomen farmers of the cotton belt, the yeomen of the upper piedmont only occasionally bothered to grow cotton in order to secure ready cash. In general, they 'scorned accumulation for speculative purposes', and distrusted 'unbridled competition and the excesses of a market controlled in the interests of a few'; instead, they 'stressed co-operation and the common good' (Hahn 1982: 33–39). Cotton, allegedly, was not quite the common symbol of profit we have made it out to have been.

Yet the case for anti-commercialism is in fact a weak one. Professor Hahn himself admits that, in one of his upland piedmont counties, 'farmers who persisted from one census year to the next occasionally acquired additional land and perhaps a slave or two': is this not accumulation or at least competitive enterprise? We are not told why those yeomen farmers who did not persist from 1850 to 1860 moved away; could they have sought better and more lands elsewhere? Nor are we given much evidence of the thoughts of the yeomen themselves. To raise some sensible manifestations of community co-operation into a fully fledged belief-system not only goes beyond the immediate evidence. It creates a false contrast with a commercial agriculture which, we are left to deduce, was carried on by market-dominated, profit-motivated, property-fixated, and compulsively individualistic planters and small farmers who had swallowed the planters' ethos and values. Again, in conceding that some of his yeomen farmers increased their holdings from 1850 to 1860 and even perhaps acquired a slave or two, Hahn immediately adds 'but virtually none did well enough to cross class lines and become planters' (Hahn 1982: 42–4). Yet the notion of 'class lines' that could be 'crossed' makes something altogether too rigid of differences in wealth and status which were usually elusive and shaded. Finally, accounts of the alleged 'alternatives' to commercialization do not spell out how many Southerners opted out of the market system. Wright argued, for the Cotton South, that only 28 per cent of farms did not grow cotton (Wright 1978: 18–19). And the failure to grow cotton may have been as much the result of a need to concentrate on food-stuffs, of a lack of sufficient land, or of inadequate labour, as the product of an anti-commercial ideology. Even for the upper piedmont, we remain ill-informed as to the number of yeomen who stayed put in this non-market setting.

Cotton created its own 'habits of mutuality' as well as stimulating the expansion of the entire Southern economy. A study of a large region in the hinterland of Augusta, Georgia, shows that nine-tenths of all farms had fewer than 500 improved acres and about four-tenths had fewer than 100 improved acres. Such farms grew corn and raised hogs as well as producing cotton for market. But cotton cultivation offered whites a community of interests. Small farmers and great planters alike shared the annual routine of preparing their land, planting, ploughing, hoeing, picking, ginning and baling. Planters remained immersed in the details of cotton production; they provided ginning and marketing services and advice to their neighbours. Slave labour may have been hired out for some purposes. Such services could be described as merely profitable. But, equally plausibly, they could be placed within a pattern of social relationships shaped also by churches, political parties and extended kinship. Only by segregating 'planters' as a separate (and poorly defined) class is this pattern overlooked. Cotton cultivation created a common interest in price trends, in trans-shipment possibilities, in crop types and diseases, in the weather (which made the farmer's life 'an emotional roller coaster'), and in prospects for finding and opening new lands to cotton (Harris 1981: 12, 17, 22–4). Southern commercial agriculture was a complex world of activity and discussion, participation in which was, even if at a modest level, extremely widespread. Instead of erecting contrasts between co-operative hill-country yeomen and aggressively competitive cotton-belt farmers and planters, perhaps one should recall the Principle of Self-Interest Rightly Understood; that principle, according to Tocqueville, guided Americans into restraining their individualism and joining together to advance their mutual interests. It seems to have been a principle applicable to cotton belt entrepreneurs and piedmont yeomen alike.

How, then, are we to strike a judicious balance in considering the Cotton Kingdom? Some characteristics were distinctive: the large numbers of enslaved field-hands; the use of a small and much abused cadre of overseers; the sheer volume, bulk and value of the cash crop; the greater average improved acreage per farm (97 for the slave states generally and 130 for the Cotton South) as compared with 69 in the free states (Wright 1978: 52); and the existence of substantial plantations whose land and slaves represented huge capital outlays. Yet, if cotton made prominent fortunes and brought mass-production methods to select fields, it did not squeeze small farmers out, or necessarily require slave labour, or concentrate slave-holdings only in planters' hands. Instead, as it carried Southerners across the Appalachians and beyond the Mississippi, cotton helped keep white society fluid, mobile, enterprising, as well as drawn together by mutual commercial interests and racial pride. It set the annual time-table of agricultural events, shaped the distribution and use of land and underpinned the cash economy. Not without reason has it come down to us as the ubiquitous symbol of the antebellum South.

Chapter three

INDIANS

I

Extensive access to land – be it for plantations or modest family farms – forced Southerners from the 1610s to the 1830s into a predatory relationship with the Indians. Indeed, the fundamental social requirements of Southern agriculture created demands for land and labour which impelled whites to seize the first from the aboriginal inhabitants and to extract the second from imported Africans. By the 1850s, of course, the Indians had been cleared from the vast region to the east of the Mississippi and the relationship between whites and blacks was the dominant element in Southern racial thinking. Yet, if we are to understand the making of Southern whites' consciousness and the forging of a Southern white identity, it is worth pausing to consider the Indians' impact upon whites. For not only had whites experienced two centuries of conflict with the Indians up to the 1830s, an important enough legacy in itself; whites living in the Deep South continued to feel an Indian presence, and sometimes an Indian threat, until the 1830s and early 1840s. Whites over forty years of age in much of the Deep South in 1860 retained a living memory of the 200 years' struggle for the lands of their region. This was an experience largely alien to the North, where the Indian frontier was far more limited and far less populous than the Deep South's in the 1830s. The survival of the five so-called 'Civilized Nations', of Cherokees, Chickasaws, Choctaws, Creeks and Seminoles in the Deep South strengthened the whites' sense of race mission and their contempt for the blacks, gave them a political cause – Indian removal – in the late 1820s and early 1830s, and stiffened both their state pride and their military ardour. The Southern Indians thus offered, as a negative reference group, a multifaceted legacy to the generation that was to embark in 1860–1 upon secession and war.

For many decades, the Indians have been the invisible people of Southern history. Although their place-names have remained as the descriptive labels for towns, rivers and states alike, and although there has long been an interest in their very early history and the archaeology of their pre-historic settlements, the Indians' role in the nineteenth-century South has, until very recently, been largely ignored by writers of 'mainstream' Southern history. Those three volumes of the *History of the South* published by Louisiana State University Press which deal with the years 1789–1861 scarcely mention Indians at all (Abernethy 1961; Sydnor 1948; Craven 1953); and Clement Eaton's *The Growth of Southern Civilization 1790–1860* refers fleetingly to the Indians on a couple of pages. These omissions are surprising. Admittedly, the Indians were already by 1790 the least numerous of the three broad racial groups – whites, blacks and reds – living in the South. Perhaps only 100,000 or so of them inhabited the South east of the Mississippi compared with 690,000 blacks and over one and a quarter million whites. But the Indians were widely distributed across the land, taking as their terrain an expanse of territory and hunting ground far, far greater than their relative numbers would indicate and, as it was to transpire, far, far greater than they were able to hold against white rapacity and land hunger. Yet, despite the weakness of their grasp, the Indians were squeezed out of their lands east of the Mississippi only gradually and only with difficulty.

Eighteenth-century gradualism continued into the early nineteenth century. In 1796, Tennessee, for instance, still had three-quarters of its land area claimed by Cherokees and Chickasaws. A series of treaties in 1798, 1805, 1806, 1817, 1818 and 1819 ceded the overwhelming bulk of that land to white settlement. The Chickasaw Purchase of 1818, for example, opened the western quarter of Tennessee and the entire area bordering on the Mississippi river to formal white ownership. After 1819, only a small area of south-eastern Tennessee, a mountainous corner, was left in Indian hands (Folmsbee *et al* 1969: 145–7). Farther south and even to the east, the Indian nations remained reasonably intact until the great years of removal, 1826–38. Between 1826 and 1836 about 40,000 Indians – including 18,000 Creeks, 15,000 Choctaws and 6,000 Cherokees – were removed from their homes east of the Mississippi to the west (Schoolcraft 1851: 377). In 1838 the forced removal of 16,500 Cherokees to what is now western Arkansas and eastern Oklahoma, began to be completed in 1839. At the same time, in 1838, the first phase of the Second Seminole War was concluded to the disadvantage of that people, whose nation was finally broken in 1842. Together with the final assault of 1838–42 in Florida, the removals of 1826–38 turned Georgia, Florida, Alabama and Mississippi from being states at least one-third or half 'Indian' into states fully open to white settlement. Yet, if an era of Southern history drew to a close, its influence was to endure.

II

Indians contributed to whites' notions of racial hierarchies and of blacks' inferiority. It cannot be said that Southern whites afforded much deference to Indian susceptibilities. They tended to lump them all together; the name Indian was itself an alien designation concocted by Europeans (Berkhofer 1978: 3, 15–20, 26–9). They blamed tribes for the misdeeds committed by outcast or renegade individuals, and ignored the limited nature of much Indian warfare, which emphasized the avenging of particular wrongs or atrocities rather than the execution of large-scale or long-sustained campaigns (Reid 1979: 33–4, 38; Perdue 1979: 111–12). They gave little practical expression to the eighteenth-century drawing-room cult of 'primitivism', the idea that a 'savage' or 'primitive' society was, by virtue of its closer contact with the 'natural' world, morally superior to more civilized societies. And, being themselves so physically mobile and so little fixed geographically, whites disregarded Indians' religious, mythological and tribal attachment to their surroundings and treated them as being far more nomadic than they truly were.

Even so, the Indians won a degree of grudging regard from whites which exceeded that given to the blacks and which served to accentuate black inferiority. Although slaves mounted a few spectacular uprisings in the period 1790–1840, blacks' resistance to whites was always infinitely greater in prospect than in actuality. In contrast, Indians had to be kept down by properly organized and often considerable force. Innumerable local expeditions embodied hundreds of militia troops. The battle at which the largest number of Indians fought and were killed was Horseshoe Bend, in Alabama in March 1814, where 1,000 Creeks were defeated by 1,400 whites and 600 Cherokee and Creek allies under Jackson. In all, Jackson commanded about 2,600 white troops in the Creek campaign (Rogin 1976: 156). Such forces were far from being insignificant; as a comparative yardstick, Jackson's army at the battle of New Orleans against the British was a hastily assembled and highly assorted crowd of 5,000 men (Williams 1981: 132). And the Second Seminole War of 1835–42 cost $30 millions, 1,500 'American' lives, and the services, at one time or another, of 30,000 militiamen and volunteers (Williams 1981: 142).

This long record of formal confrontation elicited a respect for the Indians never paralleled by any similar respect for blacks. The romantic and historical novels of William Gilmore Simms, pre-eminent among the South's indigenous antebellum fiction, well illustrated this difference in status. To an extent, Simms, writing from the 1830s, was simply following the literary example set by Sir Walter Scott in describing historical events which combined elements of warfare and of culture clash between one civilization on the decline and another progressing to an assured and prosperous destiny. Just as Scott dealt with the contest between Highland clans and the more individualistic, urban and entrepreneurial Lowlanders of eighteenth-century Scotland, so Simms, when he was not writing of the Revolutionary Wars, described – sometimes with sympathetic understanding – the Indians' demise as a potent force in North American affairs. The novel *The Yemassee* (1835) recounted the story of that important South Carolina nation's humiliating and thorough defeat in 1715. Simms, condescendingly no doubt, put the following thought into the head of one Yemassee chief, Sanutee:

> It is in the nature of civilisation to own an appetite for dominion and extended sway, which the world that is known will always fail to satisfy. It is for her, then, to seek and create ... Conquest and sway are the great leading principles of her existence, and the savage must join in her train, or she rides over him relentlessly in her onward progress.

While this description offers no very subtle insight into an Indian leader's thinking, Simms acknowledged that Sanutee's determination not to yield 'the territory of his forefathers without further struggle' was an honourable one. The Yemassee themselves were worthy of more general respect. 'They were politic and brave – a generous and gallant race'; indeed they formed 'something of a republic' (Simms 1964: 29, 39, 92, 107). Given their moderately advanced social and political development, the Yemassee's perception of growing white contempt and high-handedness drew a sympathy to these Indians far exceeding any white sympathy for the supposedly passive and uninteresting black slaves.

Indians contrasted with blacks in other respects. One Southern writer confidently declared a widely held belief that the Indian's mind 'is superior to that of the negro' (Mills 1826: 113–15, 119–20). Marriage with Indians, while hardly condoned, did not draw upon whites such obloquy as intermarriage with blacks attracted. Indeed, intermarriage between frontier whites and Indian women flourished, with the bizarre consequence that one meets men such as Alexander McGillivray as a late eighteenth-century Creek chief. When a census was taken of the Cherokee nation in 1835, some 17 per cent of Cherokees had white ancestors. Indians' status was even further buttressed by their involvement in slaveowning; some 8 per cent of Cherokee household heads were slaveowners in 1835, though it must be admitted that the Cherokees were exceptional even among the five 'civilized nations' for their permanent settlements and their advanced political organization (Perdue 1979: 115–18; Persico 1979: 92–109).

If Indians were deemed to be less inferior than blacks, they were still subject to high-handed and at times brutal treatment. This was especially true of the years 1826–38 when Southern whites came together to enforce the removal of the last human impediments to white agricultural settlement east of the Mississippi. Removal was an almost inevitable alternative to extinction. As Washington wrote in 1796, 'scarcely any thing short of a Chinese Wall, or a line of Troops' would keep whites off Indian lands (Sheehan 1973: 268–9). A Democratic congressman told President Van Buren in November, 1837, 'the country people in the new states waking or sleeping or working never think of anything but "Land"' (Young 1961: 186–7). Uncontrollable white permeation into tribal lands merely demoralized the Indians. By the late 1820s, Thomas L. McKenny, the head of the Indian Office within the War Department, rationalized removal from the Deep South partly on the grounds that such a course offered the only mode of tribal salvation. Of the Creeks he wrote in 1829, 'There is no sketching that can convey a clear perception of the misery and degradation in which this tribe is involved. If ever mercy pleaded, it pleads now ... to get these to their fertile Country West of Arkansas' (Sheehan 1973: 3–11, 250–4).

In various ways, removal was depicted as part of the quest for an enlightened policy to deal with the Indians. It was promoted as a humane measure in the Indians' best interests. It was also advocated as a means of combating frontier vice. In January, 1828, Mississippi's General Assembly petitioned Congress, urging federal removal of Indians within the state:

> a large portion of the most valuable territory within the chartered limits
> of this State is occupied by savage tribes intersperced [*sic*] with
> disorderly whites whose vicious and intemperate habits give the example,
> and afford the facility of indulging in intoxicating Liquors, a practice
> rapidly extinguishing their numbers, and entirely hostile to the progress
> of Civilization.

Mississippi's legislators suggested that the federal government remove the disorderly whites and enter negotiations with the tribes for Indian removal to 'a region more congenial to their nature', and remote from 'the influence of vicious example'. This comment not only displayed underlying racial prejudices, but also proffered, for the first time in Mississippi's legislature records of the 1820s, an 'official' comment on intemperance as such. In making that connection between Indian depravity and white frontier immorality, the legislators also linked the cause of general improvement – the sweeping aside of frontier irregularities, misconduct and uncertainties – with Indian removal (Memorial passed 21 Jan. 1828: RG 47 Legisl. vol. 19 MDAH).

These comments suggest why the removal of the remaining Indians from the Deep South in 1826–38 united whites. Respectable opinion sought a long-term solution to the problem of preserving the surviving nations, while ridding the states of messy and perhaps immoral frontier conditions. Some of the 'roughs' engaged in creating those conditions had every reason to welcome removal as an opening to advantageous land speculation. And land-hungry Southerners of all types cast greedy eyes upon the tribal domains. Even a nation that did not 'degenerate' was the object, from 1828, of a fierce campaign for removal. The elaboration of a more formal Cherokee system of government, the consolidation of Cherokee villages, the spread of slaveownership among wealthier Cherokees and the founding of a Cherokee newspaper printed in the Cherokee language fuelled Georgians' appetites for the Cherokees' patrimony rather than encouraged thoughts of a local condominion between red and white states as the Indians desired (Davis 1979: 129–44).

Although it has been argued that Indian expulsion reflected not the wishes of the Southern plain folk but the designs of the wealthier land speculators and their political allies (Rogin 1976: 220–1), white Southerners' support for the chief Indian remover, Andrew Jackson, was as warm and widespread as their subsequent enthusiasm for settling the newly opened Indian lands. When the state legislatures of Georgia, Alabama and Mississippi in 1828–9 petitioned the federal government for removal they were tapping popular support for that policy and exploiting the possibilities opened up for removal by the election of President Jackson. As Michael Rogin has written, 'Jackson was the moving force behind southern Indian removal' in the years 1814–24. He was responsible for nine of the eleven treaties ceding Indian lands in the South which were concluded in that period. These treaties transferred Florida to the USA, and to the whites no less than three-quarters of Alabama, one-third of Tennessee and a fifth of Georgia and Mississippi, as well as small slices of North Carolina and Kentucky. Such services 'helped make him the southern candidate for President' in 1828 and 1832 (Rogin 1976: 165). Jackson translated that appeal into reality by sweeping the Deep South. In 1828, Georgians gave all their presidential votes to Jackson, while over 80 per cent of Alabama's and Mississippi's voters did the same. South Carolina, the only other Deep South state in that year, declined to provide for popular participation in the selection of presidential electors, but its electoral college votes went without exception to the general. His reputation as an Indian fighter was essential in 1828 to his securing 81 per cent of all popular votes cast in the South; and his stand on Indian removal helped him win 88 per cent of Southern popular votes in 1832 (Cooper 1978: 5–6, 11, 22).

Indian removal was so extensive in the 1820s and 1830s that its fruits were distributed broadly. Land companies and large-scale speculators reaped a bumper initial harvest from their dealings in the new federal domain of Mississippi and Alabama. But the sheer quantity of land available prevented them from driving up prices or monopolizing land holdings. True to the pattern of earlier western settlement, Indian removal created neither vast estates nor a white tenant class; instead, it opened the way, as any observer would have predicted from the past record, to the settlement of formerly Indian lands by small white farmers (Young 1961: 69–72, 102, 113, 122–4, 136–7, 186–90). And the justification for removal remained traditional and highly populist, harking back to the sixteenth and seventeenth centuries' doctrine that hunters had no territorial rights in the face of cultivators, while also enlarging upon ordinary whites' race pride and an even more venerable sense of Providential mission. Governor George Gilmer of Georgia (a state which vigorously pressed for removal) reasoned:

> Treaties were expedients by which ignorant, intractable, and savage people were induced without bloodshed to yield up what civilized people had the right to possess by virtue of that command of the Creator delivered to man upon his formation – be fruitful, multiply, and replenish the earth, and subdue it (Berkhofer 1978: 161).

Gilmer's reference was, of course, to Genesis. Thus the request for new lands and the displacement of allegedly 'primitive' peoples – even though they were not as footloose as they were so typically depicted – profited from divine authority.

III

Finally, the Indian 'threat' fostered whites' patriotism and service to their states. In most Southern historical writing in the mid nineteenth century (as we shall see in Chapter 5), readers' attention was directed to the record of persistent and successful struggle against Indian foes. Prominent Indian fighters such as President Jackson, Judge Daniel Boone and Congressman Davey Crockett won sectional and national repute. But on a less illustrious plane, individual states boasted their own warrior founders; a good example was John Sevier, a humble but ambitious militia colonel of the 1780s who became Tennessee's first governor and served in that capacity in both 1796–1801 and 1803–9 (Ramsey 1853: 700, 709–11).

Nor was state pride and patriotism sustained simply by leisurely contemplation of the conflict-ridden past. The Second Seminole War of 1835–42 involved the participation of some 30,000 irregular troops, volunteering for periods of three or six months. These volunteers were raised within the states, with a speed and enthusiasm which may be illustrated by what happened in Georgia in 1836.

Georgia had a history of trouble with the Seminoles in Florida. After some years without Indian scares, Georgia's administration in 1812 responded to the outbreak of war with Britain by warning of the danger posed by 'numerous tribes of restless and warlike savages of doubtful faith' in Spanish Florida. A committee of the state legislature asserted that the British, aided by their Spanish allies, would excite 'the merciless savages, red and black, to their accustomed and atrocious deeds of murder, rapine and desolation' (J. of Sen. Ga. 1812: 6, 24–5). If the War of 1812 brought no dramatic conflict between Georgia and the Seminoles, dangers remained. In 1818, 1,000 of Georgia's militia participated under Jackson's leadership in the First Seminole War, which engaged 2,800 white militia and regulars, yet another substantial force by contemporary American standards (Williams 1981: 140).

Far more seriously, at the end of 1835, just after Georgia could celebrate the final agreement on Cherokee removal, a serious Seminole uprising occurred in Florida. The federal territorial governor asked Governor William Schley on 7 January 1836 to provide military assistance. By the end of January, Schley was receiving a steady flow of replies to his public call for volunteers. He was informed by one colonel in Augusta, 'You must have learned through official returns, with how much spirit the citizens of Augusta have volunteered, for service in Florida. The whole community promoted it, by the most liberal contributions and every other species of zealous encouragement.' One volunteer told the governor in February, 'Whoe ever has the good of his country at heart is willing to goe any way' to relieve 'his fellow man who is suffering the fortunes and pains of scalping knife and tomahawk of the savage'. And a junior officer reported in February on an eagerness to get on with the fight: 'the men are in a great state of suspense and if we could get marching orders quick, it would be in a great many respects very much to our advantage. My men are mostly farmers and it is a critical time with them. They do not know how to arrange their affairs.' An early war – and the speedy completion of voluntary service – would free these farmers for the planting season. (Letters to Govr. from Jn°. H. Eaton, 7 Jan. 1836; Col. William Cumming, 27 Jan. 1836; Capt. W. U. Anderson, 18 Feb. 1836; Capt. E. N. Calhoun, 26 Feb. 1836: Georgia. Govrs.' papers. William Schley, TCC Box. 50)

By the sleepy standards of the 1820s and 1830s, Georgia's government suddenly came alive in 1836; the governor's correspondence – at least that which is preserved – swelled to a volume far exceeding that for any other topic or episode during those two decades. The prospect of fighting in Florida sent adrenalin flowing through Georgians' veins as no other issue did.

Of course, not all correspondence with the governor was simply patriotic and enthusiastic. The most interesting social problem raised by the war was the balance of residual power within Georgia. If too many whites volunteered immediately, and if the war continued to such time as a draft was required, then white manpower would be dangerously reduced. Colonel William Cumming argued that Augusta's Richmond County should be excluded from a later draft. Augusta had a militia regiment whose paper strength was 1,000 men. Since 166 men had volunteered by the end of January, a later draft of one man in ten would deplete the town of 266 men of military age, a quarter of those potentially available. Such a drain threatened the whole system of law and order: 'When we consider the number of our slaves, and the temper of the times, it must be obviously impolitic, unless in cases of greater emergency, to strip any district of so large a part of its effective force.' Similar fears of slave rebelliousness arose elsewhere. General L. L. Griffin asked the governor to maintain a cavalry company at Macon because the town had lost men heavily through emigration to Texas and through volunteering for the war in Florida. Yet the river-port and its surroundings had a large black population, and three large boating companies in Macon employed substantial numbers of blacks, drawn widely from the countryside. Any idea of a future draft was opposed from Fort Gaines in February on the grounds that men were needed locally to ward off Indian depredations and because 'The negro population is considerable, and from the restlessness manifested, in that portion of our population, apprehensions of a serious nature naturally arise.' Such fears came not solely from towns. A predominantly plantation county, Madison, similarly resisted a heavy draft upon its manpower resources because it held such a small white population in proportion to its blacks. And in rural Bryan county the same fear obtained (letters to Govr. from Col. William Cumming, 27 Jan. 1836; Genl. L. L. Griffen, 4 Feb. 1836; John Dill, 8 Feb. 1836; Col. Stewart Floyd, 2 Feb. 1836; R. J. Arnold *et al.,* 18 Feb. 1836. Govrs.' papers. William Schley, TCC, Box 50).

These expressions of concern for the policing of the home front in war afford rare examples of whites making direct comparisons between Indians and blacks. They testify to white fears that an inadequate presence of white men of military age would allow black hostility and resentment to explode. Yet they suggest that, while Indians were self-evidently a foe to be assailed manfully and adventurously in battle, the blacks were simply a potentially restless labour force to be cowed and to be worried about only when white manpower was otherwise engaged.

Whatever light the call to military service threw on whites' racial attitudes, the popular response to the Seminole emergency of 1836 was swift and enthusiastic. A substantial force was rapidly raised. By late 1837, for example, the federal commander in Florida had an army embarrassingly large for his military tasks, composed as it was of some 9,000 men, including 4,100 volunteers. Of the latter, at that time, full battalions had come from Florida, Georgia, Louisiana, Missouri and Tennessee, while only companies had been levied in New York and Pennsylvania (Mahon 1983: 88–90). Although the last and the most draining of the Indian wars east of the Mississippi was not solely a Southerners' war, it was very largely one. Such military service provided a precedent and a model for later actions. During the Mexican War, for example, three-quarters of the volunteers came from the Southern states, a number wildly exceeding the proportion of the Southern whites in the total American population (McPherson 1983: 240). When secession came, Southern patriots emulated not merely their

Revolutionary ancestors, but their immediate forebears whose attachment to their states and their sense of racial destiny had been deepened by Indian removal in 1826–38 and the Seminole War of 1835–42.

Throughout the antebellum years, Southerners wrote proudly of their achievements against the Indians. John Drayton (1802: 14) enthusiastically described the transformation of the region east of the Occonees:

> Instead of the sword or the scalping knife, which were often wielded over these grounds, and of the war whoop's shrill tone, and the death song, which often echoed from the mountains, implements of husbandry are the only weapons which strike the soil; and the cheerful song of the husbandman the best music of its glades.

And Southern historians of the 1840s and 1850s, as they plotted the rise and filling out of their states, gave great weight and prominence to the Indian past (Ch. five). Such historical memory was signally reinforced in the Deep South by the far more immediate experiences of the 1830s. Both together perhaps encouraged the younger generation of the 1850s to live up to their folk traditions of military prowess and self-assertion. Southerners by 1860 had long been telling themselves that their ancestors had fought for, justly won, and, faithfully to God's commands, made civilized their vast domain. The displacement of the Indians was thus a living, evocative and unifying part of Southern whites' heritage.

Chapter four

BLACKS

I

The black presence was self-evidently a defining characteristic of the South. If the South was created by stripping the Indian of his land, it was sustained by dispossessing the black of his freedom. Black slavery became legally entrenched increasingly from the 1660s; it became numerically more important from the end of the seventeenth century. By 1790 the South contained 1,271,500 whites, 657,500 slaves and about 32,000 blacks who, while free, hovered in an unhappy no-man's land of debased status and second-class citizenship. Seventy years later there were 8,097,500 Southern whites, 3,953,700 Southern slaves and a very polyglot community of 262,000 Southern free blacks; one in three Southerners was black. In the Lower South (defined to include Alabama, Arkansas, Florida, Georgia, Louisiana, Mississippi, South Carolina and Texas) the blacks' presence was even more striking; 2,943,200 whites faced 2,423,500 slaves and 37,000 free blacks (Berlin 1974: 46, 136, 396, 399). Not surprisingly, therefore, the last generation of historians has rebelled against a century of neglect and condescension and concentrated enormous attention upon the examination of black, especially slave, customs, folk-lore, religion, marital habits, family ties, work, diet and resistance. As a result and somewhat ironically, we now know more of the slaves' *mentalités* and material life than we know of the Southern ordinary whites'.

What can be said about the blacks themselves is not, however, our concern here. The blacks enter this discussion of white attitudes and social bonding for the effect they had upon white society. Their existence was, as the crude population figures demonstrate, a major and obtrusive fact of white life, and contributed to a racial mix that was unique in the mid nineteenth century world. Two problems naturally stem from this fact. First, how was slavery justified morally and intellectually in an age of powerful Romantic humanitarianism and strong democratic and libertarian beliefs? Southerners by the 1850s were, after all, isolated from European official opinion over slavery – for European governments had abolished slavery in their colonies – in a way that they had not been a generation and certainly two generations earlier. Second, and flowing from the first question, how did so blatant a form of property ownership and so firmly entrenched an economic interest as slavery come to be acquiesced in, accepted and defended by the Southern white majority who were not slaveowners?

II

The intellectual justification of slavery served in itself to strengthen white fellow feelings. At one level, slavery struck many slaveowners as an historical legacy to which they had to reconcile themselves. Puritanical austerity was a part of their make-up. One of John Donne's meditational poems well expressed a resignation to suffering consonant with many Southerners' other-worldly devotionalism: 'affliction is a treasure, and scarce any man hath enough of it'; man was 'made for God' by affliction. Viewing blacks as innately too inferior, too bestial and too dangerous to be allowed their freedom en masse within the USA, even the more liberal-minded Southerners of the 1820s and 1830s saw little alternative to slavery other than the colonization overseas of freed blacks (Fredrickson 1971: 9–12). Once blacks declined to embrace colonization – as they did, for instance, in Virginia during the 1830s – then, given the whites' racial beliefs, slavery seemed an inescapable social necessity. Since labour itself was regarded as a God-given duty, slaveowners, or at the least the reflective among them, regarded themselves and their slaves as bound to a Calvinist tread-mill of toil which ultimately and eternally benefited both. Such an air of historical resignation accentuated Southerners' resentment against abolitionist outsiders' interference with the intertwined relationship of slaves and slaveowners. Work ethic as well as profit, religious conviction as well as racial prejudice insulated slaveowners from the most compelling humanitarian arguments proposed by abolitionists (Jenkins 1960: 200–12, 242–84).

It is unlikely that most Southerners came to rationalize their acceptance of slavery by invoking complicated divine purposes. Straightforward and aggressive racism doubtless loomed larger in popular thought. Here is a description of Africa penned by Samuel Cassels (1838), a graduate of Franklin College (the forerunner of the University of Georgia), and included in a volume of poems dedicated to the officers and members of that college's alumni association in 1838:

> Her kings are despots, and her gods are fiends,
> Her worship orgies, and her music screams.
> . . . .

Her winds blow hatred, and her rain is blood,
Her leagues are ruptures, and her friendships rude.
Satan's dread kingdom spreads from far to near,
Whose sun is darkness, and whose hope, despair

Such opinions, very firmly implanted by the 1830s, condemned the blacks to a past that was unremittingly base. They perhaps strengthened the dogma that arose in the early nineteenth century that all Africans arrived in America as slaves (they were not, that is, destined for indentured labour) and had already been degraded to slavery in Africa. Such opinions also encouraged whites' self-congratulatory belief that whatever regime prevailed in America was an improvement upon any conceivable African alternative, since slavery introduced both God and a sense of earthly purpose to the Africans. They furthermore stimulated white fears that blacks freed in large numbers would regress to a barbaric norm. And, finally and ironically, they may even have contributed to the free or freed blacks' rejection of colonization in the 1830s by creating a distinctly unappealing picture of Africa and the Africans.

Southern whites' analyses of the blacks were not unambiguous. Some Southern clergymen, publicists, and politicians adopted emancipationist ideas in the 1780s or promoted the cause of wider private manumission. In 1807 Southerners recognized, implicitly, the horrors of the trans-Atlantic slave trade by accepting its abolition; few and feeble demands were voiced thereafter for the reintroduction of that traffic (Takaki 1971: 160–99). Moreover, even the reservations about emancipation expressed by Thomas Jefferson in the 1780s acknowledged that it was the intense suspicions and resentments entertained by *both* races of each other – and not merely black inferiority – which made an amicable co-existence of freed black and enlightened white in a post-emancipation South so extremely difficult to visualize. Nor did Jefferson imply that black suspicions and resentments were anything but reasonable; 'Deep rooted prejudices entertained by the whites; ten thousand recollections, by the blacks of the injuries they have sustained, would make emancipation impossible without either the blacks' expulsion or the "extermination" of one of the two races.' (Peterson 1977: 186). Yet, just as Jefferson's emancipationist dreams of the 1780s were to remain dreams still at his death in 1826, whites began to elaborate and even to apply notions of racial stewardship to the treatment of slaves.

Managerialism and moralism combined, especially in the 1840s and 1850s, to inspire numerous articles and books, many of them associated with the New Orleans editor, statistician and Southern separatist, J. D. B. De Bow, on how owners should best treat slaves and on what should be provided for slaves in diet, housing, clothing, work regimen and punishment. Standards of good conduct so amply ordained then fed backwards to increase still further whites' sense of paternalism and of blacks' dependency upon white paternal instinct. Governor Hammond of South Carolina even wrote of slavery as being founded upon a 'compact' between master and slave:

> no saner or more just agreement was ever made working to the mutual benefit of both and charitably inclined in favor of the weaker party. The master exacts of the slave obedience, fidelity, and industry; and places him under just so much restraint as insures compliance with his regulations. The slave in return has far more certainly insured to him *peace, plenty, security,* and the proper indulgence of his social propensities – freed from all care for the present, or anxiety for the future with regard either to himself or his family (Jenkins 1960: 112, original emphasis).

More generally, and from the late eighteenth century, whites set out to convert slaves to Christianity. They thereby unleashed forces they subsequently failed entirely to control, for slave preachers acquired a standing, influence and authority within the slave community independent of the planters and outside their paternalistic ethos (Genovese 1975: 255–79). Slaves also gained a certain moral force from the whites' impulse to proselytize. And that moral force, supplemented by purely personal interactions, weakened the general impression of blacks' innate licentiousness and depravity.

Yet it would be wrong to exaggerate these humane tendencies, for slaves, even when well favoured, were treated most typically as children to be disciplined or dependents to be indulged rather than as potential equals. And struggling side by side with the Christianized slave and the 'happy' house servant were the rebel and the runaway, who neither submitted to white rule nor derived sufficient 'moral' authority from religion to counteract their disaffection. Such opposition to what whites at least purported to believe was a paternalistic system in turn fostered white fears of bloody racial strife, and reinforced white commitments to slavery as a safeguard against potential black violence.

Antebellum writers' preoccupation with paternalism should not distract us entirely from self-interest. As one slaveowner confided to his wife in 1848: 'If we do commit a *sin* owning slaves, it is certainly one which is attended with *great conveniences*' (Oakes 1982: 121, original emphasis). The most compelling and wide-ranging defences of slavery were advanced by slaveowners or by writers who wooed the planters for approval and profit (Faust 1977: 12–14, 24–44). The possibility of heavy losses of property and a dislocated plantation economy inspired many such defences. These began to sprout particularly from the 1830s, in response to Northern abolitionist attacks. They coincided both with the increasing use of state rights theories, convenient in arguments against federal interference with slavery, and, notably, with a powerful cotton boom.

The most effective Southern criticism of slavery came in the 1780s, long before the paternalist case was developed. Plantation labour in that decade, and into the early 1790s, apparently (the figures available are contestable) faced important economic difficulties. It seems that tobacco output in seaboard Maryland and Virginia became less profitable in those years and consequently depressed slave prices. This drop made slavery less financially attractive just when Revolutionary concern for equality and natural rights and religious agonisings over servitude flourished. As a result of these pressures on pocket, thought and conscience, three Southern states, including Virginia, lifted their colonial prohibitions upon personal manumission. By 1790 all Southern states except North Carolina permitted owners to free their slaves (Berlin 1974: 29). Before that, and going back to the early eighteenth century, individuals' right to dispose of their property in slaves at will had been curtailed in colony after colony in order to protect the common 'good' against an unregulated surge in free black numbers.

Yet if Revolutionary enthusiasm and religious disquiet produced a personal commitment to dispense with slavery – Virginia's manumission law of 1782 was highly regarded in this respect – antipathy to slavery soon ran dry. Between 1782 and 1790, Virginia's free black population grew from 3,000 to nearly 13,000. By the early 1790s, however, progress to freedom faltered. In 1793, free blacks were forbidden to enter Virginia, an eloquent enough testimony to the central tension between unease with slavery and hostility towards a biracial order consisting of free blacks and whites. That tension led to further action in 1806 to contain the undesirable impact of manumission upon white society as a whole; Virginia decreed that slaves manumitted in the future should leave the state after one year or when they attained their majorities. Responding hurriedly to Virginia's law, the nearby slave states of Maryland, Delaware and Kentucky banned free slaves' entry into their jurisdictions if those freedmen sought permanent residence. These laws together put a very considerable strain upon the humane impulses of Virginians who wished to free their slaves, for such manumitted slaves could legally be forced to move far from their familiar environment (Russell 1913: 61–82). By prescribing departure, and by making departure northwards to the border slave states illegal, state laws may have tainted manumission in both slaveowners' and slaves' eyes.

Virginia's decision to expel slaves manumitted from 1806 onwards was significant for two reasons. First, it was a political compromise that showed how far legislative opinion had retreated from the bold future imagined, and hoped for, in 1782. In 1805 and 1806, the state legislature nearly abolished the right of private manumission; the proposal to do so failed by 77 to 70 votes in 1805 and by 75 to 73 votes in 1806. Expelling manumitted slaves, therefore, offered a compromise between those who upheld the rights of individual slaveowners to maintain unfettered power over their property – to the point of ridding themselves of it – and those who asserted that Virginia's social fabric would be endangered by individual acts that excessively expanded the states' free black populace.

But, secondly, the law of 1806 was more a threat held in reserve than a police measure promptly and purposefully adopted, for little effort was made to enforce the new law. Even so, it remained as a powerful source for white control and intimidation of free blacks residing in Virginia, and whites indeed reduced free blacks to an often tormented and normally insecure status in the nineteenth century. It also discouraged manumissions. Quite numerous in Virginia from 1782 to about 1800, manumissions fell off in the 1800s and 1810s and then sank lower still from the early 1830s as pro-slavery thought became more astringent and slave prices boomed. A slave's relative chance of being granted his or her freedom therefore dropped markedly between the years 1782 and 1800 and the late antebellum period (Russell 1913: 66–71, 82, 156). This reaction was the more noteworthy because Virginia had a less pressing need for more slaves than did, for example, the expanding and brash south-west; and because Virginia had been richly endowed in the 1780s with such Enlightened thought, paternalistic impulses and religious awakening as quickened and gave voice to anti-slavery feeling.

Experiments with manumission and dreams of emancipation were short-lived. If the switch from tobacco to cereals in parts of Maryland's and Virginia's plantation belt had encouraged both, anti-slavery sentiment was probably sagging before 1793 and the commencement of the boom in upland cotton which guaranteed slavery's prosperous future. It was sagging before the slave rising in Saint Domingue in 1792 and Gabriel Prosser's conspiracy to seize Richmond in 1800 fanned white fears of free blacks as threatening the social order. This is not to deny that the impulse, while it lasted, achieved nothing of moment after the 1780s. In 1790, 5.5 per cent of all blacks in the Upper South were free; in 1810 10.4 per cent were. But the impetus and enthusiasm for the extension of manumission failed to gather pace from the mid 1780s. And from 1810 to 1860, the proportion of the Upper South's blacks who were not enslaved rose only modestly, to 12.8 per cent. Nor did anti-slavery sentiment spill very generously into the Lower South. The free black contingent there represented only 1.6 per cent of the black population in 1790, 3.9 per cent in 1810 and 1.5 per cent in 1860. Even the bulge of 1810 was sired not by home-grown conscience but by foreign-bred imports; mulattoes fled to South Carolina from Saint Domingue after the rising and bloodshed in that French Caribbean island; and the Louisiana Purchase of 1803 added more French-speaking free blacks to the Lower South's small existing free black population (Berlin 1980 provides the figures). Already, then, in the 1790s and 1800, the incidence of manumission provided a test of Virginia's moral influence which the Lower South failed to pass; already Upper and Lower South diverged in their treatment of slaves. But that failure and divergence does not mean that the test was a very stiff or a continuing one, or that the contrast was, for practical purposes, a dramatically striking one after about 1810.

Whites' contemptuous treatment of free blacks illustrated how pro-slavery thought affected behaviour towards all people of colour. Admittedly, some free blacks climbed the social and economic ladder; some even held slaves. Many became craftsmen, small businessmen and skilled service workers in the towns. In 1850, just over half the free blacks of the Lower South lived in towns of over 2,500 people; the Gulf ports offered an environment favourable to black enterprise and to modest black autonomy; even in older established Charleston, three-quarters of free blacks held skilled jobs. But it was in the Upper South that the majority of free blacks lived, and there they constituted a far more significant proportion of the population than in the Lower South.

Two-thirds of the Upper South's blacks lived in the countryside, where most of them sank, or were pushed, to the meanest manual jobs, as labourers or ditchers, often on very harsh work contracts (Berlin 1980). Even free black farmers lived under severe pressures; for their civil rights were constricted, their residency in a state could be scrutinized and terminated and their dwellings could be invaded by white patrols searching for runaway slaves. Virginia's response to overcrowding in its state penitentiary in 1822 illustrated the contempt in which free blacks were held. To ease pressure on prison space, the legislature decided to keep free black felons out of the penitentiary by substituting whipping and sale into slavery for imprisonment as a stock punishment for free blacks convicted of serious crimes. So salutary did this arrangement strike Maryland's and Delaware's legislators that they copied Virginia's example, adding the refinements that free blacks' punitive sale into slavery would be for a fixed number of years and their terms as slaves would be served outside the state. These laws did not last long; they were offensive enough to provoke opposition and repeal in Maryland and Virginia (Berlin 1974: 183). But they were brazenly discriminatory at a time and in a context when humane standards for criminal punishment were being extended. The whole intention behind the construction of state penitentiaries was to dispense with cruder, indeed avowedly 'barbaric', methods of retribution and to provide for possible reformation through imprisonment. Legislatures in the Upper South, if briefly, had no trouble in cutting free blacks off from this humanitarian concern. Although the enslavement of free black felons was a transient case of intense racism, free blacks more generally continued to encounter abuses intolerable to whites. They were whipped, sometimes legally, where whites by the mid nineteenth century were not. They suffered, usually without redress, a good deal of vigilante molestation. In Tennessee (1834) and North Carolina (1835) they were formally stripped of the vote just as universal white manhood suffrage was being celebrated by the 'Jacksonian' system of mass political parties (Berlin 1974: 190–1, 334–8).

Free blacks failed to combat such treatment. Many barriers to protest or action divided the handful of wealthy urban blacks from fellow blacks who were common labourers, or the mulattoes of Charleston's exclusive Brown Fellowship Society from the small farmers of piedmont Virginia, or even the black elites of such diverse cities as Baltimore and creole New Orleans from each other. Few points of unity joined black artisans from town to town. Although some jobs – particularly those such as barbers, carpenters, plasterers, blacksmiths, bricklayers and shoemakers which were in the service sector and which required little initial capital outlay – had the reputation of being black men's jobs, those trades tended to be conducted on a limited scale and to depend heavily on white clients. They did not offer bases for free black organization. Specific trades were not uniformly regarded as debased, 'black' callings. For example, draying was left mainly to blacks in Norfolk, Virginia, but was actively monopolized by whites in Baltimore and St Louis. Again, in 1860 Richmond possessed no black tailors, whereas 40 per cent of tailors in Charleston were blacks. Such particularity worked against free black unity of action or protest, even if action or protest had been feasible in the racial climate of the antebellum South. And not even whites established trade unions of more than an extremely local kind (Berlin 1976: 217–49).

Whites grudgingly recognized a free black *demi-monde*; even if freedom itself represented an individual, perhaps idiosyncratic, gift from whites, the result of gratitude to a 'faithful' servant, of guilt or love towards an illegitimate child, of a death-bed atonement for a lifetime's benefit from slavery. Some of the harshest penalties laid upon free blacks provoked white opposition. The disfranchisement of free blacks in Tennessee and North Carolina during the mid 1830s was much objected to; and one reason for the failure of Virginia's expulsion law of 1806 was most whites' refusal to enforce or heed it. When white working men in the 1830s and 1840s occasionally opposed the employment of free blacks as apprentices, an obvious riposte was that free black labour was much needed in the South (Russell 1913: 148–9, 154–5, 157, 176–7). In 1860, at a time of acute tension within the section, Arkansas ordered its free blacks to leave the state or face enslavement. Arkansas was not customarily looked upon as a pacesetter among Southern states, but the legislatures of Florida, Mississippi, Missouri and Tennessee (not all Deep South states) pondered similar moves and some of them passed Bills following Arkansas's example. Yet in each case expulsion was vetoed by the state governor or was thwarted in the late stages of the legislative process. And in Maryland a referendum turned down a proposal to enslave all free blacks (Berlin 1974: 372–80). These steps were considered, obviously, in an atmosphere of uncertainty, and perhaps of fear, over how free blacks would respond if and when the Republicans won the presidency and started to organize their anti-slavery party in the slave states. But, even at so late a stage in the relationship between free blacks and whites, the recurrent tension between brutal measures and humanitarian restraint surfaced once more. If Virginia's free blacks in 1806, or the free blacks of Florida,

Maryland, Mississippi, Missouri and Tennessee in 1860, did not feel the full weight of white power, they were yet reminded of their dependence upon white caprice, a caprice only just counterbalanced by the strength of white conscience, or by white calculations of free blacks' value to the South.

The treatment handed out even to free blacks and the suspicion that they would, if too numerous or unconstrained, pose some threat to a slaveowning society suggests the extent and depth of Southern white racism. Alternatives to slavery were canvassed, but they gained limited persistent support. And every so often free blacks came in for some sharp reminder that their freedom was distinctly conditional upon whites' approval and legislative benevolence. In that fashion, the blacks acted as a powerful negative reference group to all classes of whites.

III

It is easy to understand how the case for slavery was embellished from the 1830s. Writers seeking political approval or planters' patronage turned their pens to the defence of the South's peculiar institution. The sheer weight of precedent bore down upon white Southerners who were encumbered, as they repeatedly said they were, with an historical legacy which was difficult to remove and with a religious faith which did not put worldly perfectionism at the top of its list of moral imperatives. Profits discouraged manumissions, while racial intolerance and fear of blacks' possible rebelliousness made manumission even more socially unpalatable than it was economically feasible after the 1780s and 1790s. Evangelical religion from within and abolitionist attacks from without subsequently stiffened prominent slaveowners' and publicists' resolve to promote stewardship rather than colonization. And so, instead of very largely ignoring slavery as had been their forebears' habit until the last few decades of the eighteenth century, mid nineteenth-century whites proclaimed the most elaborate and wide-ranging case for fettering blacks to servitude. Slaves were happy and well treated, went one argument, more so than they would be if left to fend for themselves. Their lot might be hard, ran another, but their labour met God's purposes and their transportation from barbaric Africa hauled them within range of eternal life thereafter. Freeing them, reasoned yet a third argument, would expose the South both to a crisis of labour – for blacks were too idle by nature to work fruitfully – and a crisis of confrontation; for ex-slaves would avenge themselves upon the whites. Some Southern publicists, such as George Fitzhugh, not necessarily those most listened to, extolled slavery for underpinning a Southern upper class in the best European mould. Most insisted that full white equality in social relations and in political rights depended ultimately upon the open and complete subordination of the black labouring under-caste. Overall, the pro-slavery case lacked internal consistency. But its range, depth, force and liveliness were formidably sufficient for the slaveowners' intellectual, religious and political needs.

What remains unexplained, however, is why the non-slaveowning whites accepted these arguments and why, indirectly, the blacks thus constituted a social bond to white society.

The most obvious mystery is why poorer whites did not challenge slavery. Non-slaveowners' radicalism, aimed against privilege in all its manifestations, including the most glaring one of slavery, indeed bobs elusively in and out of many histories of the slave South. The pre-eminent historian of the antebellum free blacks, Ira Berlin, wrote of the Southern anti-slavery movement of about 1790: 'While patrician slaveholders disparaged slavery but did nothing about it, non-slaveholding farmers, artisans, and tradesmen filled the ranks of the antislavery movement ... Class antagonism, long masked under a veneer of racial solidarity and deference politics, suddenly struck against slavery.' This suggests the stuff of which great crusades were made. But, having been told that ordinary whites were about to assail slavery, we soon learn that, 'Even in the Upper South, anti-slavery sentiment was fragile and confined to a small group of men and women' (Berlin 1974: 28–9, cf. 84–5, where the evidence for class antagonism inspiring anti-slavery is drawn from the same, single individual who is cited earlier). Such anti-slavery support as existed may have been drawn largely from the non-slaveholding ranks; but it was limited in extent and may have been essentially urban in complexion. More concrete episodes than this rather vague supposed upsurge of anti-slavery feeling occurred in the antebellum South. But no tangible gains were won by slavery's opponents.

Two examples may suffice. The first is the more compelling, the better explored and yet the more puzzling. In 1831–2, Virginia's state legislature extensively debated the possible introduction of emancipation. The debate has been described since as a watershed in the Southern analysis of slavery, provoking as it did Thomas R. Dew to publish the first full-length defence of the institution; Dew's book did not so much deploy novel arguments as, by heaping assorted arguments together, raise the pro-slavery propaganda effort to a new level. The whole affair thus apparently closed the period of anti-slavery criticism and hope and opened one in which the 'positive good' argument for slavery won growing popularity. Yet Alison Freehling has recently argued that Virginia's discussion of emancipation in 1831–2 was more heavily charged and more seriously threatening to slavery than had earlier been claimed. She sees the debate as part of a running contest over representation and internal improvement between non-slaveowning western Virginia and the slaveowning tidewater and piedmont areas.

This contest generated much regional antagonism in the 1810s and 1820s, antagonism in turn assuaged only partly in 1830 with a modest redistribution of state legislative seats towards the western counties. The state constitution of 1830 still gave undue legislative weight to the slaveowning east, and so, according to Freehling, left the westerners still dissatisfied – indeed 'ablaze with discontent' – in 1831–2. Once the debate began, it soon revealed that 'Slavery in Virginia was more than a sectional issue between east and west; it was also a class issue between slaveholding and non-slaveholding whites on both sides of the Blue Ridge.' This conclusion is based upon sentiments expressed in legislators' speeches, extrapolations from the constituencies legislators represented, the membership of anti-slavery groups and the occupations of anti-slavery petitioners. Moreover, the majority by which emancipation was rejected – 73 votes to 58 – largely reflected the maldistribution of state legislative seats in the slaveowners' favour; and the fact that so sizeable a minority of representatives opposed slavery in 1832 was remarkable. Finally, even Virginia's legislature was prepared, by 67 votes to 60, to pass a preamble condemning slavery and looking forward to eventual emancipation (Freehling, 1982: 80, 176, 160–9). Such, then, is the evidence for slaveowners' dissatisfaction with the prevalent order, for their determination to overthrow it, and for the inadequacy of viewing a legislative session which mouthed criticisms of slavery as a rapid breeding-centre of the 'positive good' ideal. Yet, why did nothing much follow from these auspicious, supposedly angry, beginnings?

A sketchy answer is discernible. Within a few years of the debate, Virginians of all persuasions on the question of slavery's future were deploring Northern abolitionists' implicit intervention in Virginia's affairs; even Southern anti-slavery critics resented such meddling from north of the Mason–Dixon line. Yet, if such were the case, the fact that state loyalty superseded moral distaste for slavery showed how allegedly deep regional and class resentments among Southern whites were readily dispelled. Another explanation is that hopes for gradual emancipation became increasingly unrealistic as blacks themselves resisted the colonization schemes of the 1830s and so confronted Southern emancipationists with the unpalatable fact that freed slaves would stay within the South. Modest voluntary schemes were indeed tried after 1832; but why their failure should have deterred whites truly intent upon emancipation and removal, and prepared to use state power to back up both, is unclear. More generally, and rather more in the future than in the years immediately following 1832, the regional division of forces within Virginia was complicated by the growing use of slaves in parts of west Virginia – especially the Shenandoah Valley – during the three decades after 1830. The more straightforward regional alignments over slavery in 1832 became more confused; at the same time, the western counties in 1851 secured representation almost completely equivalent to their share of the state's population. The formal inter-dependence of political privileges and slaveownership disappeared (Freehling 1982: 229–31, 170–228, 234–41).

But this answer, while clearly containing much in it that more widely explains Southern non-slaveowners' lack of anti-slavery zeal, fails to explain specifically why non-slaveowning Virginians, who were so bitterly alienated in 1830–32 and so agitated by the eastern politicians' indifference to equal representation and intransigence over slavery, were so readily bought off by the hazy and distant reassurances about possible future emancipation that were incorporated into the legislative preamble of 1832. When the state election occurred in April 1832, 'both candidates and press largely sidestepped this explosive issue' (Freehling 1982: 201). National politics captured the attention of both, and, if a pamphlet battle over slavery's and Virginia's future rumbled on, that verbal joust scarcely gripped non-slaveowners' attention. It may be that the theatrical diversion of national party politics in 1832 was enough to turn aside the blazing anger of the previous year. Debates over internal improvements financed by the federal government – a favourite theme with Henry Clay, President Jackson's opponent in 1832 – touched Virginia's western malcontents, to whom better communications with the east were of grave concern. And the presidential election was followed in the winter of 1832–33 by the crisis over South Carolina's nullification of the federal tariff. But, while there were other political matters in 1832 which deservedly absorbed attention, the fact that attention was so distracted from slavery suggests that non-slaveowners' resentments were more rhetorical than real, more perennial than persistent, more manageable than menacing. The debate of 1831–32 fired off an explosion of pamphlets, speeches and newspaper editorials. These naturally painted the issues in lurid colours. They revealed natural resentments which not surprisingly came to the fore in such a debate over slavery's future. But those resentments failed to be translated into any coherent, organized political movement against slavery. In short, they lacked the depth and intensity to edge their way permanently into the political arena.

Virginia's debate merits discussion because it was a rare, and an unusually well documented, exploration of slavery's place and future in the antebellum South. After the early 1830s, only Kentucky, in 1849, re-examined the issue of slavery, and, indeed, put the possibility of extremely gradual emancipation to a popular referendum. Kentucky thus went farther than Virginia's legislature agreed to go in 1832. Yet the result was similarly anti-climactic, a heavy defeat for emancipation in a state where non-slaveowners outnumbered slaveowners, where anti-slavery leaders were men of prominence and even political weight and had long campaigned against slavery, and where, as far as we can tell, there was a free vote. Class apparently affected anti-slavery less than did attachment to the Whig party, for Whigs aimed principally to promote economic diversification and saw slavery as an impediment to that cause. Kentucky's anti-slavery men thus deployed 'generally conservative and cautious' arguments against slavery, rather than posed as the advance guard in a non-slaveowners' freedom fight (Degler 1974: 90–6).

These two examples were the most prominent occasions when emancipation was publicly debated in the South during the period 1830–60. Both were in the Upper South and neither stimulated any persistent anti-slavery activity. The facts that no comparable debates occurred in the Lower South, and that those of the Upper South fuelled no non-slaveowners' campaign against slavery, lend credence to Professor Fredrickson's contention that a *herrenvolk* democracy prevailed in the South. Democracy, in other words, for a white superior class rested upon the forceful, unremitting and, in some aspects, totalitarian subordination of the inferior blacks. And the democratic rhetoric of the 1830s, which coincided with the explosion of well-developed defences of slavery, served to bind whites together by preaching political equalitarianism for whites while contending that blacks were excluded from the precepts of the Declaration of Independence (Fredrickson 1971: 55–70; 1981: 69–70, 154–5). Attempts to prove that non-slaveowning yeomen were moving in the late 1850s towards an anti-slavery position and were on the verge of challenging the slaveowners' hegemony fall down from the sheer lack of satisfactory evidence to sustain such a beguiling hypothesis (This is the defect of Johnson 1977 and Hahn 1979). In 1860–61 very little opposition to slavery arose from the non-slaveowning areas; presumably because, as the Northern writer Frederick L. Olmsted found when he travelled in the Cotton Kingdom in the 1850s, non-slaveowning whites who conceded to him no love for the institution still saw slavery as the best means of controlling the blacks (Olmsted 1971: 191–2). Later hostility, during the Civil War, to the war effort and to the secession cause, and arising overwhelmingly from non-slaveowning regions, constituted not a demonstration against slavery as such but a protest against the extraordinary burdens of taxation, army service, privation and requisitioning of food supplies imposed upon people totally unaccustomed to obtrusive or revenue-hungry government. The war as a crisis in itself was sufficiently grim, costly and widely felt to provoke dissent from and resistance to the Southern cause when the defence of that cause levied so heavy a toll in men and material upon the non-slaveowners. Non-slaveowners' grievances were neither humanitarian nor anti-slavery but practical and self-serving, the product of the war itself; more important, they were, again, not especially pervasive.

Before the war, slavery's acceptance became enmeshed in a complex of larger national causes: in the safeguarding of Southern and state rights, in denunciations of Northern interference, in resentment against so-called Yankee Puritan hectoring, in the maintenance of cotton output as a vital component of America's overseas trade. While the resultant Southern patriotism had its roots in concern over slavery, that patriotism created a multi-faceted populist ideology, not simply a pro-slavery creed. Granted, that creed was vigorously disseminated; but the populist ideology incorporated more ideas in it than the claim that slavery was a positive good for Southern whites.

The latter notion – whose origins went back to early eighteenth-century ideas that white political freedom might be extended rather than qualified by slavery's existence – must be placed also in the political and social context of the 1830s and 1840s. For one thing, no biracial society existed as a possible model for Southerners to follow; Latin America merely served as evidence, to Southerners, of decay engendered by biracialism. And Americans were generally worried about reconciling open democracy, territorial expansionism, individual physical mobility and economic prosperity with a stable and orderly constitutional and social environment. These ingredients seemed potentially disruptive enough without adding racial prejudices and supposed incompatibilities by encouraging the growth of a free black population. In addition, when Southern politicians in the 1830s and 1840s spoke of economic privilege they located it more commonly in banking than in plantation houses. Finance capital represented exploitation, profit without labour and economic amorality. Senator Robert J. Walker of Mississippi in 1839 denounced the whole system of paper currency 'as destructive to the morals, dangerous to the liberties, and ruinous to the true interests of the American people'. And in Arkansas during the mid 1840s, Governor Archibald Yell urged that the state's rural producers would be best off without elaborate credit institutions (Sharp 1970: 67, 117–19). It was perhaps no mere coincidence that Southern consciousness began to be propagated when, from the early 1830s to the mid 1840s, banking issues were prominent in national, and often also in state, politics; and when banking's worst abuses were alleged to flow from Northern centres of capital. Later, in the 1850s, the complaint *Southern Wealth and Northern Profits* (the title of a book by Thomas P. Kettel 1860) encouraged Southerners to depict themselves as honest producers of the important cash crops – cotton, tobacco, sugar and hemp – from which Northern financiers, merchants, insurers, and shippers – the 'vampire capitalist class' according to George Fitzhugh – sucked their life-giving and scarcely earned riches.

Casting the North, however vaguely and crudely, in the role of financial villain matched the disparagement of the North as a hot-bed of interfering anti-slavery moralism. Both these characterizations were handed down for mass consumption from politicians, publicists and intellectuals above. Marxian historians of the South, notably Eugene Genovese, have argued from this that the Southern non-slaveowners were misled by a planters' racist ideology developed and articulated to buttress security of property in an age of increasing democratic and anti-slavery thought (Fox-Genovese and Genovese 1983: 167, 249–64). To say that the ideas supporting slavery were formulated by the intellectual elite tells us, in fact, very little, for a whole range of doctrines and invocations was so worked out. Who else, after all, unfolds arguments and advances ideas but those taking to the stump or taking up the pen? Numerous courses of action were recommended to the white masses without very obvious success: to conduct themselves temperately, to behave more as God ordained, to patronize Southern literature, to diversify economically, to improve their agricultural methods. The Upper South even had its own anti-slavery movement which was capable, in 1831–2 and in 1849, of presenting its case cogently and to a large audience. The proper test of these various recommendations' and doctrines' effectiveness was not where they came from – for they all came from above – but how well they squared with their audiences' prejudices and perceptions. Intense racism existed independently of the planters' self-serving ideas. As a report of the Connecticut Colonization Society noted in 1828:

> In every part of the United States, there is a broad and impassible [*sic*] line of demarcation between every man who has one drop of African blood in his veins, and every other class in the community ... The African in this country belongs by birth to the lowest station in society; and from that station he can never rise, be his talent, his enterprise, his virtues what they may (Fredrickson 1971: 17).

Given the national consensus on black inferiority, Southerners did not have to take a long step to arrive at a plausible justification for enslavement. Olmsted's ordinary non-slaveowners were not brainwashed by the far-ranging pro-slavery case with its references to classical, Biblical, anthropological and medical reasons for slavery. They simply accepted slavery as the best method of controlling blacks, for whom they entertained an abiding abhorrence. Indeed, decades earlier, from the 1780s to the 1810s, Jefferson and Madison, leaders of the intellectual and political elite, had recognized popular racism as the chief obstacle to their hopes for eventual emancipation.

Moreover, just as there were many kinds of slaveowners, some very rich, most merely affluent but hard-working and hard-pressed farmers, so non-slaveholding conferred no uniform status. Appreciable numbers of non-slaveholders were, or saw themselves as being, upon the threshold of obtaining a slave or two. Thus, for example, non-slaveholders in the south-west in 1860–1 probably supported secession because they believed that the expansion westwards of slavery offered them improved prospects of eventual slaveownership (Barney 1974: 296). Finally, as Professor Degler points out, Genovese's argument that planters established a hegemony in the South by diffusing their own ideas among the non-slaveowners does not allow for any proof that non-slaveowners genuinely agreed with the pro-slavery creed; it simply asserts that the non-slaveholders, in so far as they submitted to the system of slavery, displayed a 'false consciousness' of their true class position. Yet a correct appreciation of the white masses' interests is defined only as that proffered by Marxian analysis; the theory feeds back upon itself. And even Genovese concedes in one instance that mutual self-interest among slaveowners and a significant portion of non-slaveowners may have kept slavery going (Degler 1977: 71–6).

In sum, therefore, why non-slaveowners and slaveowners came together in denying rights – even sometimes humanity – to blacks remains a controversial question to answer. Undoubtedly a powerful and full pro-slavery case was amassed. But deliberate efforts were, very occasionally, made in the Upper South to overturn that case, only to meet rejection. To a very large extent, defending slavery became entangled with other issues of public concern in the years 1830–60: with states' right to control their own affairs, with sectional jealousies of Puritan preachings from Boston pulpits, with rural producers' resentments against the finance capitalists of speculation-mad New York and Philadelphia, with anxiety for securing territorial and economic expansion while guaranteeing social stability. For these reasons, and because slavery underpinned the Southern economy, attacks upon slavery came to be regarded as assaults on something increasingly defined as the Southern way of life. And that nebulous phenomenon, for whatever cause, secured loyal support from all ranks of white Southerners.

IV

Defending slavery was a principal but not the solitary aspect of white racism. Subjugation of Indians elicited strong racist self-justification; and free blacks as well as slaves were vigorously discriminated against. Indians and blacks together thus boosted whites' sense of unity and common purpose as well as their racial pride. But race pride alone – or even taken in conjunction with an interest in cotton cultivation and with a need to displace the Indians – does not fully explain white Southerners' commitment in 1861–5 to their section (Fox-Genovese and Genovese 1983: 250–1). Southern whites were drawn together by other unifying factors than racism: their interest in an historical past that encompassed more than slavetrading, their habit of self-government, their commitment to family, their social rituals and, more tenuously, their sense of respectability. Each of these factors helps take us beyond the view that *herrenvolk* democracy alone 'explains' the resilience of white society under the pressure of political and later military attack in the mid nineteenth century.

Chapter five

HISTORY

I

The early nineteenth century witnessed an upsurge of interest in the historical past. This was related, first, to eighteenth-century concerns for theme and direction in historical writing, a genre which was increasingly intended to illustrate the march of progress, if not always the triumph of Providence. It was related to European historicism and its impulse to trace the past roots of contemporary phenomena. It was fostered by the spread of Romantic literature. Indeed the novels of Sir Walter Scott had as much to do with promoting historical awareness in America as did any single indigenous intellectual impulse. But American interest in historical writing, and historical novels, was more specifically stimulated by the Revolution, which swiftly became a grand and heroic event in itself, and by a newly perceived need to trace and to explain a national heritage. America's greatest early historians described the birth of a nation, instead of merely recounting the political and social evolution of individual colonies. This preoccupation in the early nineteenth century with the heroic, the romantic and the national, especially among the most widely read American historians, did not, however, displace more particularistic investigations and state interests. Quite the contrary, groups came together in eleven states during the 1820s and 1830s to follow earlier examples set in Massachusetts and New York and founded state historical societies (Boyd 1934: 19–22). In historical study and in imaginative literature, an interest in locality and state benefited greatly from the wider public interest in the 'national' past. Many writers – including the South's pre-eminent novelist, William Gilmore Simms – argued that local and state patriotism and awareness were essential and complementary to growing national pride (Simms 1840: 319). Until at least the 1840s, Southern literary men typically argued that state and Southern consciousness were merely one necessary part of a larger nationalism. While, therefore, the best-selling historians of the early and mid nineteenth century customarily addressed themselves to national issues and national events – notably the Revolution – their widely read and highly profitable work served also to draw serious attention to state history.

Southern historians were not distinguished, pioneering or prolific in the period 1790–1860. Historical writing, the publication of original documents and the establishment of state historical societies all proceeded first and more rapidly in New England than in the South. The premier Southern state historical society – Virginia's – was not established until 1831, to be followed by Louisiana's in 1836 and Georgia's in 1839; yet by 1831, eight Northern societies were already in existence (Boyd 1934: 21). While it would be wrong to equate institutional expansion with intellectual growth, or historical societies with purely historical investigation – for these societies were often gathering places for the variously learned and generally inquiring – this sluggish institutional development epitomized a more general backwardness in the South. Indeed one reason for the emergence, especially in the 1830s and thereafter, of Southern historical inquiry was a Southern belief that New England had made too much running in the race to discover a national heritage, and that the American past was too explicitly the record of one region's achievements and of one region's Puritan culture. In response, therefore, individual Southerners, sometimes, as in Georgia in the late 1820s and in 1837–39, with modest state government backing, attempted to correct what they regarded as an imbalance in historical portraiture. As a result, although Southern state histories were available before the 1830s, and although accounts of Southern states' past also appeared in gazetteers, weightier and more systematic state histories tended to come after the 1830s, when historical investigation was given a certain edge by sectional competitiveness.

Historical writing rendered to its practitioners neither the outward esteem to be gained from the ministry nor the profit to be secured from the law. Moreover, and paradoxically, the social message conveyed by state histories was not as obviously relevant to the developing Southern cause in the 1840s and 1850s as was the social message emitted by Biblical studies or by much medical and anthropological research. For scholarly work on these subjects buttressed the pro-slavery case, giving it apparent intellectual depth and firmer appeal. Yet, curiously, the bulk of Southern historical writing scarcely mentioned slavery at all. If slavery merited mention, it came in as a minor matter, certainly not as a subject to be analysed in the way that theologians, lawyers and medical authorities were analysing and defending it by the 1840s and 1850s (Simms 1840; Pickett 1851; Ramsey 1853). It is presumably for this reason that historical writing as such has been so relatively little discussed by those seeking to define the 'Southern mind' on the eve of the Civil War (Jenkins 1960; Eaton 1961). For, in trying to define the 'Southern mind' so-called, twentieth-century historians have naturally tended to concentrate more on the 'Southern' than on the 'mind'. Yet the existence of a body of thought and writing little concerned with slavery does not mean that Southern historical publications promoted national or proto-national sentiment. Quite the reverse. Antebellum Southern historical writing was important not because it showed how slavery issues failed to penetrate all Southern discourse, but because it provided an extra element – the historical heritage – in the close bonding of white society.

II

It cannot be said that Southerners were quick in initiating or sophisticated in advancing their historical inquiries. Mississippi, for example, was a boom state during the 1850s and boasted America's richest community in Natchez's Adams County. It had become a state in 1817 and enjoyed a moderately complicated past splattered with French outposts and Indian tribes of resilience and antiquity. Indians remained in possession of about half the state's land area until the 1830s. Yet only very tentative steps were taken to supply a coherent picture of the state's history. When William Gilmore Simms, an outsider admittedly, wrote of Mississippi in his novel *The Border Beagles* of 1835, his story was of outlaw gangs and frontier violence all set in the wooded and scarcely passable riverine swamp lands of the west. When J. F. H. Claiborne, the most dedicated and distinguished of Mississippi's early men of letters, began his quest to provide a state history, the record of his journeyings of the early 1840s merely laid biographical foundations for an understanding of the past. Claiborne took some interest in social conditions, stressing for example how generally prosperous, law-abiding and contented the poorer whites of the piney woods were. But real contemporary history for him was equated with the doings of eminent, or at least vaguely heard of, state politicians (Claiborne 1906: 487–538). Claiborne went on to become Mississippi's first genuine historian, after he had joined with others to establish the state historical society. Yet that society did not come into existence until 1858 (Natchez, *Mississippi Free Trader* 22 Nov. 1858). By comparison, Iowa, only settled from the 1840s, and New Mexico, still a territory in the 1850s, got their societies in 1857 and 1859 respectively (Boyd 1934: 21–4). Given the value of these societies as meeting-places, pressure groups for the preservation of historical documents and other materials, publishers of documents and original papers, founders of libraries, and propagandists for historical awareness, the fact that Mississippi, despite its affluence and its not altogether uninteresting past, was so slow to create such a society indicates a more general Southern lack of early or probing historical inquiry.

Admittedly, not all Southern states were so sluggish. Georgia in the late 1820s played a major role in starting federal government efforts to gain American access to British official records bearing upon the individual states' colonial past. And this pressure in turn came from Georgia's first official historian, appointed in 1824 partly because Governor George M. Troup had been appalled at the sorry condition in which the state records were kept. Although the state historian won this opening battle to get access in London, he failed to obtain sufficient financial backing from Georgia to enable him to transcribe all the relevant documents available. Only in 1837–9 was a more concerted effort made to secure copies of Georgia's colonial records deposited in the imperial capital. From this evidentiary base, William Bacon Stevens, encouraged by the Georgia Historical Society (of 1839 provenance), wrote the first scholarly history of Georgia in two volumes published in 1847 and 1859 (Coulter 1964: 73–4, 81, 86, 121–6). So, too, though in less substantial fashion, J. G. M. Ramsey was aided by a Tennessee historical society with his massive chronicle of that state's past, published in 1853 (Ramsey 1853). But Georgia in the late 1820s and in 1837–9 was probably exceptional rather than typical; and even in Georgia the state's aid and interest was not to be relied on for any length of time.

Once individuals bestirred themselves, their state histories tended to fall into an obvious pattern of narrative, of battles largely against Indians, of treaty-making, of tangled diplomacy with the French and Spanish, and of Anglo-American advance, ineluctable and beneficent alike. These historical narratives of eighteenth-century events – the very recent past was mostly avoided – offered detailed accounts of power politics and of military and militia endeavour. But the story was further complicated, enlivened and indeed made heroic by the Revolutionary Wars. Anti-British sentiment was thus played up in historical writing; and remained an important facet of Southern consciousness.

William Gilmore Simms turned his fluent pen to history, as distinct from historical novels, in 1840. His *History of South Carolina* was an avowedly 'popular' work and one that formed part of Simms's attempt to lift Southern consciousness and pride. Yet the pivotal event in South Carolina's history was the Revolutionary war. And Britain was a properly abominated enemy, even in South Carolina where there had been a good deal of wartime support for the British. The reasonableness of the Revolutionary cause was fully displayed, according to Simms, in 1780–82 during the British occupation of Charleston:

> Every passion of the tyrant had they shown in turn; haughty scorn,
> contemptuous hate, reckless lust and groping and grinding avarice. They
> had trampled upon its sensibilities, shed its best blood in wantonness,
> and gleaned it of its treasures. The last lingering hour of their stay was
> distinguished by the ravages of a spirit still as greedy of gain as they had

shown at their first coming. Thousands of slaves, stolen from the
plantations, swelled the flying train of the British officers. For these the
spoilers ultimately found a profitable market in the West Indies.

Simms asserted that South Carolina was stripped of no less than 25,000
slaves by the British during the course of the war: a telling measure
indeed of British rapacity (Simms 1840: iii–iv, 313). Such disparaging
sentiments were reinforced both by lively historical romances
concerning the Revolution published in the 1830s and 1840s and by the
War of 1812, which appeared in some at least of the mid nineteenth
century state histories. Andrew Jackson, the victor of the battle of New
Orleans (1815) as well as a determined, indeed exuberant, Indian fighter,
won a particularly enthusiastic following in the South. Mississippi's new
state capital, designated in the early 1820s, was named after him. He
swept the South in the presidential elections of 1828 and 1832. Jackson
day, the anniversary of New Orleans, was the Democratic party's special
day of commemoration and celebration. And Anglophobia was kept
alive in more practical ways by Jackson's followers. During the 1840s,
anti-British sentiment encouraged the annexation of Texas (to forestall
British meddling in that area) and inspired Jackson's sub-lieutenant
from Tennessee, President James K. Polk, to declare that, in the Oregon
boundary dispute, America's position was '54° 40' or fight' (Sellers 1966:
52, 235–8, 340–3).

Unfriendly noises recurred in the 1850s. In 1858, for instance, Senator
James H. Hammond of South Carolina's boast that 'Cotton is King' did
not merely warn the North to stop provoking the South; it proclaimed
Britain's economic dependence upon Southern cotton and so her
inability to intervene on the Northern side in any potential sectional
show-down in the USA. In 1851, Representative Robert Toombs used
the anniversary of Washington's birthday to remind his fellow
Georgians that 'British emissaries are stirring up fools, fanatics and free-
negroes' in the North 'to resist the will of the American people as
constitutionally expressed in their public laws' (Phillips 1913: 228). On 4
July 1856, a keynote speaker at Georgia's Democratic state convention
reminded his audience that the American colonists had fought the
British for the right of local self-government; and he lauded the
Democrats' presidential candidate, James Buchanan, for 'his successful
resistance to the pretensions of England' and for 'the diplomatic skill
with which he seemed to master the arts of Palmerston and Clarendon',
the British prime minister and foreign secretary (Stiles 1856: 10, 33).
When Southerners were not recording Britain's past aggressions, they
could fulminate against Britain's present claims. In the summer of 1858
an Anglo-American dispute arose over the British claim to a right to
search on the high seas. This was a subject of perennial annoyance. But
some Southern newspapers and politicians urged that America resist
British pretensions forcefully. The Richmond *Whig,* not a typically
bellicose journal, argued that war with Britain would not only be

71

beneficial domestically – by arousing American patriotism and by burying slavery disputes, at least for a time – but would yield swift and easy American gains, in Canada, in the Pacific and in central America. More generally, 'A war with America will be the first step in England's decline. She has already reached the culminating point' (quoted in Natchez, *Mississippi Free Trader* 5 July 1858). There was nothing very consistent in these views. Hammond was asserting in March 1858 that Britain's reliance upon Southern cotton would aid the South in any sectional confrontation. Yet in July some Southerners were contending that a war with Britain offered an excellent chance to soothe sectional antagonisms. But lack of consistency is not the point here. Anti-British sentiment, reinforced and justified by an ample body of historical precedents, was clearly commonplace in the antebellum South.

Eccentric and individual responses also illustrated the pervasiveness of such sentiment. When a neighbour of Nat Turner's owner first heard gun shots that heralded the slave rebellion of 1831 in Southampton County, Virginia, he thought that the firing signalled a British landing and attack (Boney 1974: 452). His mind presumably went back to the coastal raids staged by the British during the War of 1812. In 1863 a British army officer travelling in the Confederacy found an hospitable and open reception virtually everywhere. But his hosts commonly regretted Napoleon's defeat at Waterloo (Lord 1954: 96). When James H. Hammond, then a former governor of a proud and not very democratic state, visited Britain in the 1830s, his sensibilities were offended by the treatment he received as something of a colonial bumpkin (Faust 1982: 188–90). Personal experiences and foreign policy disputes thus served to give immediacy to the Anglo-American antagonism which emerged from the history books. In that sense, if not in relation to slavery, historical writing emphasizing the Revolutionary conflict was 'relevant', or at least resonant, history.

In another respect – the South's bounteous natural endowment – the past was linked to the present. We have already noted how Colonel Claiborne, who published his state's first full and scholarly history after the Civil War, had, in his travels about Mississippi early in the 1840s, commented upon the healthiness and abundance of the piney woods, the region populated generally by poorer and less permanently settled Mississippians. The idea of natural abundance, and the healthiness of the environment in much of the South, was vigorously spread by the nineteenth-century historians of their states' eighteenth-century past. This emphasis had a long and not merely scholarly or Romantic history. As Professor Breen has noted of seventeenth- and eighteenth-century Virginia, great promotional play was made of the luxuriance of nature within the South and the readiness with which that luxuriance could be made to yield its agricultural fruits (Breen 1980: 170–95).

Tracts were published to lure settlers to the land of easy plenty. In 1732, one such pamphlet urging the merits of settlement in Georgia announced, 'In America there are fertile Lands sufficient to subsist all the useless Poor in *England,* and distressed Protestants in *Europe.'* Another such publication in 1733 stressed that Georgia, as well as the Carolinas:

> abounds with provisions. Vast numbers of Cattle, as well as Hares, Rabbits, and Deer. Fowls and Fish of various Kinds; Fruits of the best sort. *Indian* Corn and *European* Grain of every Kind in vast Abundance. The Climate is Known; the Air very clean, healthy, and almost always temperate, and there are Men to instruct in the Seasons, and in the Nature of cultivating that Soil, which is a very rich one.

These enthusiastic words were meant both to stir poor settlers to migrate and to stimulate wealthy patrons to make such migration financially possible (Reese 1972: 69, 179). Similarly, a good deal of promotional literature was disseminated in the nineteenth century. Samuel R. Brown's *The Western Gazetteer* (1817) referred, for example, to the new state of Mississippi as yet unnamed:

> The country bordering on the Tennessee frontier resembles that of the best parts of Kentucky ... the country bordering on the Tennessee river, for 100 miles above and below the Muscle Shoals, and for forty miles north and south, I consider as the garden of North America, and unquestionably the best adapted to longevity and human enjoyment (Brown 1817: 223).

North-eastern Mississippi had numerous rivals for the title 'The Garden of North America'. Bishop Stephen Elliott, Jr., addressing the Georgia Historical Society in 1844, reminded his audience that 'Georgia, especially, was proclaimed as the garden spot of the earth'. Even though immigrants had been proceeding to the New World for nearly two centuries, Georgia from the 1730s held out an enticing prospect as a land 'of perpetual spring and ever-blooming flowers and exhaustless life' (Elliott 1844: 7). In 1859 an historian of South Carolina's upper country noted that 'this region of romance' afforded a wealth of forests, prairies and rolling hills which 'was not surpassed in picturesque beauty and grandeur, by the best portions of Texas of the present day; and its virgin soil was not then inferior to that of the same boasted state' (Logan 1859: I, 1–7). In the 1840s and 1850s travellers in regions as widely separate as the Appalachian mountains of Georgia and North Carolina and the prairies of Texas just across the Rio Grande from Mexico recorded privately and publicly their astonishment at the magnificence, romance and bounty of the land around them. And in the mid 1830s one army officer objecting to the war being waged against the Seminoles described the countryside around St Augustine, Florida's largest town, as 'a perfect Eden' (Potter 1836: 3).

Historians, gazetteers and promoters alike – or the same men merely switching roles – commented warmly, even eloquently sometimes, upon

the South's attractive and attractively bountiful environment. Attitudes
to the informal, frontier society which this environment underpinned
were, however, far from being unambiguous. For one thing,
Southerners, like Americans more generally in the nineteenth century,
were living with an unfolding, changing and ill-defined frontier. By
reflecting upon what they thought were past conditions in an under-
developed society, writers were often influenced by a contemporary
tension between frontier and eastern seaboard conditions. Moreover,
statements about contemporary opportunities for social advancement
offered by the abundant land often reflected the historical experience by
which colonial Americans had improved their lot. Secondly, there was a
great deal of mid nineteenth-century moral ambiguity about 'frontier
society' in the recent past. By the 1830s and 1840s a realist strand in
Southern writing had emerged, to recount the virtuous and earnest
simplicities of frontier days. Yet such accounts usually wobbled between
ritual regret for lost innocence or enterprise and complacent self-
congratulation at the moral advances achieved by Southerners since the
late eighteenth century. The earlier frontier thus acquired a somewhat
confusing image: a luxuriant garden of Eden inhabited by the serious,
the struggling and the familial; or an abode where subsistence came
altogether too easily to Fallen Man as he romped or tottered his way
through every manner of grubby depravity.

Governor John Drayton made the connection between plenty and
opportunity in *A View of South Carolina* (1802). He pointed out:

> Unlike European countries, whose inhabitants are restricted by imposing
> tenures, the soil of Carolina is possessed by the people, in a manner the
> most encouraging to industrious labors ... few lands are holden on lease;
> or if they be, the leases are for short terms, and liberal conditions: and,
> in general the lands are possessed and tilled by the rightful owners of the
> soil. Hence every improvement made, enhances the pleasures, and
> independence of its owner.

Land was available for as little as $1 to $6 per acre in upland areas, the
exact price being related to situation and proximity to navigation;
'Hence, men possessing any capital whatever, may settle themselves
independently; upon lands which descend to their posterity; together
with every improvement made thereon, by their industrious labour.'
Here, of course, Drayton was pressing a contemporary parallel with
venerable roots; for the typical eighteenth-century British farmer was a
tenant obliged to pay high rents in expansive times, unable to pass on a
solid and well secured inheritance to his off-spring, and reaping no
profit from farm improvements made during his tenancy. Moreover,
farmers in South Carolina were free of complex patterns of manuring
and rotation such as obtained in less favoured lands, while agricultural
implements required there were 'few and simple'. Such ease, plenty and
simplicity naturally conduced to a state of virtue. When Drayton noted

that the poorest whites lived in log and clap-board houses of one or two rooms, he added: 'it is here that health and independence dwell. And a crop of a hogshead of tobacco, or a bag or two of cotton, forms an income, which pays the taxes and expenses of the farm; and makes a family happy and contented.' In drawing such a picture and such conclusions, Drayton was making an historical comment on the rural life of eighteenth-century America, in contrast to that in Britain, as much as he was describing a contemporary scene (Drayton 1802: 109–13, 140). Yet the world of frontier simplicity was soon thought to be fast receding.

A prominent theme of historical writing was regret at the passing of the frontier life-style. J. G. M. Ramsey's contrast between late eighteenth-century and mid nineteenth-century Tennessee displayed a typical nostalgia; 'the early occupants of log cabins were among the most happy of mankind'; frontier woman found her 'true glory' in being a hard-working housewife and mother, finding as she did 'all her joy, all her happiness, in the merited approbation of the man she loves'. By implication, mid nineteenth-century women were not nearly so hearth-centred. Their menfolk were also unworthy of their late eighteenth-century predecessors. Ramsey's Tennessee frontiersmen flung themselves into 'manly, athletic, or war-like' sports, so building up their self-respect, patriotism and love of individual independence:

> In those purer days of the Republic, patriotism was not an echo merely. With the pioneers of Tennessee, it was a principle, deep, strong, active, full of vitality and vigour . . .

> The *principles* held by the men of that day were their *convictions*, the convictions of a deliberate judgment and of a pure and unselfish patriotism . . . The tactics of the partisan and the factionist were unknown, and the manufactories of public sentiment were confined to the common good sense of the people themselves, rather than their passions, their interests and their prejudices.

If illiterate, these frontiersmen had the requisite good sense, sufficiently inquiring minds and a strongly enough established oral tradition to encourage them to reflect upon politics and to immunize themselves against fanatical and extreme nostrums. Enabled also to participate in public affairs, Tennessee frontiersmen exhibited such a 'lofty State pride' that it became 'a passion':

> The Tennessee pioneer can be exceeded by none in fondness for and admiration of his own country. His valour acquired, his enterprise subdued it. It has become the symbol of his heart, the home of plenty, of quiet and security. Its greatness excites his admiration, its beauty his pride, its character his enthusiasm; its unstained escutcheon is the theme of his boast and glory.

Historical writing of this stripe was clearly directed as much to fuelling myths and to erecting a standard by which to judge contemporary state patriotism as it was to evaluating the past (Ramsey 1853: 717, 720, 729–37). But the myths were nothing if not potent and lingering ones.

J. W. M. Breazeale's *Life as it is,* published in Knoxville, Tennessee in 1842, similarly attributed Tennessee's conversion from 'a vast, howling wilderness' into a prosperous state to 'bold, fearless and intrepid' leaders among the early settlers. Breazeale detected in frontier society a vital element of liberation and social fluidity:

> In old, wealthy and densely populated communities, family rank, and opulence, exercises an influence which bears down and overrides the poor, obscure and indigent, however talented and enterprising they may be. Hence, the bold, talented, intrepid and aspiring amongst the lower ranks, many of whom are frequently the most virtuous and highly gifted individuals of the community, will seek a theatre for the display of their energies, and the exercise of their genius where they can be useful to their country, and acquire rank and honor for themselves.

One exemplar of this adventurous spirit was Colonel John Sevier who led expedition after expedition against the Indians in Tennessee from 1779 to the early 1790s. Beginning life humbly elsewhere, Sevier attained pre-eminence in the new state (Breazeale 1842: 7, 32–81, 101).

The flush times of the 1830s brought similar opportunities to self-making men in such booming south-western slave states as Mississippi and Alabama. According to their chronicler, Joseph G. Baldwin, writing in 1853:

> In a new country the political edifice, like all the rest, must be built from the ground up. Where nothing is at hand, every thing must be made. There is work for all and a necessity for all to work. There is almost perfect equality. All have an even start and an equal chance ... The rewards of labor and skill are not only certain to come, but they are certain to come at once.

Having thus emphasized the scope given to talent, especially legal and professional talent, in the opening of new territories – and much of Mississippi and Alabama in the 1830s was freshly seized from the Indians – Baldwin contrasted that frontier condition with the restrictions operating upon young professionals in the eastern seaboard states (1853: 227–31):

> An old society weaves a network of restraints and habits round a man; the chains of habitude and mode and fashion fetter him: he is cramped by influence, prejudice, custom, opinion; he lives under a feeling of surveillance and under a sense of *espionage*. He takes the law from those above him. Wealth, family, influence, class, caste, fashion, coterie and adventitious circumstances of all sorts, in a greater or less degree, trammel him; he acts not so much from his own will and in his own way as from the force of these arbitrary influences.

This was an unusual and extreme contemporary criticism of the seaboard plantation order. Notably, it occurred in the context of a lengthy, even somewhat impassioned, discussion of the social dynamics of frontier settlement and of the creative legal and political skills called forth by westward movement. Moreover, it, like so much of the other commentary on the virtues of frontier life, appears almost as a recessional, sharpened by regret at the ending of an exciting, challenging, and fulfilling era.

The demise of frontier society was not entirely regretted by Southern historians and observers. If, as one speaker to the Georgia Historical Society in 1843 urged, the study of the past provided 'lessons of encouragement or of warning' for the present, so the creation of an historical record was equivalent to establishing 'a moral laboratory' (King 1843: 5–7). If studying the eighteenth century revealed a relative decline in state patriotism, looking backward also documented moral improvement. Augustus Longstreet writing in 1835 of Georgia's plain folk and Joseph G. Baldwin writing in 1853 of Alabama and Mississippi were not, strictly speaking, historians. But their comments on the fading of a frontier, face-to-face society, which Longstreet located at the turn of the century and which Baldwin placed in the 1830s, had an obvious historical dimension. Early frontier life revolved around the local 'doggery' or cross-roads drinking places, regarded by Baldwin as 'those haunts of vicious depravity'; it fell into a demoralizing round of spontaneous horse races, shooting matches, individual brawls and gambling on cards, cock-fighting or quoit-pitching (Baldwin 1853: 109, 127). From such a portrait of frontier life in Georgia, Longstreet (1835: 66) drew at least one cheering conclusion:

> Thanks to the Christian religion, to schools, colleges, and benevolent associations, such scenes of barbarism and cruelty, as that which I have been just describing, are now of rare occurrence: though they may still be occasionally met with in some of the new counties.

This note of approval for the passage of frontier conditions did not, as has already been stressed, reflect any consensus view among mid nineteenth-century Southerners. Far from it. J. G. M. Ramsey not only concluded his voluminous history of Tennessee with a panegyric on the frontiersman's patriotism and state pride: he also underscored the co-operative aspects of frontier life, in which settlers joined together to build cabins and chop wood and defend themselves against Indian attack; and he saw no reason to be condescending about the spontaneous and intense merriment to be drawn from simple entertainments (Ramsey 1853: 717, 724–30, 737). So, an ambiguity remained between those who found frontier manners barbaric, if perhaps also quaint, droll or ridiculous and those who saw more homely virtue than crude vice in frontier ways. Historians and contemporary

observers alike, however, agreed that an important part of Southerners'
heritage had disappeared since the late eighteenth century.

What message comes down to us from those who were reflecting on
the Southern past in the early and mid nineteenth century is neither
consistent nor unambiguous. But certain themes in it stand out. There
was a resilient strain of anti-British feeling much nurtured by Romantic
novelists' and historians' absorption in the events of the Revolutionary
Wars, and by subsequent, if far less concentrated and considerable,
attention given to the War of 1812. There was a continuing fascination
with the story of America's natural bounty and a widely shared notion
of America as richly endowed by an approving Providence. Finally,
though this perhaps was less a subject that united Southerners, there was
a belief that frontier society was rapidly disappearing, that important
cultural changes had occurred between the late eighteenth century and
the 1850s, and that territorial expansion offered impressive
opportunities for individual social advance and, controversially, general
social improvement. What no-one disputed, however, was the need to
tame the 'vast, howling wilderness' of the trans-Appalachian west, or
the pride which Southerners should feel at their recent ancestors'
western achievements.

III

When early nineteenth-century historians became mesmerized by the
need to base their historical writing firmly upon documents, they
naturally reinforced an earlier tendency to concentrate on military and
diplomatic rather than on less well or fully documented events. One
result of this fixation with the formally written record was neglect of the
Southern blacks' story. Such was not the case for the Indians.

For example, Albert J. Pickett's *History of Alabama* (published in
1851) gave enormous attention to the ethnic mosaic of that state's past.
Volume I described the mores and history of the Muscogees, Creeks,
Alabamas, Natchez, Choctaws, Chickasaws and Cherokees separately
and at length. A further substantial portion of that volume investigated
the French presence in Alabama and in neighbouring Mississippi
(Pickett 1851: I, 54–179, 180–303). The second volume recounted the
battles and rivalries of the French and British and of the Revolution; it
also devoted 132 of its 445 pages to the War of 1812, although, not
surprisingly given the geographical setting, more was written of Indian
wars in those years than of Anglo-American conflict. Pickett rounded
off his history by providing full biographies of Alabama's founding
fathers at the statehood convention of 1819 (Pickett 1851: II, 240–372,
400–45). This pattern of emphasis – on the varied ethnic background of

the eighteenth century, on the struggle for supremacy and on biographical political history – was, broadly speaking, the normally acceptable pattern adopted by other Southern historians. For instance, Colonel B. L. C. Wailes became the first chairman of the Mississippi Historical Society in 1858 (Natchez *Mississippi Free Trader* 22 Nov. 1858). Four years earlier he had written a 100-page historical introduction to his *Report on the Agriculture and Geology of Mississippi, Embracing a Sketch of the Social and Natural History of the State,* which was published by the state government. That introduction ended with thirty pages on the Spanish hand-over of Mississippi to the USA in 1796–8. Despite the book's proclaimed interest in both agriculture and social history, the historical outline of political and military happenings mentioned blacks and slaves only half a dozen or so times, and omitted all reference to their uses and to the agriculture associated with them (Wailes 1854: 17–116). Southern historians thus followed a broadly familiar model of composition. They all virtually ignored slavery. They all gave much attention to the white man's heroic struggle against the Indian. In that sense, historical writing provided a useful point of cultural consensus.

Historians and reporters upon contemporary affairs alike expended much energy in distinguishing between Indian tribes. But they also argued from the experience of the eighteenth century that all Indians were on a course to ultimate degeneration if not extinction.

John Drayton, in describing South Carolina in 1802, recognized the jostling and fluid quality of eighteenth-century Indian life. He recognized, too, that Indians had been victimized by rapacious whites. But he also attributed Indian decline to inherent racial defects. Once defeated, the Catawbas fell speedily 'into a state of insignificance and drunkenness'. And the Indians' record of 'assassinations and barbarities' deservedly drew upon those people massive, and often cruel, white retribution (Drayton 1802: 92–4, 99). So, too, a staff officer of the 1830s, who deplored white transgressions against the Indians, could not help but admire the courage and enthusiasm displayed by white soldiers volunteering to counter Indian aggressions. Woodburne Potter, in *The War in Florida* (1836: 124), thus described the response in South Carolina, Georgia, and Alabama to a call for volunteers:

> with a spirit which does honour to the American character, hundreds of the bravest sons of those states flew with eagerness to the standard and superseded the necessity of drafts being made. Meetings were organized in Augusta, Savannah, Darien and Charleston, at which the most enthusiastic feeling was evinced, and a few days after nearly 2,000 volunteers were ready to embark at a moment's warning for the theatre of war.

In such fashion, race pride overwhelmed humanitarian sympathies. Looking back from 1851, Albert Pickett, who wrote his history of

Alabama as a pastime (admittedly an onerous one) and a public service, saw 1818 as a vital year in Alabama's progress; Creek resistance to white expansion broke down in that year, thus bursting open the 'flood-gates' of immigration (Pickett 1851: I, viii, II, 384). Not only were Southerners convinced of their right to the land; they were persuaded that it was their duty to seize it. Bishop Elliott, in addressing the Georgia Historical Society in 1844 on 'A High Civilization: The Moral Duty of Georgians', stressed that the whites had justifiably cleared the state's Indians from their lands, and that the story of Indian decline and removal illustrated the steady triumph of civilization over backwardness (Elliott 1844: 8–9, 13–15).

Individuals were singled out for their stalwart contributions to Southern expansion over time. It is a familiar fact that such frontiersmen as David Crockett and Daniel Boone, the one becoming a US Congressman, the other a federal judge, won enduring fame even in their own day. Yet humbler individuals also achieved a certain degree of recognition for their pioneering troubles.

In 1831 Mississippi's General Assembly petitioned the federal Congress to grant a section of land to Amos Moore, a blind man dependent for subsistence upon his poor and aging mother. The grounds for this request were the services rendered by Moore's father, 'one of those adventurous and enterprising men, who having spent the youth and manhood of his life in advancing the boundaries, and protecting the improvements of civilization' left little for his family, especially his son who was blind from the age of four. The Mississippi legislature expanded upon Moore senior's 'life of toil and danger and public usefulness':

> In the early settlement of Tennessee, and when that country was a
> wilderness infested with fierce and savage barbarians, he was among the
> foremost of those hardy adventurers who extended the settlement and
> repelled the appalling dangers which were in that country the only
> impediments to the advancement of civilization.

Later, but still in the even newer state's formative years as a territory, he moved into Mississippi (Memorial passed 10 Dec. 1831: RG47 Legisl. vol. 20, MDAH). A cynic might argue that the politicians of Mississippi were simply trying to relieve themselves of a possible burden on public relief by pleading so eloquently with Congress. Yet, whatever the motives behind their rhetoric, it should also be noted that they fully acknowledged the part of the ordinary and materially unsuccessful individuals – not just pioneers who became governors and generals – in the South's great historic mission. If a large measure of the South's history as formally chronicled concerned militia colonels and their conquests, that history served also to immortalize deeds with which the Moores of the unfolding South could identify. The role of the folk hero was, after all, to exemplify actions in which others had participated and/or could take pride.

And this was the service which historical writing, of all kinds, could render. Bishop Elliott (1844: 20–1) drew this lesson from the excitement stirred by Sir Walter Scott. In combining Scottish history with imaginative literature, Scott had not merely transformed the past. He had aroused patriotic interest in the Scottish present and future:

> Who can calculate the concentrating and harmonising effect which such a writer as Scott has produced upon his country? He has invested every glen, and crag, and loch, and mountain, and ruin with a *world interest,* and in doing this has made every Scotchman prouder that he is one and linked his heart to his home by ties stronger than any distance or time can obliterate. He did what we are striving to do — caught every tradition as it floated by and gave it permanence.

This accurately defined the ambition fuelling the chronicle-writers of the antebellum South: to catch every tradition and give it permanence and thereby confirm the heroism of the eighteenth-century past and stimulate interest, pride and patriotism in the mid nineteenth-century present.

IV

The South's history taught no simple lessons. Some leading Southern intellectuals were either dissatisfied with what had happened or wanted to break away from the habits of the past. J. D. B. De Bow used his *De Bow's Review* to trumpet arguments for Southern economic diversification and industrialization. While remaining an emphatic proponent of Southern separatism, De Bow also asserted the need for the South to make itself economically self-sufficient by breaking with its overwhelming agricultural past. Some businessmen took up the challenge, and one of them, William Gregg of Graniteville, became both a successful industrialist in the 1840s and 1850s and an energetic propagandist for Southern industry (Eaton 1961: 243). For such men the lessons of the frontier past – and certainly nostalgia for it – were scarcely relevant to present economic needs. Other writers, not however dedicated to industrial expansion, regretted the way in which Southern society – or the Southern society they condoned – had been steadily weakened and diluted by the influence of an open and somewhat wild frontier. This was a view common in Charleston intellectual circles, especially towards the mid nineteenth century. Ultra conservatives and ultra modernists thus voiced different objections to the expansionism of frontier society.

Despite such disagreements, Southerners interesting themselves in history – and an increasing number of them did so – found within the historical record certain basic themes to propound. Writers of history did not see fit to devote much attention to slavery or to blacks. But they still emphasized such aspects of the mainly eighteenth-century past as served to strengthen white Southerners' self-confidence and patriotism: the steady, desirable and almost inevitable displacement of various Indian tribes; the complex and hard-fought thwarting of French designs by the British; and the overthrow of British imperial rule. An historical background and folk culture of that kind reinforced race pride and Anglophobia, reminded Southerners of the need for martial skill and military preparedness, and lent an heroic tone and Providential purpose to the otherwise fairly mundane story of Southern agricultural expansionism. The remembrance of things past was not the most vital bond holding Southern society together. More obviously immediate pressures – from the potential rebelliousness of slaves and enticing opportunities offered by physical mobility, land availability and a flourishing household economy – exerted greater influence than the past. But the Southern states' history was delineated at fuller length and with greater accuracy as the nineteenth century progressed by men who generally believed they were uplifting, inspiring and uniting their Southern fellow-citizens. Simms most blatantly in South Carolina, Ramsey in Tennessee, Pickett in Alabama and Claiborne in Mississippi were obvious examples of historians who viewed their scholarly writings as serving a public and useful purpose. And when the secession crisis finally broke, secessionist leaders appealed naturally and with confidence to the Revolutionary past as justification and example.

Chapter six

MOBILITY

I

When David Potter sought in 1954 to explain American exceptionalism, and the distinguishing hall-mark of American civilization, he entitled his book *People of Plenty*. A bounteous nature and vast material resources had, he argued, helped create a peculiarly non-European society, certainly a society more fluid, more open in opportunity and more aggressive and optimistic than modern European societies. Plenty, in this case of space and a general ease of cultivation, played as large a part in the shaping of the South as it did in the making of an 'American' civilization. The quest to become independent yeomen farmers inspired white Southerners from the rude, intractable, indentured servants of the 1620s to the gaunt, struggling yet persevering share-croppers of the 1930s. Even the blacks, after the Civil War, viewed yeoman independency as their principal economic and social objective. The four great military actions supported or engaged in by Southerners from the 1770s to the 1860s – the Revolution, Indian removal, the Mexican War and the Civil War – were in part at least brought on by this persistent itch for individual improvement, predicated in Southern circumstances upon access to western lands. For those lands were destined to become, if not always immediately, then at least very quickly, the raw materials for the seemingly endless creation of modest family farms. Space and plenty, and the physical mobility fostered by them and necessary to their full exploitation, contributed as much to the viability and bonding of Southern white society as to the realization of a more generally American dream.

Given such space and the urge, energy and ruthlessness to seize it and to fill it in, what did physical mobility do for Southern whites? Mobility eased social tensions and resentments that undoubtedly existed; it produced a certain amount of residential differentiation between some of the exceedingly wealthy and the extremely poor; and it prevented widespread pauperization and/or the advent of manufacturing within a constricted eastern seaboard South. The mass, largely westward, movement of the Southern population between 1790 and 1860 probably did not greatly alter the distribution of wealth; it did not produce a new South, although it *may* have contributed to the creation of a politically more egalitarian South; it did not conjure up new classes or divest old ones of their economic, social and political power; nor did it transform Southern thought or the section's ethnic mix. Instead, mobility ensured that the South remained as Southerners generally wanted it to remain, an agricultural and fairly fluid society.

Madison had warned the federal convention of 1787: 'In future times a great majority of the people will not only be without landed, but any sort of property.' He referred then as much to the South as to the country as a whole; and he continued to worry over this impending threat, even to such a new state as Kentucky in the 1790s (McCoy 1980: 129). The prospect of these propertyless masses forming a manufacturing work-force was so distinctly repulsive that Madison and other Southern leaders of his generation worked for decades to maintain a transatlantic division of labour. America's reliance upon British manufactured goods was no mark of subservience to metropolitan capitalism, but rather a happy escape from Americans' potential reduction to the demeaning and impoverished ranks of urban wage-slavery. The celebration of this escape continued as a dominant theme in Southern political economy throughout the antebellum period, reaching a crescendo of sorts in the 1850s with George Fitzhugh's violent condemnation of virtually all wage labour as, in effect, slavery (Fitzhugh 1960). And it remained an important theme thereafter. But the means of escape were not solely the South's successful resistance to high federal tariffs, designed as the latter were to protect and succour Northern industry. Mobility offered another escape route; for without mass movement to the west, pressure upon eastern seaboard lands would have created severe pauperization in the early nineteenth century; and that in turn would presumably have added practical weight to the theoretical case for introducing factory production. Plenty in itself and the availability of 'the People's Empire' to the west did not create an American and Southern social ethic. Rather the wide, but Indian, spaces of the constantly receding west were thrown open to settlement to sustain an ethic already fully accepted and articulated.

II

The facts of mobility are well known and simply demonstrated. In 1790 Southern whites numbered 1,271,488. Within two generations, by 1850, there were 6,222,418 white Southerners, of whom 1,933,153 lived in seven states that were uninhabited in 1790, or were then but modestly settled areas beyond America's control. Even in 1810 these seven states of 1850 – Alabama, Arkansas, Florida, Louisiana, Mississippi, Missouri and Texas – contained only about 75,000 whites. As these new regions attracted settlement, the eastern seaboard inevitably declined in relative importance. Kentucky held 61,133 whites in 1790; by 1850 its 761,413 whites made it the second most popular abode for Southern whites after Virginia, with 894,800. And if the old dominion retained its pre-eminence as the white homeland, only one white Southerner in every seven lived there in 1850, whereas one in every three had done so in Virginia's more glorious epoch, in 1790 (De Bow 1854: 45).

Of course, not all Southerners of the 1850s had been born in the South; some immigrants arrived from the North and from overseas. But the influx of foreign immigrants was not nearly as hefty as that flowing to the North. And immigrants anyway flocked to the cities and towns. Table 2 shows the leading Southern cities' foreign-born population in 1860. In none of the states containing the cities listed in Table 2 did the foreign-born in the population outside those cities exceed 7 per cent of the total non-metropolitan population. For example, while 61 per cent of St Louis' free people in 1860 were foreign-born, only 7 per cent of the free people in the rest of Missouri were born abroad.

As far as Northern immigration went, there was very little of it. For the South as a whole in 1860, only 3.4 per cent of the native-born population had been born in the North. Indeed, the South lost slightly through interregional migration among the native-born. In 1860, 655,496 Southern-born free people lived in the North – overwhelmingly in Illinois, Indiana and Ohio in that order. Only 355,811 Northern-born free people resided in the South (*Statistics* 1866: lviii, lxv). Yet Southerners' northward wanderings did not necessarily imply criticism

TABLE 2. Leading Southern cities' population in 1860

	Total free population	Foreign-born (%)
Baltimore	184,520	28
St Louis	157,476	61
New Orleans	144,601	44
Louisville	61,213	37
Richmond	23,635	20
Charleston	23,376	26
Mobile	20,854	34
Wilmington	19,044	21
Memphis	18,741	37
Savannah	13,875	33

of or dissent from slavery; nor were they necessarily the outcome of thwarted material ambitions. For those who had migrated to Kentucky in the early nineteenth century, or those born there, or in Tennessee, and for many Virginians pushing out to the west, movement into the southern areas of Ohio, Indiana and Illinois was neither illogical nor uncongenial, except, of course, to slaveowners. It was often easier to move in that direction than to press on to Missouri. Nor were such migrants a complete 'loss' to the South in her time of need during the 1850s; the southern areas of Ohio, Indiana and Illinois supported both a staunchly conservative faction of the Democratic party and the political conciliation of the South. Some Southern emigrants were alienated by the section's institutions and beliefs – most notably, fugitive blacks. But the emigration generally stiffened the Southern cause in national politics.

This process of westward movement has been so amply and variously illustrated with statistical and biographical evidence, so enthusiastically chronicled by re-tellers of the frontier saga, and so thoroughly embedded in Americans' collective consciousness, that it ceases almost to be a matter of comment or debate. Yet the scattering of Southerners widely across the trans-Appalachian West – like the splattering of so much machine-gun fire across a broad field of battle – was an accomplishment sometimes hazardous and often difficult to achieve; and its success certainly kept the South buoyant and socially viable in the mid nineteenth century. Movement to the West meant that material failures in youth in one locality might be compensated for by an acquisitive middle age in another; that resentments at the social mix or social order at place of birth could be eased by a major change of residence; that the cramping of opportunity where land prices were high could be counteracted by migration to less costly regions of settlement, or to altogether more fluid areas where squatters flourished without the niggling formalities of title deeds and land purchase; and that speculative opportunities could be pursued where cheaper or more readily tilled lands beckoned. To say all this is, in essence, to parrot the safety-valve thesis. Yet perhaps what physical mobility most effectively permitted was the maintenance of the yeoman farmer ideal – and its reality – in a period of rising consumption standards, exploding population and growing expectations that economic opportunities would be open to all.

If all men were mobile, the poor were more mobile than others. A whole range of local studies shows that it was the less wealthy who most failed to persist within the localities between decennial census years. For example, in St Mary's county – a mainly tobacco county in southern Maryland, and one facing stagnation from the late eighteenth century – a sample of 450 migrants revealed that 90 per cent of the emigrants in the 1790s were landless, and 67 per cent lacked taxable property. And landowners who did leave the county in the 1790s consistently owned smaller farms on average than persisters. The emigration, mainly to Kentucky in the 1790s, was neither random nor unorchestrated. County newspapers' advertisements in the years 1789–99 gave notice of a total of 480,000 acres being available in western regions, especially in Kentucky and available on easy terms or by lottery. By 1810, the ultimate destination was less clear-cut; Kentucky waned and some migrants even began venturing to the south-western territories; and wealthier emigrants, when such curiosities emerged, preferred well-established plantation areas in southern Maryland or tidewater Virginia (Marks 1979: 303, 316, 329, 332).

Such differing levels of mobility, related to wealth, recurred throughout the South and throughout the antebellum period. A plantation county in Alabama's lushest cotton lands – Dallas county – manifested a similarly differential pattern of migration. The following were the rates of persistence between 1850 and 1860 of heads of households according to their wealth as assessed in 1850:

	(%)
Over $25,000	58
$1,000–24,999	41
$1–999	34
0	24

Dallas had been organized only in 1818, but was already, by 1860, a thoroughly developed plantation community, with 77 per cent of its people being slaves. Even so, it was far from being a static community. Of white males aged twenty years or more in 1850, 66 per cent had left its principal town, Selma, ten years later; and 49 per cent of such men in *rural* Dallas county departed during that decade (Barney 1981: 34–7; Barney 1982: 148). A rather less wealthy and planter-dominated county was Clarke in Georgia's piedmont. It began to take settled shape at the turn of the century. In the early 1800s, Georgia's state university was placed in Clarke's frontier town of Athens. As in Dallas county, the urban population by the 1850s was more fluid than the rural populace. Between 1850 and 1860 the actual number of white males aged twenty years or more rose only slightly in Athens; but in 1860, 62 per cent of white male residents aged thirty to fifty-nine were newcomers. In a large, sample section of rural Clarke county, the number of white males aged twenty years or more fell slightly in the 1850s; even there, however, 54 per cent of white male residents aged thirty to fifty-nine in 1860 were newcomers to that area. In demographic terms, Dallas and Clarke, which were essentially wilderness or frontier in the 1790s when St Mary's county was experiencing such a vigorous exodus, were facing broadly similar problems of slowing real population growth rates by the 1850s. But their populations were not simply losing men; men were entering and leaving these counties in revolving door fashion. And this restlessness was much related to affluence. For Clarke county as a whole, 58 per cent of landowning farmers aged thirty to fifty-nine persisted from 1850 to 1860; a markedly higher rate of persistence than that of all men in that age group (Huffmann 1980: 239–51).

To-ings and fro-ings of this frequency and type were found as much on the frontier and in the West as in the maturing or even stagnating plantation areas of the East. For instance, the non-slave population of Phillips county, Arkansas, rose from 4,344 to 5,936 between 1850 and 1860. Yet only 32 per cent of farm-operators and landowners persisted in that decade; and a mere 18 per cent of rural labourers and non-landowners did so. Phillips county was one of the earliest parts of Arkansas to be settled, but its inhabitants had scarcely sunk their roots by 1860 (Moneyhon 1981: 159, 170). Even more freshly established was Nodaway county, Missouri. Organized as a county in 1845, Nodaway was mainly prairie; its population soared from 2,048 in 1850 to 5,123 ten years later. Although Northern settlers were attracted to it, 68 per cent of its people in 1850 and 56 per cent in 1860 had been born in slave states. Yet only 32 per cent of males aged fifteen years or more in 1850 were still there in 1860, even despite the dynamic growth in the county's population and the availability of land. Again, though, persistence was related to wealth. Of those reporting real estate worth at least $1,000 in 1850, 43 per cent stayed throughout the subsequent decade. Of those without real estate in 1850, only 25 per cent persisted. These proportions were remarkably similar to Dallas county's rates of persistence: 41 per cent for those with wealth of $1,000–24,999, and 24 per cent for the propertyless (Manring 1978: 389, 392, 401, 405–10). And this in spite of the strong contrast in length of settlement, type of agriculture and relative importance of slavery between the two counties.

These facts about mobility suggest the most powerful reason for mobility; yet high mobility itself makes discussion of mobility's practical impact difficult. No historian so far has been able to trace the fortunes of the nineteenth-century migrants who left one county possibly for a neighbouring county, a nearby state, or to leapfrog to some distant and fresh area of new settlement. But the rates of persistence already mentioned point to economic discontent and economic ambition as the spur to mobility. The landless and the propertyless moved on at a demonstrably higher rate than did the landowners.

This was not invariably the case. A detailed study of a sub-region of typically 'yeoman' agriculture in north-central Alabama shows that in the late 1820s and 1830s the planters and slaveowners were far more mobile than their less affluent neighbours. Slaveowners hurried to exploit the land boom of those years by crossing the border into very fertile lands acquired from the Indians in Mississippi. As these lands came on to the market, Alabama planters gobbled up excellent land especially attractive for slave labour at low prices. Their westward movement in turn provoked an exodus of small farmers from these developing plantation areas, particularly during the economically depressed 1840s. Some at least of such small farmers moved eastwards to the very area just abandoned by the entrepreneurial planters. Thus, for example, one in ten households in Alabama's yeoman Marion county in 1850 was headed by an immigrant from Mississippi's plantation belt. A disproportionately high level of migration by planters in this manner altered the social complexion of north-central Alabama. But this sharp contrast between yeoman and planter areas softened in the 1850s, as high cotton prices encouraged slaveownership and cotton production, and drew slaveowners into the yeoman sub-region. By 1860, 35 per cent of Marion county's *slaveowners* had entered the county since 1850 (Allman 1979: 297–308, 365–9).

More generally, the higher levels of persistence displayed by the planters and substantial farmers did not mean that such groups were immobile, or that they so monopolized local resources as to squeeze out the poorer whites, or that they uniformly formed tightly knit and permanently fixed local ruling elites. There were examples of local planter elites whose dominance carried on over the generations. Such planter groups formed a cousinage of family influence rather than a well defined aristocracy of inherited privilege and power. In Burke county, North Carolina, a mountain area settled in the 1770s, some dominant, persisting and wealthy families soon emerged. During the period 1777–1865 a McDowell went from Burke county to the state General Assembly for 29 sessions of the 77, an Avery for 17 and an Erwin for 13. A McDowell owned the county's most highly assessed plantation in 1860 and an Avery was the largest slaveowner in Burke before 1860. These men stood out in a county where only one in eight farms had over 100 improved acres on the eve of the Civil War. Yet even these leading and persisting families were hardly grandees. The McDowells' seat and the Averys' house were substantial dwellings; but nothing more than ample farm-houses (Phifer 1979: 14–19, 75–6, 95). And these families' heavy representation in state politics did not parallel the continuous hold which British gentry families exerted over the localities where they were pre-eminent.

More generally, while some planter families obviously stayed put and stayed dominant, others roamed geographically and slid in and out of the elite. A sample drawn from five 'black belt' counties in Alabama's most prosperous plantation area shows that of the 236 very wealthiest families in 1850, 47 per cent were still present in the richest 236 ten years later. (This estimate of persistence takes heirs into account; it is not a measure of persistence among the 236 wealthiest individuals.) Yet the sample group constituted 8 per cent of all landowners, a substantial icing on the social cake (Wiener 1978: 8, 10). In a more narrowly defined elite (amounting to the wealthiest 4.5 per cent of the landowners in 1860), only 30 per cent of the very richest planters in a sub-region of south-west Georgia in 1850 were still there ten years later. Admittedly, this area had not been settled for as long as Burke county had been; it was wrenched from the Creeks in the 1830s. But its mobile (either down or out) elite shows that, if the affluent were less footloose than the landless, they were still fixed in neither place nor status (Formwalt 1981: 410–19).

If the quest for better, cheaper or more land exercised planters and poor farmers alike (though more so for the latter), harsher and more pressing reasons for geographical mobility operated, especially, though not exclusively, upon poorer farmers.

A classic, if possibly exaggerated, example of the push of worsening circumstances as against the pull of alluring prospects acting upon immigration came from the tobacco area of southern Maryland during 1790 to 1840. As the prices of tobacco fell in the 1790s and 1800s, prospects for tobacco farming dimmed. Tenants and small-scale farmers could just about make a profit, but only if their costs were low. But from the 1810s for tenant farmers, and from the 1820s even for landowners, real depression set in. Land was in short supply; persisters began to lose wealth, not gain it. Where successful adaptation to tobacco's troubles was possible and was effected, on the more fertile lands and in the 1810s, the switch to wheat increased the size of farms and reduced the population among landowners and tenants alike. There was simply insufficient high quality land available for a universal conversion to wheat farming (Marks 1979: 343, 355–6, 396–7, 445).

So, too, elsewhere, fertile land was either exhausted in the short-term agricultural cycle or insufficiently abundant to meet the yeoman-farmer ambitions of a burgeoning population. Debts, as well as falling prices or contracting land supplies, encouraged migration. A novel written in 1859, by 'A Southern Country Minister' in South Carolina, told the story of a Baptist minister and farmer of 300 acres being obliged to sell his farm and seek cheaper lands in the west when a neighbour failed to pay a debt for which the minister stood security. Yet the unfortunate minister remained optimistic: 'Blessed America! whose broad prairies and fertile woodlands, lofty mountains and green valleys invite the landless and houseless to independence, to happiness, to homes!' (A Southern Country Minister, 1860: 9–12, 152–66). This experience, of selling land in fertile and well developed areas to pay debts and then moving to areas of cheaper land, was not simply a fictional conceit. Even for those not in debt, but who wanted bigger farms or more easily cultivated land, geographical mobility offered an enticing prospect. One agricultural journalist, impressed by recent travels in Texas, declared in his *Affleck's Southern Rural Almanac and Plantation and Garden Calendar, for 1856:*

> let those who may feel dissatisfied with their present locations; who are
> not realizing a fair return for their investment in kind and labor or
> whose family, white and black, increase more rapidly than their means of
> support; let them go and take a leisurely look at Texas.

Especially attractive bargains in land could be obtained in areas at some distance from major roads. But it was not solely these low land prices prevalent in Texas that made that state so alluring. Affleck recorded his frustration with conditions at home:

> We have been industriously engaged for more than a dozen years in cultivating and improving the worn and washed hill lands of Southern Mississippi. No means have been left untried to render our farming profitable. But we cannot say we feel encouraged to persevere. The labor is incessant and never-ending. Improvement, when effected, is not permanent. After expending skill, labor and money in bringing a tract of land into a productive state, the utmost vigilance is needed to keep it so.

In contrast, cultivation in Texas was relatively easy; purchasable land was not so heavily timbered as to be difficult to clear; and the lie of the country militated against the washing away of the soil. This meant that environmental conditions in Texas did not operate against permanent and comfortable settlement to the extent that they did in southern Mississippi. Upland areas there demanded so much effort from yeomen farmers, in clearing woods, in breaking new fields as the highly friable soils gave out, and in trying to raise crops, that limited time and energy, and indeed incentive, given the rapidity of soil exhaustion, remained for ordinary farmers to construct adequate and permanent dwellings. They had no compelling reason to be tied to their prevailing lot in Mississippi (Affleck 1856: 7–9, 11–12, 15).

Stepping westwards was not simply a response to economic decline, impending impoverishment, or debt. It was also part of a quest for opportunity among the young, for if the wealthier persisted to a far greater extent than did the poor, the old persisted more than the young. Of wealthy planters possessing fifty or more slaves in Georgia, Alabama, Mississippi and Louisiana, only 22 per cent were under forty years old in 1860 (Menn 1964: 176). These were the people most likely to be immobile. Yet the vast mass of white males aged twenty or more, 65 per cent in fact, were twenty to thirty-nine years old. The less wealthy were also often the young. In Texas in 1860, of those whose wealth was valued at under $500, 38 per cent were in their twenties, and 72.4 per cent were under forty years old. Of those worth $20,000 or more, 70.6 per cent were forty years or older (Campbell and Lowe 1977: 61). The plight of the propertyless and the 'enforced' mobility of the poor should not be exaggerated where about two-thirds of white men over twenty were still in their twenties and thirties (*Population ... 1860*: 592–3); where a sizeable minority (38 per cent in one regional sample) of men in their early twenties were unmarried *and* lived with their parents (Harris 1981: 81); and where a majority of white males remained unmarried at twenty-five years of age. Much mobility was a rural, Southern response to Horace Greeley's urban, Northern call, 'Go West, Young man!'

III

Whether mobility improved the economic lot of the mobile is difficult to prove. Over the long term, recent research suggests that the aggregate distribution of wealth did not alter much. Alice Hanson Jones has attempted to ascertain the distribution of wealth in the colonies in 1774. Her estimates, which are based on both complicated procedures and not unimpeachable evidence and assumptions, point to a situation in which the top 10 per cent of free adult wealth-holders ('roughly heads of free families') held 47 per cent of all physical wealth. The top 20 per cent together held 70 per cent; the poorest 30 per cent held 1.6 per cent (Jones 1980: 313–14). Nearly three generations later, in 1860, the position, as depicted by Gavin Wright, was very broadly similar, but with a more marked concentration of wealth in the top decile of wealth-holders. Taking total wealth, Wright calculates that the top 10 per cent accounted for 58.6 per cent of all wealth in the *cotton* South (not the South as a whole). Taking agricultural wealth, Wright finds that the richest 10 per cent owned 53 per cent, whereas the poorest 50 per cent owned 5.6 per cent (Wright 1978: 26, 30). Allowing for deficiencies in the data, and for the fact that different areas were sampled, these figures at best indicate that mobility and expansion had not fundamentally altered the distribution of wealth. So, too, a variety of local studies for the 1790s and 1800s and a wider analysis for the 1850s by Lee Soltow suggest a general sameness in the distribution of wealth (Soltow 1975, 1980, 1981). If this seems a weak conclusion, one stresses that the evidence is elusive, that the geographical areas sampled are often not precisely the same, but display very differing agricultural interests and characteristics, that the population expanded enormously between the 1770s and 1860, and that the concentration of wealth at the top end reflects also the age profile of this very youthful population.

The fullest and most accessible figures for wealth distribution come from the censuses of 1850 and 1860. These reveal considerable gains in the wealth of slaveholders, somewhat at the relative expense of the non-slaveholding farmers and labourers; although the proportion of household heads who were slaveholders declined in the 1850s, the share of total agricultural wealth in slaveholders' hands slipped almost imperceptibly. Professor Wright estimated that the average wealth of slaveholders in seven regions of the Cotton South climbed from $8,887 in 1850 to $25,058. The average wealth for non-slaveholders in the period also rose, but not at such a rapid rate: from $753 to $1,764. Obviously the real gap widened greatly (Wright 1978: 36). This occurrence has encouraged some general speculation on the social dynamics of the late antebellum South. Steven Hahn, from his research on selected upper piedmont counties in Georgia, concluded: 'Over time, slave prices and land values rose, thereby narrowing prospects for social mobility. Evidence indicates that the late antebellum period witnessed a growing concentration of wealth and increasing social stratification.' And this differentiation, between very noticeably increasing wealth in plantation areas and yeomen areas left behind as slaveowners accelerated away, contributed, according to Hahn, to the secession crisis of 1860–1 (Hahn 1979: 15–16, 57, 117–18; Hahn 1982: 36, 40, 46–7). For yeoman disaffection made political separation attractive to the planters in power, as a way of forestalling a potential alliance between disgruntled Southern yeomen and Northern Republicans.

This argument remains hypothetical. Mention was made among secessionists in 1860–1 of possible yeomen disaffection. But it was a very minor point beside the predominant concern for the defence of slavery and Southerners' right to control the future fate of slavery. Moreover, the facts of wealth distribution themselves afford uncertain evidence. We cannot extrapolate belief or behaviour from them. We need to be careful to assess their true significance. Much, for instance, has been made of the long-term drop in the proportion of Southern household heads who owned slaves, from 36 per cent in 1830 to 31 per cent in 1850 to 25 per cent in 1860 (Wright 1978: 34). Yet these figures are sometimes treated as if they can scientifically be regarded as pointing to a trend, which three figures cannot be harnessed to do. And they are also cited without full and necessary warning that the census of 1860 was taken in the midst of a mini-boom in the Cotton South. Following a national credit squeeze in 1857–8, the South especially enjoyed high raw-material prices in 1859 and a record cotton crop. Slave prices rose as a result. Clearly, the assessed wealth of slaveowners and planters with prime cotton lands was enviably high in 1859–60. But the assessment reflected very specific conditions. By contrast, in 1850 the South was beginning a steady recovery from the price deflation and general economic depression of the early and middle 1840s. From the simple circumstances of when the censuses were taken, one would expect a widening gap in wealth to have emerged between non-slaveholders and slaveholders in 1860 as compared with 1850.

The boom conditions of 1859–60, however, did not necessarily mark a major trend that would continue in future. Moreover, if, as Wright makes clear, the actual wealth of non-slaveowners rose appreciably in the 1850s – though not quite as rapidly as the slaveowners' average wealth – then this fact was of as much importance to ordinary non-slaveowning farmers as was the fact that the rising cost of slaves made the purchase of slaves increasingly difficult. As long as purchasing power was not eroded by inflation and as long as access to land was open, then the essential buoyancy of Southern society remained. Southerners themselves, after all, were unaware of the fine details of overall wealth distribution; but they certainly knew what their cash flow looked like.

There is little reason to doubt that access to land remained open. The percentage of Tennessee's farmers who owned their own land rose fractionally in the 1850s as shown in Table 3. In Mississippi, admittedly, the proportion of household heads who were landowners dropped slightly in the same years (Table 4). But, given the inevitable inaccuracies and misreporting in the original census returns; and that these figures do not refer to the same people but to a shifting population, of whom perhaps only 40 per cent persisted from 1850 to 1860; and given minor shifts in the agricultural circumstances and fortunes of the sample counties in Tennessee and Mississippi upon which these regional generalizations are founded, it is justifiable to conclude that no notable constrictions upon landowning arose in the 1850s (Clark 1971: 27–9, 9; Weaver 1945: 64–71). Indeed, Wright shows that statistically trifling changes occurred in the aggregate distribution of improved land between 1850 and 1860 (Wright 1978: 30).

TABLE 3. Landowning among Tennessee farmers

	1850 (%)	1860 (%)
Eastern Tennessee	approx. 60	approx. 60
Middle Tennessee	66	71
Western Tennessee	68	73

Moreover, if total wealth was concentrated in the South, landowning was not. In the early years of settlement, big landholdings were often acquired by prominent politicians, or Revolutionary War generals, or consortia of investors, for speculative purposes. In a sample survey of nine of Tennessee's counties for the period 1787–1812, Lee Soltow found that among 12 people holding 10,000 acres or more, only 1 was a resident; a mere 68 of 3,800 taxpayers held 2,000 acres or more, and only 21 of them were residents (Soltow 1981: 281). In Phillips county, Arkansas, 88 men (of a white population of 5,936) in 1860 held 1,000 acres or more; but only 1 in 4 of these men, according to the census at least, held *improved* acres (Moneyhon 1981: 163–4). Such lands were for

TABLE 4. Landowning among Mississippi household heads

	1850 (%)	1860 (%)
Delta Loess region	89	86
North-eastern hills	83.5	74.5
Pine barrens	78	77.5

speculation or grazing. By the 1850s, under 1 per cent of Tennessee's landowners held more than 5,000 acres; about 5 per cent held over 1,000 acres; a majority owned 200 or fewer acres; and a majority of non-slaveowning farmers held 51–200 acres (Clark 1971: 39–40, 46). It is little wonder that a whole generation of patriotic Southern historians have written warmly of a yeoman society or of the plain folk as the true back-bone of the antebellum rural order (Owsley 1949; Clark 1971; Weaver 1945). Even in the excellent cotton-growing area around Augusta, Georgia, nine-tenths of all farms had under 500 acres of improved land. Tenancy was relatively unimportant; it varied from county to county in that region, from a high of one-quarter to a low of one-tenth of all farms; so, too, labourers headed from 11.7 per cent of county households to a tiny 1.5 per cent (Harris 1981: 17, 208–11). And where, very exceptionally, tenancy was common, tenants were not necessarily, by local standards, poor. Covington county, Alabama, was one such odd place; 58 per cent of household heads in 1850 were tenants, but 95 per cent of tenants owned animals and 65 per cent of them possessed livestock worth $100 or more (McWhiney 1978: 19). If slaveownership became rarer in the late 1850s, land was still readily available and tenancy was little known.

A lack of slaves did not condemn non-slaveowners to individual poverty or inertia. A study of settlement in Texas in 1860 shows that immigrants into the state from the Gulf South moved into the cotton-growing, slaveowning regions of eastern Texas. But immigrants from Tennessee, Kentucky, Missouri and Arkansas moved into the north-central and central regions where they pursued their own farming practices and interests, untroubled by the usually obtrusive presence of cotton, slavery and the plantation regime (Jordan 1979: 211–14). Moreover, even in the hill country of Arkansas or the mountains of North Carolina, non-slaveowning farmers could grow cotton as a cash crop. In one Arkansas highland county, 47 per cent of slaveless farmers raised cotton in 1860 (Otto 1980: 51). It was not unknown beyond the plantations for even farmers' teenage daughters to work in the fields when required at harvest time. More generally, the sheer space available, the ease and frequency of physical movement, and the opportunities for herding and for killing game, all contributed to the making of an acceptable, if not affluent, standard of living.

This last consideration, moreover, raises a question which has not so far been answered. Historians have been mesmerized by wealth statistics, largely because these can be culled readily from the federal censuses of 1850 and 1860 (earlier censuses being of limited use on this score). Yet one may object, first, that these analyses of wealth-holding are largely presented without reference to the age structure of the wealth-holders. Such a lapse is especially serious when the male population was as youthful as the South's; for example, in 1860, about 40 per cent of rural Alabama's white males over twenty years old were also under thirty (Allman 1979: 377). Wealth did increase with age, yet age is omitted from most studies of wealth-holding. Secondly, a fixation with wealth-holding at arbitrarily determined times creates a false impression of reality, an ignoring of the fundamental economic distinction between a stock concept and a flow concept. Most people pay closer attention to their flow of income than to their stock of assets. Yet our knowledge of Southerners' income and income distribution is exceedingly sketchy. Although wealth and income are interrelated, they are not necessarily tightly linked. One can think of a farmer owning two infant slaves and a female slave of advanced years capable of nothing beyond mild household chores. The infants would certainly add to his estimated wealth; but the possession of three slaves would add nothing, for many years, to his income. Nor is this a merely fanciful putative case. In a sample of four yeoman counties in Alabama in 1820 and 1830, one in five white households owned a slave; but a majority of these slaveowners held only one to three slaves. As measured by their stock of assets, these slaveowners belonged to a local elite (Allman 1979: 195–6). In terms of immediate income, they could well have been no better off than their slaveless neighbours. Until we know a great deal more about individuals' income, as well as the profile of wealth-holding at scattered and artificially determined points, we need to be suspicious of bold and unambiguous claims about the rising and declining fortunes and expectations of such vast and crudely defined groups as planters and yeoman farmers, slaveowners and the non-slaveowning majority.

At root, the principal achievement of nineteenth-century expansionism and mobility was to sustain the ideal-type of Southern farming society that had emerged by the late eighteenth century; a society in which, if there were some large plantations and if about 30–40 per cent of white men were landless and probably, though not necessarily, poor, the broad mass of white households obtained at least small farms and the opportunity to labour long and hard at the plough.

IV

E. P. Thompson, in a frequently quoted passage, once complained that static analyses of social 'structure' and quantitative efforts to define class were inappropriate, since 'class itself is not a thing, it is a happening' (Thompson 1965: 357). Something along the same lines might be said of the habit of mobility and of the South itself. Despite many changes from 1790 to 1860 in crop specialism, in the practice of agriculture, and in the physical environment where agriculture was carried on, the distribution of wealth within the South, the social mix there and the underlying commitment to yeoman farming and small plantation cultivation remained constant. Southerners – policy-makers and ordinary men and women alike – evinced a marked reluctance to seek their fortunes in, or shift their families to, what towns existed in the South. Such protest as there was against the Southern economic order was directed against speculators, distant finance houses, inflation-fuelling, note-issuing banks and more occasionally planter power. The latter, the most obvious target for home-grown attack, was rarely subjected to any sustained indigenous onslaught. The agrarian ideal maintained its appeal. And mobility afforded a more ready, easier and probably more effective means of individual economic improvement than internal redistribution promised. Moreover, mobility took on the qualities of a virtue in itself, as Southerners were intent on becoming rather than merely being. Given the fact that the aggregate distribution of wealth remained fairly constant during the geographical and population expansion of 1770–1860, physical mobility and the conquest of new resources clearly provided material gain for vast numbers of whites.

This past success, conditional upon physical mobility and, in its assumption of the easy cultivation and easy accumulation of land, conditioned by physical mobility, lay behind the political anxieties of the 1850s and the Southerners' considerable unity in insisting upon slavery extension during that decade. But those anxieties and that unity were related also to future prospects. For in 1850, 54 per cent of the white population in six of the seven Deep South states that led secession ten years later were under twenty years old. Nearly 52 per cent of all American whites in 1850 were of that age (De Bow 1854: 51). But the South generally, and the Deep South perhaps especially, did not provide for or encourage migration to the towns as a means of material self-advancement. Only fresh farmlands, and the guarantee of future movement into them, would answer the future economic needs of so root-less, so young, and so determinedly agrarian a people. It was not surprising that the contest over slavery in Kansas, and in the new West generally, precipitated the sectional controversy that led to war. For a denial of western expansion came, rightly or wrongly, to symbolize for Southerners a denial also of that geographical mobility which was a saving technique, a habit and almost a virtue in itself.

Chapter seven

GOVERNMENT

I

It was fashionable in the 1850s for Northern opponents of slavery extension to assert that the dynamic for expansionism came from within the Southern class system. Expansionism was at the behest of the planter elite, and was promoted to preserve slavery in the long term. Southern political leaders countered with the claim that slavery itself boosted white unity and that the only class within the South was the class of whites differentiated for ever and in every way from the debased and degraded blacks. This dispute, often made more sophisticated and detailed with time, has continued ever since the 1850s. We have already argued that it would be wrong to see the Southern state governments of the 1850s as dominated by the planter elite. On the other hand, we have also argued that the difference between planters and slaveowners is an impossible one to define in the neat statistical fashion so habitually employed by historians. What can be stated categorically is that the slaveowners dominated Southern politics, even if most slaveowners were men of middling wealth and humble attainments and aspirations. The questions which naturally arise from this fact are: Were there fairly readily detectable signs that slaveowners systematically used power against the interests of non-slaveowners? Was there an underlying slaveowner–non-slaveowner antagonism within Southern society?

At one level, the slaveowners generally used their power for entirely selfish and defensive purposes. In most Southern states by the 1850s there was at least some residual bias towards slaveowners left in the state systems of representation. In the most blatant cases, legislative seats were distributed according to total population; in less blatant instances, they were distributed according to the federal ratio, thus counting a non-voting slave as three-fifths of a person; and in other cases, legislative seats went according to a combination of white population and taxes paid. To some degree or another such methods of representation inflated slaveowners' powers. But it must be said that these hang-overs from an eighteenth-century struggle to reconcile the representation of interests with that of persons were being steadily eroded by the 1850s. In Virginia, for instance, a long contest against the legislative over-representation of the slaveowning east by the largely non-slaveowning west won some – very reluctantly yielded – practical concessions; these took the form of state funding of internal improvements beneficial to the west granted by the legislature in the late 1810s and 1820s. The contest culminated in 1830 and 1851 in constitutional changes which greatly reduced the east's privileged position. If the campaign for more equal representation was a long one, it achieved much in 1830. And it must be seen against a backdrop of very considerable anxiety among eastern slaveowners that the non-slaveowning western Virginians would not so much try to abolish slavery as raise state taxes in order to finance internal improvements projects helpful to the west. While, therefore, one should not pretend that full equality of representation had been accomplished by the 1850s, one should not rush to the opposite extreme of equating unequal representation with anti-republicanism; there was a perfectly sound republican tradition that interests should be protected within a system of representative government. Moreover, the inequalities were usually not, by the 1850s at least, glaring. Virginia's reformed constitution of 1851 provided for apportionment of house seats solely on the basis of white population; and it opened the principal state offices to popular election. Yet it also retained existing and somewhat arbitrary senate districts that greatly favoured the heavily slaveowning tidewater and piedmont areas; and it made a concession to slaveowners by fixing taxes on slaves against price inflation. These conservative features of the settlement of 1851 were not, however, very striking. The western regions enjoyed a majority when the two houses of the legislature together elected the US senators. And the popular will could be expressed very readily in voting for the state governor and other leading officials (Freehling 1982).

By international yardsticks, Southern state governments, with the exception of South Carolina, were thrown wide open by the 1850s. In 1839 the British Chartists – an organization very heavily supported and led by the skilled working classes and the lower middle classes – demanded six major constitutional reforms. Some of these were obviously already anachronistic in contemporary America: there were virtually no property qualifications for office-holding, and congressmen, unlike British MPs, were already paid for their services; universal manhood suffrage was more or less accomplished for Southern whites, even though it was very far from having been achieved in Britain even as late as 1914. The British Chartists also demanded annual parliaments, to ensure that legislatures were fully responsive to popular will; American federal and state elections were already very largely at least biennial. The only real component of the Chartists' ideal which was not already realized in the South was the establishment of equal electoral districts.

But even here, as has been indicated, the movement of constitutional change by the 1850s was running very markedly in that direction.

By British nineteenth-century standards, therefore, the Southern states had achieved a high degree of constitutional democracy. This fact, however, still does not disprove the assertion that the slaveowners were peculiarly privileged and very effectively entrenched in power.

More specifically related to this point are two further facts. One is that *some* Southern states – for example, Alabama – had very open democratic systems of representation and government. Slaveowners there enjoyed no reserved power. Yet non-slaveowners' political pressure did not burgeon, to assail slavery. And the demands for Southern, and slavery, expansionism were as forceful and persistent and popular there as anywhere else in the antebellum South. The extent of truly 'popular' state government appears to have had little impact upon states' policies towards slavery or their demands for slavery extension. Secondly, although there may have been occasions when non-slaveowners resented slavery and, more particularly perhaps, resented slaveowners' power, there were few occasions when non-slaveowners launched vigorous and long-term campaigns against the slaveowning interest. One explanation for this is that slaveowners were never quite strong enough to forestall some concessions being made to the non-slaveowners. But another is that non-slaveowning farmers – generally the poorer farmers anyway – took scant interest in state government. As long as government was limited and unobtrusive, as long as taxes were low and land was available and inexpensive, then the non-slaveowning electorates were apathetic and acquiescent.

State governments were, then, firmly in the political hands of the slaveowners. Yet the non-slaveowners had ready and frequent access to power; and it was up to them to choose their representatives from the middling classes. In the Virginia house of Delegates in 1831–2, for instance, when the possibility of very gradual emancipation was vigorously and closely debated, 22 of the 133 members were planters, according to the formal definition of a planter as the owner of 20 or more slaves. But 33 delegates owned no slaves, and 17 owned only one or two slaves (Freehling 1982: 272–8). Even in Virginia the maintenance of slavery lay in the hands of a legislature which could include many very small slaveowners or non-slaveowners in its membership. Given this fact, was there much evidence that state governments suppressed or thwarted the 'popular' will, acted merely as bulwarks for slaveowners' property interests, deliberately avoided taking action on welfare issues in order to keep slaveowners' taxes down, or became so mesmerized by national slavery issues that they failed to tackle other problems closer to home? In order to answer this question, the state governments of Georgia and Mississippi, both of the Deep South and both important secessionist states in 1860–1, will be examined in closer detail.

II

A study of the surviving records (and it must be admitted that not a vast quantity of relevant records survive) suggests the following conclusions for Georgia's government. The institutions of the state were weak. Yet the case for state action was made at the very top. One might cynically say that there was a gubernatorial convention that state governors should mouth their beliefs in state action to provide schooling and to promote economic development, comfortable in the knowledge that legislators would disregard their ritual exhortations. Yet some governors said nothing about positive government; the option of silence existed. And others did try to innovate. The point is that the ideology which governor after governor passed down for the ordinary voters to absorb was not one of negativism and quietism. Not only did governors urge the citizenry to regard the state governments as their own. They also pressed the legislators to expand public services. If the non-slaveowners or ordinary slaveowners wanted to find a cause, it was often the state governors who were offering one for them to adopt. This situation is quite the opposite to that which Marxian historians depict. Doctrines disseminated from above were not those of complacent conservatism. The energy and ideas for reform – ultimately thwarted by the slavocracy, in the Marxian view – did not seethe up from below.

First: the state institutions. Amanda Johnson, in her history of Georgia, long ago documented the repeated complaints made by governors in the years 1827–55 about the feeble organization and equipment of the militia (Johnson 1938: 372–4). Here was an institution of prime importance to a white populace sitting on the powder keg of slavery. Yet throughout the period 1800–60, and not just in the years 1827–55, governor after governor pleaded with the legislature to reform and improve the state militia. In 1802 Governor Tattnall grumbled about the inadequacy of the militia laws based upon the Act of 1792. Officers and privates alike, he claimed, found these complex and contradictory laws incomprehensible. Ordinary citizens, especially those in the upper country, could not afford the muskets and accoutrements prescribed for purchase (J. of Sen. Ga. 1802: 5–6). In 1811 Governor Mitchell repeated Tattnall's recommendation that the state should equip the militia: 'The hardy laboring class of our citizens are unable to bear this expense, and hence we see how few of our Companies now established are able to man even one field piece' (J. of Sen. Ga. 1811: 11). Nothing much happened.

Nor did the fault solely result from a system which threw the expense of armaments upon the militia soldiers themselves. One retiring brigadier in 1836 reported to the governor on the indifference towards militia service on the part of the 'best men' locally, who refused to run for election as officers:

> It is with regret that I have for some time been witnessing the growing indifference of the people on the subject of military affairs; and the low estimate in which the service is held. The better qualified of the citizens will not consent to hold an office. The consequence resulting from such a state of things, men of loose morals or intemperate habits are elected and appointed, who serve in such a manner as to throw the service into disrepute, and thereby a large portion of the people, feel no interest in the institution (Aaron W. Grier to Govr., 15 Nov. 1836: Ga. Govrs.' Papers. William Schley, TCC, Box 50).

This variation on the perennial theme that there are no bad privates, only bad officers, came, surprisingly, at a time when large number of Georgians volunteered to serve in the Seminole War. But such a response to an emergency did not compensate for long years of neglect. In the mid-1850s Governor Herschel V. Johnson was vainly urging a total reorganization of the militia; and haplessly acknowledging that governors had long pleaded for such reforms. In 1858–9, the legislature's only response to Governor Joseph E. Brown's reformist pleas was the passage by the House of Representatives of a resolution favouring the establishment of an armoury. Brown in 1859 went so far as to describe military training in Georgia as the worst in any of the original thirteen states; but to no avail (J. of Sen. Ga. 1855–6: 34; 1857: 20–1; J. of H. Ga. 1858: 32–33; 1859: 24; Johnson 1938: 374). When national events stimulated wider interest in military preparedness in 1860 the South generally displayed an amateur spirit of enthusiastic volunteering that well showed how fragile were the states' existing militia institutions. In November 1860, for instance, J. F. C. Settle raised a militia company in Mitchell county, Georgia, and became captain of it. He promptly wrote to Governor Brown asking for speedy despatch of 'such arms and accoutrements as may be at your disposal, for forty men'. He asked also for advice on military organization – and in turn offered the governor some – but did so while wondering whether any such organization existed in the state. None of this correspondence suggested that the militia organization had reached deep into Mitchell county (J. F. C. Settle to Govr. 10 Nov. 1860. Ga. Govrs.' Papers. Joseph E. Brown. TCC, Box 55).

The ineffectiveness of state militia arrangements and the inefficiency of state militia musters were much commented upon – indeed frequently parodied – by contemporaries. Why was nothing much done? Governors returned repeatedly, from 1802 to 1860, to the subject. Yet legislatures failed to bestir themselves. They may have wished to avoid raising taxes. They were probably, and not unreasonably, satisfied with the local vigilante arrangements for coping with runaway slaves and recalcitrant blacks. But they also respected local jealousies of state government interference. Such caution in the face of customary rights was best expressed in November 1847, by Governor George W. Towns. Captain A. Wilson had asked the governor for an appointment as a battalion colonel if he raised a mounted battalion in Georgia. Towns declined to meddle with the customary right of volunteer soldiers to select their own officers:

> If the right of the volunteer to choose his field officers is secured to him by law or usage, I care not which, it is of that delicate nature that should not be infringed, if it be possible to avoid it, and the cases must be rare that would render it proper for the Executive to interfere (A. Wilson to Govr. 9 Nov. 1847, Geo. W. Towns to Capt. A. Wilson, 12 Nov. 1847. Ga. Govrs.' Papers. George W. Towns. TCC, Box 54).

Such attitudes were not, of course, simply Southern. Localism tugged hard against military efficiency on both sides during the Civil War. But such respect for citizens' customary rights and local initiative makes nonsense of excessively formalized ideas of 'state power' in a Southern setting.

The disparity between what a rational and reformist governor might desire and what the legislature and the localities would dispense was again evident in Georgia's disputes over schooling.

In 1816 Governor Mitchell requested state financial assistance for schooling. This suggestion – for once – struck a responsive chord. A legislative committee in 1817 endorsed the idea of establishing free schools by citing the grandest political arguments. 'As the legitimate end of government is the good of the governed, those who are entrusted with the sovereign powers of the state, are under the most sacred obligations to consult and promote the general welfare.' Whereas arbitrary governments kept their populations ignorant and subordinate, free governments' basis lay in a favourable public sentiment, since 'the more pure and enlightened is the public judgment, the greater is the perfection of the institution, and the stronger is the interest which binds together the various parts'. Since the state's principal resources were the minds and morals of the people, the state itself had a duty to diffuse knowledge and thereby develop those resources. In effect this meant aiding the poor: 'The children of the wealthy will find opportunities of education somewhere, but there is a large proportion of the community whose means are limited, and whose minds must forever remain uncultivated, unless they receive the paternal care of the government' (J. of S. Ga. 1816: 6; J. of S. Ga. 1817: 34). In the economically buoyant conditions of 1817 the legislature advanced $250,000 to establish a school fund; a further $250,000 was appropriated in 1821 (Johnson 1938: 245). This generous beginning was followed in the 1830s by less happy consequences. The monies allocated for schooling were placed in a separate education fund, from which, in turn, sums were invested in various enterprises, such as banks and railroads. These enterprises were either badly or corruptly run or simply unsuccessful; by the 1830s the education budget was steadily depleted. A new school fund had to be created in 1836–7 (Heath 1954: 245–9). But in 1852 the revenue available from the state was the interest on only $300,000, and that revenue had to be distributed among counties according to the number of poor children returned by the county ordinary or clerk (Coulter 1925: 2–3).

The 1850s – a decade largely of prosperity – witnessed renewed interest in educational provision. In 1853, the commissioners of common schools for Chatham county (which included Savannah) argued that 'a great and perhaps the chief impediment' in the way of state aid to public education was the use of 'poor' in describing the fund and the schools. Instead the school system should be 'popularized as much as possible ... in such a manner as to interest all classes in the system itself' (A. Porter *et al.* to Govr. 9 June 1853. Ga. Govrs.' Papers. Howell Cobb. TCC Box 54). This argument was certainly repeated; but Governor Herschel V. Johnson in 1855 and 1857 was more concerned to combat the illiteracy found among the poor than to introduce a comprehensive school system. As had been the case in 1817, Johnson's urgings were couched in the political language of the Enlightenment. If the people were to be capable of true self-government, they required 'intelligence, to know how to govern, and virtue, to give that intelligence proper direction.' To furnish education – 'an indispensable qualification for good citizenship' – to the poor, Johnson in 1857 recommended that the counties be divided into school districts, which would then be empowered to raise money through taxation (J. of S. Ga. 1855–6: 27–8; J. of S. Ga. 1857: 22–4). His successor, Brown, went further in arguing to the legislature that the schools had for too long suffered from paltry financing and incompetent teaching. He wanted democratic schooling for a democratic white society:

> let every free white child in the State have an equal right to attend and receive instruction in the public schools. Let it be a Common School, not a Poor School System. Let the children of the richest and the poorest parents in the State, meet in the school-room on terms of perfect equality of right. Let there be no aristocracy there but an aristocracy of color and of conduct (J. of H. Ga. 1858: 20–1).

Such boldness made some headway; in 1858 the legislature ear-marked $100,000 per annum from the receipts of the state-owned Western and Atlantic railroad for educational purposes. In this fashion, extra state taxes were avoided; and the possibility existed of having an increasing flow of income available from the railroad. At the same time, the counties were authorized to raise their own taxes, expressed as a percentage of the state tax, to supplement the revenue they obtained from the state education fund. Yet in 1858 only 84 of the 132 counties bothered to raise these supplementary taxes and the amount so gleaned was a mere $65,000; the tax counties imposed upon themselves ranged from a low of 5 per cent of the state tax to a high of 50 per cent.

Confronting such a patchy and parsimonious response to his earlier recommendations, Governor Brown returned to the subject in 1859. He wanted the counties to raise $100,000, not $65,000, and the state grant to be doubled to $200,000 (J. of H. Ga. 1859: 35, 39). Nothing much ensued. The counties were less than enthusiastic. In 1860, 30 of the 132 counties failed to return to the governor's office basic statistics on the number of children and on the number of those in school during 1859; 18 of the rest did not report any local tax-raising to supplement the school fund, so bringing the total of the lethargic to 48 of 132 counties. And the state legislature failed before 1861 to establish a public school system. Even as late as 1860, about 18 per cent of adult whites were illiterate and at least 35 per cent of children aged 8–18 years did not attend school (Johnson 1938: 429; J. of H. Ga. 1859: 39).

The reasons for failure are fairly obvious. Professor E. Merton Coulter argued that administrative inefficiency prevented educational improvement; county ordinaries or clerks were not paid for educational supervision and lacked the time to tour their counties to ascertain who the poor were. An act of 1854 laid the burden of collecting information on the poor upon county grand juries; these, too, according to Coulter, had no time to check through the tax lists to discover the poor and to go beyond the tax lists to find those who did not even pay taxes. Yet this does not explain *why* the local worthies bothered so little about schooling. They were not overworked. The county courts were notoriously lax about law enforcement, and grand juries cannot have been over-burdened. And local politicians were quite capable of bestirring themselves when it came to establishing or expanding railroad companies.

The most striking fact about the debate on providing education was the absence of strong local pressure in favour of it. Coulter discovered a pressure group at Columbus which published the *Southern School Journal* in the years 1853–5. The journal pressed for increased state spending on education and promoted the creation of a state teachers' association. But its circulation never exceeded 300 subscribers and in 1854 slumped to a mere 150 genuine and very tardy subscriptions. Both journal and teachers' association collapsed in 1855. Clearly the teachers themselves formed no lobby for state assistance. This may have resulted from the transient character of teaching as a career. Teachers moved from place to place (Coulter 1925: 1–33). It was easy to enter teaching; only in 1859 was a system of inspection of teachers instituted (Johnson 1938: 429). Many teachers were women who had neither a long-term commitment to the job nor political rights. Moreover, as was repeatedly stressed, the affluent paid for education outside the state-aided schools. Yet these facts did not mean that the political establishment was indifferent to education and that the poorer citizens were deprived of a political voice. As with the militia, governor after governor urged reform and increased spending only to meet local sluggishness. Nor could one say that local politics was buttoned up by the planter elite. Service on grand juries and as JPs was widely open to ordinary men, if not, one hopes at least, to the illiterate. But these localities – with some and, from the examples of Columbus's pressure group and Savannah's Chatham county commissioners' advocacy, probably urban exceptions – failed to exploit the possibilities open to them. Perhaps, at the end of the day, the argument that better education was necessary in order to equip the people more fully for the onerous and moral obligations of citizenship was repellent in its paternalism and unattractive in its failure to offer more tangible rewards than republican intelligence and republican virtue to the farming masses.

A state which did so little centrally to defend and educate its people and which deferred so readily to local custom and lethargy could scarcely be regarded as having a government capable of bold or forceful action. Yet the picture was not entirely one of governmental weakness and indifference. Welfare provision was possible at the local level and through voluntary agencies. And the state government – like most Southern state governments – came to life in the 1850s in giving financial aid to railroads.

Welfare was administered, as it had been administered in Tudor England, through a combination of central edict and local execution. An Act of 1792 empowered the inferior courts to investigate the circumstances of the poor, to bind out orphans and to appoint guardians; they could appoint overseers for the poor and levy taxes (maxima for which were laid down by the Act) for poor relief. The inferior courts also obtained, by an Act of 1817, the monopoly over licensing itinerant pedlars and traders; JPs used this monopoly to relieve seriously disabled people, for licences to become pedlars were granted mostly to blind and crippled men. The JPs were in addition empowered, in 1793, to provide for illegitimate children. They could extract a security of £150 from any man who was accused – to their own satisfaction, justly – of having fathered a bastard child. The security was for the support and education of such child until the age of fourteen and was clearly intended to prevent bastard infants from becoming charges upon the county (Cobb, 1859: 537, 542, 586–7). As population grew, so some social problems became more obtrusive and required more concerted action. This was especially true in the cities, where private philanthropy took the lead. In Savannah, for example, a Poor House and Hospital Society was incorporated in 1808; a Female Asylum clothed, supported and educated orphan girls; and an Hibernian Society helped the indigent of Irish extraction. Savannah also endowed itself with a public library in 1810, and in 1821 established a municipal tribunal to license physicians after a controversial spate of medical quackery (Johnson 1938: 240–1, 247). Not every problem was tackled promptly or well. Savannah's authorities were periodically abused by state officials in the early nineteenth century for failing to take stringent quarantine precautions against the spread of disease.

Some social problems grew to the point where state action became necessary. In 1817, after fifteen years of discussion, the state completed the construction of a penitentiary; convicted criminals could thereafter be imprisoned, and, so it was fondly claimed, both improved and made to do work that would defray the costs of their incarceration. The building of the penitentiary followed examples set in late eighteenth-century Britain and north-eastern American states: to liberalize punishments and try to reform offenders while withdrawing them from circulation in the larger society. If Georgia was rather tardy in sweeping aside punishment by mutilation and building a state penitentiary, it was extraordinarily reluctant, by any American standards, to centralize its court system. A Supreme Court was not finally established until 1845; three (regional) courts of review existed until then. On other matters also, state action arose when need eventually appeared to require it. For instance, in 1837 the legislature appropriated $20,000 to establish a lunatic asylum and subsequently increased the sum. This, again, followed a national pattern; by 1845, when the asylum was in working order, fourteen states, North and South, possessed such institutions, most of which had been founded in the previous decade or so. As with the penitentiary, though, the asylum's proponents claimed that public cost would be recouped from the wholesome if exacting work to which the institution's inmates would be put (Cooper 1845: 4–8, 15, 25).

To say that state intervention came in response to perceived practical needs is, obviously, to ignore other important factors, not least of which was the ability to pay. In 1817 the state set up a school fund, completed the penitentiary, paid up its remaining subscription to the State Bank and laid down its first comprehensive state internal improvement scheme. By that year, the state government's surplus reached $500,000, boosted by large cash injections from the US Treasury as 'compensation' to Georgia for having years earlier ceded its claims over western lands (Coleman 1977: 109; J. of S. Ga. 1817: 7). So, too, before the depression sparked off by the panics of 1837 and 1839 bit deep, Georgia enjoyed expanding revenues during the 1830s, boosted by a huge acquisition of land from the Cherokees in 1835 Thus endowed, the state government established a new school fund (1836) and its first insane asylum (1837), saw fit to make a grant to an official historian, and, far more importantly, began pumping huge sums, eventually reaching $5,000,000, into a wholly owned state railroad, the Western and Atlantic. It was the increasing revenue from this railroad that enabled the legislature to be more generous to the school system in the late 1850s. But scope for proposing schemes of state reform existed earlier in that decade, for the economic depression of the 1840s had lifted and raw cotton demand and prices were swinging upwards once more. Prosperity fed upon itself and stimulated an appetite for yet further economic development. In 1855, Governor Johnson recommended that the state foster railroad building by lending state credit to railroad companies. Four years later, Governor Brown suggested that the legislature guarantee the bonds of private companies. Both opposed further direct ownership, whose consequences Johnson criticized:

> Its tendency is to emasculate private enterprise, by removing the
> necessity of self reliance. It will complicate the state with individual
> interests, which experience teaches to be dangerous to the public welfare.
> It will increase the state debt, and consequently create a necessity for
> burdensome taxation.

On the other hand, both governors urged that private and state interests should be mixed in order to expand the railroad system. And neither – despite Johnson's comments on the evils of public corporations – advocated the privatization of the Western and Atlantic, although some of their political opponents did so (J. of S. Ga. 1855–6: 18–21; J. of H. Ga. 1858: 30–3).

The record of institutional growth in the early nineteenth century was neither impressive nor dramatic. Where historians have written of contests for power in the Southern states, they would be better advised to refer to contests for place, simply because the power available within Georgia was so very limited and so little used. Yet this condition of affairs did not arise as a result of leading state politicians' indifference. A comparison of Georgia's governors' messages of the years 1799–1822 and of 1855–60 shows some notable changes; the underlying attitude became more managerial and there was greater financial detail in the later years. But common to the gubernatorial outlook in both periods was an eagerness to extend state government activities and develop state institutions and responsibilities. In 1804 Governor John Milledge, after whom the new state capital was soon to be named, offered his vision of the state government's obligations:

> allow me to remind you how essentially necessary it is for you to keep
> constantly in view, while in the discharge of your important duties, the
> chief objects of government, and to carry into effect the whole, or such
> of them, as circumstances will permit; by providing amply the means of
> public defence; by endowments, where they may be wanting, in aid of the
> academies in the respective counties, and of our collegiate institution; by
> improving our navigable water-courses and high-ways, for the advantage
> of our agricultural and commercial intercourse; and by establishing a
> penitentiary system, with the view of softening the rigor of our penal
> code (J. of H. Ga. 1804: 4).

This view from the top was to remain – allowing for the displacement of waterways by railroads and for occasionally less promotional governors – constant throughout the antebellum period. The ideology disseminated from above was positive, promotional and often almost populist. The puzzling fact was that ordinary citizens – enfranchized and able to hold important local offices – failed to pick it up and exploit it.

III

Our general image of Southern state governments is one of very easy-going institutions and a desperate eagerness to avoid central decision-making and control. In two key respects, state governments shed their resources; land held by the states was swiftly passed into private hands, and by the 1850s the states generally were under increasing pressure to give financial guarantees to railroad companies. Where they were active, the states were energetic in transferring assets or promoting individual corporations.

Public lands were rarely retained as permanent sources of public revenue. Although Southern states held back some sections of land to yield income for schools, most public lands were rapidly disposed of. In Georgia, for instance, such lands were given away from 1782 to 1803 under a headright system that awarded 200 acres to every head of a family and 50 acres for each further member of the family up to a maximum per family of 1,000 acres. Military service – against the British or the Indians – secured an estimated 2,000 veterans another 750,000 acres in the state during the 1780s. Both systems, though dispersing land quite widely, became increasingly discredited as the 1790s wore on. Charges of land fraud carried an anti-speculation party to power, and one of its leaders, Governor Josiah Tattnall, Jr, spoke in October 1802, of his hope that,

> large monopolies by individuals may be guarded against, the baneful effects of which are already too visible in our Country; and the histories of other nations, ancient and modern, furnish abundant proof of the destructive consequences of these encroachments upon the natural and common Rights of Men. In Republics especially, monopolies should be carefully avoided; for as large standing armies are opposed to both the spirit and the safety of them, it is necessary to increase the strength of the nation by that kind of population, which will not only produce numbers, but such for defence as feel an interest in the soil (J. of S. Ga. 1802: 5).

However clumsily, the reformers were asserting that a maldistribution of land was not only wrong in itself, but hindered the build-up of Southern states' strength through numbers. A new policy was introduced in 1803, made possible by the Creek session of 1802. The cession was divided into lots of 202½ acres or 490 acres; the lots were numbered and tickets bearing the corresponding numbers, together with blank tickets, were put into a lottery. All free white adult US citizens resident in Georgia for at least one year and paying taxes enjoyed the right to one draw; special provisions were made for heads of families, for widows and for orphans. The land was not entirely free of charge; those successful in the draw had to pay a fee graduated from $9/100 acres to enter the best lands to 12½ cents/100 acres for entry into the poorest lands. Even so, it was exceedingly cheap. Further lotteries were held in the 1810s and as additional cessions were squeezed out of the Indians. Some three-quarters of all Georgia's land was distributed under the lottery system, which continued in practice until the public domain was exhausted (Coleman 1977: 105–7; Johnson 1938: 230).

This process of privatization showed two things. It revealed a marked public preference for individual enrichment over public services. The events of 1802–3 resulted from political action in response to public pressure. But they also illustrated how mistakes in the past could be rectified by expanding the available cake rather than by socially disruptive disputes over the unfair earlier distribution of shares in that cake (e.g. J. of H. Ga. 1806: 4).

So, too, the very availability of public lands encouraged a knee-jerk irresponsibility in state governments. An obvious response to demands for state action and improvement was to suggest that such demands could best be met by tapping the existing reservoir of public lands, or by asking the federal government to hand its lands over to the state.

This happened in Mississippi in the 1820s and 1830s. Under laws of 1803 and 1805, Congress made available sixteenth section lands to the states, reserved to use for schools. Under further legislation, the new state of Mississippi's county authorities received in 1818 some 661,000 acres of federal land. The county and state governments never quite made up their minds how these lands were to be administered. One supervisory agency succeeded another. And in 1833 the income from leasing these lands was funnelled into the capital stock of the Planters Bank, which collapsed in 1840 (Lucas 1973: 367–8). It cannot be said that the localities or the state managed their federal endowment with any immediate benefit to the schools. An obvious difficulty was the original federal stipulation that such lands be leased in order to generate income; renting land was distinctly unpopular in a country where so many other tracts were readily purchasable. Another difficulty, often alluded to by Mississippi's legislature, was the alleged poor quality of many sixteenth sections. In 1826, the legislature memorialized Congress to grant better lands. In 1833, this request was repeated. The legislature argued to Congress that the federal Act of 1803 operated in an unfair way:

> Where the lands are rich and valuable, there resides the independent
> Planter, who has no concern for the product of the sixteenth section; but
> where the soil is less productive and of little value, though frequently

containing as many white inhabitants as lands of better quality, yet those inhabitants are usually the least wealthy of our population, to whom a valuable school section would be of great utility.

Yet allotted lands in such poorer regions – especially the piney woods – were precisely those yielding limited revenues.

Here, then, was a clear example of Mississippi's politicians taking up a reformist cause. But two points are notable. Any proceeds from leasing the sixteenth sections were to be directed through the Planters Bank, not applied immediately to the enlightenment of the poor. Secondly, the state government looked for a solution from federal action, and, more especially, federal reallocation of Indian lands. The state asked Congress to condone a swap whereby existing sixteenth sections could be exchanged for more fruitful ones in lands just acquired or about to be acquired from the Chickasaws and Choctaws respectively. Indian removal would thus enable the federal government to 'remedy these unmerited inequalities'. Social reform was to be at Indian and federal expense, and even then was to be so managed as to extend credit facilities, through the Planters Bank, to those who were not indigent. Truly, Mississippi's political conscience was to be salved at low cost (Memorial '1826' in RG 47 Legisl vo. 17; Amendt. by Senate to Memorial and Resolns. passed 21 Dec. 1833: RG 47 Legisl. vol. 20 MDAH).

On other matters as well the legislature sought federal aid to promote state institutions and Mississippi's growth. In 1803 Congress granted a township of land in Mississippi Territory to establish Jefferson College. In 1830 the state legislature complained that this land was distant from the college and consisted of 'sterile, unproductive pine barrens' which failed to attract purchasers. It asked Congress to authorize the college to surrender its lands for equal quantities of federal land elsewhere; the implication was that such new lands would be not only nearer the college but also of better quality. In the same year, the legislature argued for thirty-six sections in Mississippi to be given to Mississippi Academy at Clinton. And it bluntly indicated the source for the new grant; 'a great portion of our state is still inhabited by the aborigines of the country' (Memorial of Dec. 1830, Resoln. of 1830: RG 47 Legisl. vol. 19, MDAH).

Regularly in the late 1820s and early 1830s Mississippi requested federal assistance in improving navigable streams. In 1827 it asked for four townships of federal land to do that, asserting that better navigation would in turn boost the value of the remaining federal holdings and make them more saleable. This theme was returned to in 1831 when Indian treaty-making whetted appetites for land. The federal government was reminded of its liberality to other states, of its duty to stimulate 'the exchange of . . . [the] present unfortunate and degraded population of red men, for a numerous, hardy and industrious one of free white men', and of its self-interest in enhancing land values through the improvement of navigable rivers. Lest these reasons seemed insufficient, the legislature added a theoretical consideration to its practical request:

> The ownership of the soil by the government and the consequent host of tenantry incident to such a state of things cannot under any aspect of the subject in which it may be viewed be favourable to our republican institutions and to that attachment of the people to the government and interest in its prosperity and perpetuity which is necessary to its stability and successful progress.

In so far as politics concerned a redistribution of wealth, that redistribution was through the agency of the states from the anti-republican grip of the general government (Memorial of Jan. 1827: RG 47 Legisl. vol. 19; Memorial of Dec. 1831, Memorial of Dec. 1833: RG Legisl. vol. 20 MDAH). By repeatedly portraying the federal government as the repository of major resources, the state politicians conveniently deflected attention from the demanding possibility that they might raise state taxes to meet state responsibilities.

These two underlying principles of state government – shed resources from state to individuals and look to federal land grants and not higher state taxes to finance new developments – were reinforced by two others. Voluntarism was expected to spearhead the creation of social welfare services and of education. And localism – the political and constitutional extension of the voluntary spirit – was deferred to.

Private provision of colleges, schools and welfare services went quite far in the nineteenth-century South. College education owed much to denominational initiative. Although the University of Georgia was the first Southern state university chartered (in 1785), it did not begin life until 1803 and was still a somewhat adolescent institution in 1860. By then a variety of private and largely denominational colleges, all of them small and many of them catering to teenage children as well as to older students, had been established. The 1830s, when private incomes were buoyant, saw, for example, the founding of Mercer in 1833 (Baptist), Oglethorpe in 1835 and Emory in 1836 (the latter two being Methodist-Episcopal) (Johnson 1938: 431–2). In Mississippi, the state university was not established until 1840 and not opened to students until 1848; before that a handful of colleges had been created, again usually taking pupils from their early teens as well as providing degree-level instruction. State institutions of higher education remained small and undistinguished. And even the private colleges tended to loose potential students to Northern or other Southern institutions in the antebellum period. In non-college education the balance was reversed. Mississippi in 1850, for example, had 6,628 pupils attending 171 academies and private schools and 18,746 pupils at 782 state-aided schools. Even so, the private effort was considerable and in many respects pioneering (Lucas 1973: 356, 358–64, 372).

Social services were generally poor. This was partly a function of size. As we have seen, Georgia set up a lunatic asylum in the 1840s. Neighbouring Florida had an insufficiently large population to venture to do so. As a result, one finds the governor of Florida in 1853 asking Governor Johnson of Georgia to admit 'an unfortunate Female Lunatic' of eastern Florida to Georgia's asylum since the only alternative in Florida itself was the county jail (Gov. James E. Broome to Gov. Johnson 2 Dec. 1853: Ga. Govrs.' Papers. Herschel V. Johnson, TCC, Box 54). But restricted social services were also a consequence of low levels of urbanization. Where towns flourished (Savannah was a good case, Natchez, despite its 'red-light' district 'Under the Hill', an improving one) voluntary services were organized and endowed. Natchez Hospital was established (1805) and run by voluntary contributions; the town's Female Charitable Society (1816) cared for orphan children; and Natchez Institute was a flourishing school founded in 1845 through an individual's donation of land. All three institutions came to request state or county financial assistance, and Natchez Institute operated in the 1850s on the basis of local tax support (Undated petition (early 1820s): RG 47 Legisl. vol. 17; petition of 8 Jan. 1825: RG 47 Legisl. vol. 18, MDAH; Lucas 1973: 370). But the initial planning, building and financing of these organizations came from affluent townsfolk. The absence of concentrated urban suffering and of concentrated urban consciences helps account for the generally low level of welfare provision in the South.

Moreover, localism did not stimulate demands for more positive state action; or if it did so, it created such particularistic counter-pulls that no coherent state provision of services was possible. Education offered a good case-study. Efforts made before the 1840s to finance public schools in Mississippi collapsed essentially with the Planters' Bank in 1840. The politicians had been too eager to do two jobs with the school money; to provide a guaranteed school income and to boost the credit facilities in the state. Following this fiasco, there was much concern to establish state schooling more securely. Governor Albert G. Brown in 1846 put a populist case for free public schools to the state legislature. But no general law stuck. Counties and townships retained initiative and control over schooling, with the result that some 125 laws were passed between 1846 and 1860 variously approving local schemes. What a general law of 1846 did lay down was that counties had to gain the consent of a majority of heads of family in the county in order to impose a tax for common schools. And that tax was not to exceed the state tax in any case (Lucas 1973: 367–73).

Yet this paucity of welfare provision did not arise because the structure of local government militated against 'public opinion'; indeed, one feature of Mississippi's political life was the relative ease with which protest was registered. The primary authorities in the counties from 1832 to 1868 were the boards of police, elected every two years by a democratic electorate. The five members of the board selected their president, whose duties included the headship of the county militia and arranging the patrol system. The boards raised taxes to care for the poor and maintained roads by requisitioning white males' labour for six days a year. Under the Act of 1846, these boards appointed school commissioners to organize county common schools. County courts of probate and state circuit courts furnished the local judicial institutions, whose work was supplemented by that, on minor offences, of JPs; JPs were all elected, many specifically, the rest in their capacity as members of the boards of police. Equally important, the only effective law-enforcement officers, the county sheriffs, were popularly elected and not answerable to any state network of command. There were no state officials to maintain law and order, except the judiciary and the militia; and the militia officers were elected by the men in their units, up to and including the brigadiers and major-generals. While, therefore, it would surprise no one if a large proportion of office-holders were slaveowners and well-established farmers, it has also to be said that local office-holding was very open, based on local consent and very far removed from offering an authoritative hierarchy, at least after 1832 (Moore 1982: 110–16, 124–5, 131–2). Given this ample provision of popular democratic institutions, what did the electorate press for? Mississippi's legislative records, in preserving a large array of petitions, offer some possible answers to this question.

IV

When the people of Mississippi – and we may take Mississippi as typical in this respect – petitioned the legislature for action they did so on a multiplicity of particularist subjects. In the 1820s and 1830s such petitions requested federal aid for improving navigable rivers and harbours, for hospitals and for school-building. In those decades and in the 1850s the state was asked to charter toll bridge companies, to incorporate banks, to plan and lay out roads, to alter county boundaries to make county seats less distant from aggrieved residents, to pay expenses incurred in such inter-county matters as sheriffs' transporting criminals between counties, to regulate and improve county governance, to allow people to change their names, to legalize inadvertently irregular marriages, to help with county schools and to lower or raise specific and special taxes. Some issues changed over time. In the 1850s temperance legislation was easily the most warmly and frequently aired issue as far as petitioners went. Yet in the 1820s and early 1830s, temperance regulations were scarcely requested at all. Some problems which we would like to believe were of contemporary importance – such as individuals' objections to the removal of free blacks – were concerns of a tiny minority. The overwhelming burden of business raised was highly individualistic or particularistic. Occasionally, petitioners peppered their supplications with general political rhetoric. But references to political ideas were rare and patently self-serving. Some of the most cogent citations of broader principles in these petitions were by Mississippi merchants protesting against state taxes that weighed upon themselves more onerously than out-of-state merchants doing business in Mississippi. References to class interests were virtually non-existent. But this did not mean that humble people felt cowed by government. Both individuals and interest-groups from humble walks of life put their complaints to the state legislature.

On education, a sample of petitions reflected the problems over financing and over the division of responsibility between state government and counties that a general description of a chaotic system has already suggested. In 1823 two dozen citizens of Warren County demanded local control of the sixteenth sections allocated for schooling. The idea behind this demand was simple, if enduring: 'public business is transacted and public works performed by agents in every instance with a negligence and extravagance that individual economy and enterprize seldom exhibit'. Just as people would not dream of allowing their 'private estates' to be managed by a board of commissioners in the state capital and agents appointed by that board within each county, so they would reject distant control of the school sections, which, in these petitioners' eyes, were 'as much their property as their private estates'. If this attitude was in some respects commonplace, it was not all-pervasive. Petitioners from Hinds county in 1829, finding that their sixteenth section was on poor land, sought (and failed to obtain) extra state cash to build a school. Yet even when requesting state aid, petitioners saw the development of anti-statist beliefs as one of the healthy consequences of state involvement in education. This was how another, earlier request for state money from Hinds county was dressed up: 'The subject of education, in every well-organized Government has been one of the most material of Legislative objects, as it affords the strongest bulwark against the encroachment of illegitimate authority, and the perfect guarantee to civil and religious liberty.' Given such assumptions, it was not perhaps remarkable that efforts at central direction, as periodically mooted, or even co-ordination, as suggested unsuccessfully in 1858 when a proposal to establish a superintendent of common schools was shelved, failed so regularly.[1]

Class rhetoric was little used in the legislative petitions. Some examples serve to illustrate how such rhetoric was actually applied. There was an overt appeal to paternalistic impulses in a petition from Hinds county in the early 1850s. The petitioners complained that everyone in the county took a pro rata grant from the education fund, even if the child or children for whom they claimed went to a private teacher or to a school outside the township. Insufficient money remained in the fund, after these disbursements, to provide 'a permanent school for the masses'. Parents able to send their children to colleges or high schools or private teachers should be obliged, so the petitioners urged, to waive their claims to money. At the other end of the political spectrum, the state legislature itself in petitioning Congress in 1831 argued for a more consciously egalitarian distribution of Choctaw lands secured by federal treaty in 1830. Those lands were 'now rapidly selling off to wealthy Capitalists'. Poorer pioneers were being excluded, being confirmed in their 'wandering and fugitive habit', and being inadvertently tempted to drift into Mexico in search of accessible lands. Congress, to assist Mississippi in 'the acquisition of a permanent yeomanry', was asked to sell 160-acre plots, at the minimum permissible price, to heads of families. More generally, class allusions occurred in arguments against allegedly inequitable taxes. A tax on sales at auction imposed in 1825 was criticized for benefiting 'the large Capitalists' and 'a few wealthy Merchants of the City'; country merchants buying their goods for retail at auction were forced to absorb the additional costs of such a tax. On a grander scale, seventy seven memorialists – mostly merchants – protested in the late 1820s against a differential limitation on legal actions over accounts; the limitation was normally six years, but merchants were not allowed to take legal action after two years from the date of any disputed accounts. This ban, they contended, should be lifted on the grounds that the Constitution was supposed to 'have a Just and Equal opperation [*sic*] on all classes of the community'. Again, forty two merchants in Natchez objected to a heavy tax on the sale of merchandise, seeing as they did no reason why 'one class of the community' should bear a disproportionate financial burden.[2]

If merchants complained against taxes devised by legislatures dominated by the agricultural interests, so too another urban group, the mechanics, could defend their own interests energetically. A grievance which emerged in 1845 in various towns – Holly Springs, Jackson, Paulding, Ripley and Salem – was craftsmen's hostility to the use of convict labour for manufacturing goods. Candidates for the state legislature from Jasper county were asked by representatives of a meeting of mechanics to pledge themselves to abolish 'the present odious system of convict labor', and to substitute in the state penitentiary 'such employment as does not come in competition with, or have a tendency to degrade the honest mechanics of this state'. Elsewhere newspapers lent their support to this protest (*Ripley Advertiser,* 16 Sept. 1843, 26 July 1845; *Paulding True Democrat,* 13 Aug., 3 Sept. 1845). And over 200 signatories sent a petition from Jackson to the legislators seeking to prevent the state penitentiary from manufacturing mechanical and agricultural implements or machines which competed with the city's free mechanics (Undated petition: RG 47 Legisl. vol. 27, MDAH). Similar protests occurred in Baton Rouge, Louisiana (Eaton 1961: 167).

None of these various assertions, or the language in which they were advanced, was especially novel or striking. But they did show that crude ideas of class interest were present, and were used in public debate. Those ideas were part of Southern political vocabulary. It cannot, therefore, be said that economic discontents could not be articulated within the normal framework of discourse or within the prevailing institutional order. Nor can it be claimed that causes touching strong emotions failed to secure a public airing and public support. The campaign for temperance reform – again, one that affected much of the South, as well as the free states in the 1850s – was one of the most emotive and lively of all antebellum 'political' movements in Mississippi.

As was customary, state and locality tussled together to sort out an appropriate policy on temperance regulation. A state law banning the sale of whisky in quantities of less than one-gallon lasted only from 1839 until 1842. It was repealed in the wake of very potent hostility. Counter-blasts from temperance reformers, however, led to the passage of a more modest, and more viable, local option law in 1854. This law devolved upon the voters the power to forbid the sale of liquor in their counties or townships. It capped a long campaign by a variety of groups. The Baptists – not predominantly a middle-class denomination – urged temperance legislation (Moore 1982: 127–8; Pillar 1973: 401). Middle-class professionals, including physicians, added their voices (*Ripley Advertiser,* 10 Feb. 1844, 9 Aug. 1845). Women unusually and prominently participated in petitioning the legislature to control alcoholic excess. Educational promoters were also angered by the impact of drinking houses, and of groceries selling liquor, on small cross-roads villages' or market towns' schools. Over 100 citizens of Pontotoc complained that the town's 'flourishing academies' had their improving work contradicted because 'the pupils are frequently compelled to encounter disorderly drunkards, and scenes of violence, upon the streets'. From Benton, in Yazoo county, came the remonstrance: 'we have struggled long to build up a school in our Town, but we now realize that all our efforts in that direction as well as all others having a tendency to improve the morals and to add to the material prosperity of this community' had been, and would continue to be, useless unless intoxicating liquor was banished (Undated petitions from Pontotoc and Benton: RG 47 Legisl. vol. 27, MDAH). As the weight of pressure accumulated, so the politicians found a compromise law that cut a path between state direction and unchecked anarchy.

Repeatedly, the petitions reveal this dual character in state public affairs; a tension between educational or moral improvement, perhaps to be directed by the state, and indifference, probably associated with local initiative and self-rule, to such ideals; and, secondly, an impatient belief that the state government existed to channel such resources as it possessed to individuals and localities, and existed in every respect as the servitor to its citizens. The legislature itself was bombarded with minor and humanitarian requests: to pay two physicians for treating poor patients; to compensate an illiterate citizen for looking after a dying and homeless indigent man; to aid an indebted man in looking after and educating an invalid son while trying to provide for the rest of his family; to award a maintenance allowance to a citizen who took in and cared for an abandoned and lunatic black girl; to pay for a deaf mute to be educated for two years at a deaf and dumb asylum in Kentucky; to license blind or crippled men to peddle free of tax or charge; to allow a wife with five children to hold property and transact business as an unmarried woman because of her husband's persistent 'intemperance and gaming'; and to permit minors aged nineteen or twenty to assume the full property rights of adults.[3] Such requests arose partly because county authorities declined to offer money for the poor and partly because the state legislature retained responsibility for many welfare matters. But the existence of these requests and the language used in them point both to a fairly informal dialogue between governed and governing and to an expectation that the legislature would ameliorate individual cases of misfortune.

Moreover, petitioners often displayed robust self-confidence in the deference due by legislators to popular wishes. In 1833, two dozen citizens of Wayne county, in the piney woods, noted that their county was about to be left without a physician. To fill that gap, they asked the legislature to pass an Act permitting a resident, David Fletcher, to practise as a physician and receive compensation for his labours. The petitioners attested to his knowledge of medicine and the benefits which this knowledge had already conferred. They noted also that Fletcher was 'a pious, moral and good citizen'. Their imprimatur, they clearly believed, was quite sufficient to secure legal accreditation for this would-be medical practitioner (Petition, 7 Nov. 1833: RG 47 Legisl. vol. 20, MDAH).

Informality thus reigned supreme. State institutions were weak; state officialdom virtually non-existent. This did not mean that a planter 'class' necessarily ordered affairs to its own ends. An alternative rhetoric of protest was available for political use. Public elective offices were open to access. By the 1850s, Mississippi, together with Alabama, Missouri, Tennessee, and Texas among the slave states, had a representative legislature based entirely on white-manhood distribution; there was little in-built planter power (Eaton 1961: 175). Campaigns for public improvement – in education and in temperance legislation – were launched and were well supported. It is not proven that they had anything very much to do with matters of class. Yet, while both causes made progress, these campaigns foundered partly on entrenched localism, voluntarism and individualism, as well as on a reluctance to pay a high cash price for 'improvement'. There can be no doubt that the rural legislatures declined to levy substantial taxes on slaves or cotton in order to finance schools, or railroads, or poor relief. When extra fiscal resources were needed, it was often the small urban middle classes – or so they complained – who were required to supply them.

Yet the legislative petitions offer no evidence, nor did the local newspapers, that any groundswell of popular protest existed to challenge this informal regime. The Jacksonian Democrats may have assailed privilege and proclaimed equality, but their programme of reform concentrated on opening opportunity by extending education and on attacking class-power in the shape of note-issuing banks. Nor does the surviving record lend any substance to an hypothesis that potential popular support existed for institutional innovation. Only in education did such pressure for reform exist; it was articulated by such notable Democrats as Albert G. Brown; and it achieved some concrete, if not complete or compelling, gains largely through local initiatives encouraged by state permissive legislation.

While, therefore, no one would claim Mississippi's antebellum government to have been a model for political scientists to study; while it is true that reformers looking for bureaucratic guide-lines found them in largely Northern examples, be they in public schools or penitentiaries; and while the state constitution and legislature repeatedly fostered localism and particularism and shied away from Utilitarian system-building, none of this meant that the regime oppressed or constricted the ordinary white populace. On land distribution and in education policy, state legislators were constantly aware of popular wishes, needs and demands. And, in every respect, after 1832 the governing institutions of the counties and of the state – the boards of police, the sheriffs' departments, the militia, the legislature, the governorship and even the judiciary – were open to contest and to election. That no 'populist' protest movements arose in the 1840s and 1850s either to challenge the Democrats and their various opponents for power, or to demand constitutional revision in the name of the oppressed 'masses', says something – admittedly, not everything – about the social consensus behind Mississippi's frame and form of open and devolved government.

V

Clement Eaton (1961: 293), pre-eminent among his generation of historians of the antebellum South, concluded a discussion of social welfare provision:

The neglect of social reform in the South was partly owing to the politicians' obsession with federal politics ... The [newspaper] editors, as well as the politicians, throughout the South had their eyes primarily on the federal capital, on the slavery and territorial issues, on the victory of a national political party – to the detriment of state issues and of social reforms.

This is an important truth about the localities. Local pride and state pride co-existed with an intense interest in national affairs. An examination of such small-town Mississippi newspapers as the *Ripley Advertiser,* the Aberdeen *Weekly Independent,* or the Monticello *Pearl River Banner* for the 1830s, 1840s and 1850s, quickly reveals that their political news was almost entirely national. They contained virtually no discussion of local politics and very little coherent debate on state questions. Much of their content was gleaned from Northern newspapers, so that a reader would have a curiously funnelled view of the country's affairs: an awareness of social happenings and economic developments in his own neighbourhood supplemented by a great deal of information on events in New York city, Philadelphia and Boston. It was as if, for the purposes of gossip, voyeurism and cultural observation, the country consisted of thousands upon thousands of rural spokes all directed to a tiny handful of north-eastern cosmopolitan hubs. But was this perspective and orientation created and fixed at the expense of state government and of greater efforts at social amelioration at home? That it was formed one of the prominent Republican charges against the Slave Power of the late 1850s; for the South's interest in national affairs was, the Republicans claimed, very much a function of its slaveowning leaders' concern to defend and extend slavery.

As far as the political and intellectual elite went, the defence of slavery – as a challenge to their talents and as a means of winning power and social esteem – became increasingly important as the Northern attack upon slavery extension and slavery itself rose in the 1840s and 1850s. Yet this defence did not dispel all other issues. Professor Drew Faust has shown – in a study of a group of eastern-seaboard intellectuals, the novelist William Gilmore Simms, Governor James H. Hammond, the agricultural reformer Edmund Ruffin, Nathaniel Beverley Tucker and George Frederick Holmes – that Southern writers felt an ambiguous relationship with their region. They were fully conscious of Southern backwardness in education. They sought to overcome it by promoting *belles lettres* and literary journals. They were conscious also of the South's economic dependency upon Britain and the North. They sought to liberate the South by encouraging more scientific agriculture and a certain amount of basic industrialization (Faust 1977: 95–100). Both these concerns were echoed by J. D. B. De Bow, who, from New Orleans, laboured in his *De Bow's Review* to stimulate Southern literary life and to foster economic diversification. But such a commitment among leading intellectuals reminds us of at least two paradoxes. One was that it was not just the South's handful of anti-slavery writers who pressed for a more varied and less agricultural economy. Some of the keenest Southern separatists did so as well. And local and state governments responded at least to the extent of affording about 55 per cent of all the investment in Southern railroads built before 1860 (Goodrich 1960: 268). Laying down railroad tracks hardly amounted to industrialization. But the advocacy for improved communications and the provision of a wider industrial base came from within the intellectual establishment. Secondly, the call for better education came from the literati, whether they favoured slavery or were critical of it. If these pro-slavery men of letters did not sit at the top of the political pole, they at least clung to the lower reaches of the totem. The case for reform, or for an expansion of education, came, therefore, from the spokesmen for the political and social establishment. In short, an ideology of opportunity – in educational provision and in the economic sphere – as well as a strident defence of slavery, formed a large part of the message sent downwards to the masses by state governors and prominent intellectuals alike.

Nor was the actual record of achievement so very deplorable. Illiteracy was, in truth, markedly higher in the South than in New England and in the North generally. Even in 1850, however, the Southern rate, of 20 per cent, meant that a great deal had already been accomplished (Faust 1977: 8). If no Southern states followed the example of the free states and founded common school systems during the 1850s, many Southern states were moving towards more rigorously organized schooling; Maryland and Virginia had widely diffused education by 1860; Kentucky and Tennessee levied education taxes from 1849 and 1854 respectively; Alabama and North Carolina established effective state superintendencies in the 1850s. As in Georgia, the pressure for better schooling often came from the political leadership. Moreover, even in free states what the state system offered was typically more impressive on paper than in reality. In the states of the old North-West, state schools were run on a shoe-string, were small, and operated frequently for but two or three months a year. While no one would suggest that Florida or South Carolina, Texas or Mississippi were doing much to educate their young, it would be equally misleading to portray the state education available in Indiana or Illinois or Ohio as impressive or complete (Welter 1962: 114, 119–20, 131). More was left in the South for private academies to do. At the same time, however, slave state governments stimulated universities in a way that the state governments of New England and the north-east did not (Brubacher and Rudy 1958: 141–4, 149).

The obvious reason for paying so much attention to educational matters is that they – unlike such questions as the care of the poor or the disabled – were widely regarded as state responsibilities. The provision of educational facilities was also viewed, consciously in some instances, as an alternative to other social reforms. Nor was it facile to argue that education opened up job opportunities (Welter 1962: 38, 93–5). But the debate over schooling in the South was ultimately somewhat inconclusive. Schooling undoubtedly opened the way to careers in medicine and the law, as well in the ministration to souls. But successful physicians and lawyers, and urban businessmen, tended to view planting and large-scale slaveownership as enterprises more rewarding and financially safer, perhaps more 'respectable', than any other careers. For well-established farmers, humble and affluent alike, there was no over-riding temptation to pursue alternative jobs to farming by acquiring an enlarged and more formal education. This does not deny that there were social reasons for becoming conversant with the classics, or for obtaining that mastery of the card-table or of the bottle, of the bordello or the duelling-ground which Southern colleges, or college-towns, frequently offered (e.g. Coulter 1928: 115). But it does stress that, throughout much of the South, there was a much less urgent pull towards urban careers customarily requiring a formal education, than was the case in much of the antebellum North.

Attention to government institutions is in some ways slightly anachronistic. The three principal successes of Southern state governments in the period 1790–1860 were very little associated with institutional development or institutional reform. First, they protected slave property in a period full of criticism of, even increasing danger to, slaveowners' rights. To the philosophical and moral objections against slavery voiced within the South itself from the 1780s to the early 1830s were added the potential dangers of slave revolts fomented, if indirectly, by the increasingly militant anti-slavery lobby of the North from the 1830s onwards. Yet the Southern states, partly through their encouragement of internal vigilantism, partly through their blustering pressure on the federal government to recapture runaways escaped to the North, succeeded in maintaining slavery very firmly intact without recourse to centralized police powers or to centrally organized militias. Southerners were militant in defence of their racial order; but the South was not a region with efficient military organizations or armed state power.

Secondly, the state governments, not necessarily in any planned or coherent fashion, managed a very important transfer of physical resources from the Indians through federal ownership to individual possession. There was little idealism in the way this transfer of land was effected. There were occasional political protests against speculation and profiteering. But if one compares what happened in the Deep South in the first half of the nineteenth century to the almost exclusive preoccupation with self-aggrandisement that marked, for instance, the behaviour in the office of the powerful councillors in North Carolina a century earlier (Clayton 1982), then the land policies pursued were smooth and unselfish. Ultimately, of course, the land was made available through federal negotiations and sometimes through federal force deployed against the Indians. But state governments generally acted to distribute these lands quickly, and, if sometimes not always planned thus, fairly equitably among the white population. The provision of land, effected by national and state governments, far transcended in importance any perceived need for education or welfare.

Finally, the state governments rode out a genuine and notable internal transfer of power. Steadily, in state after Southern state, sometimes reluctantly, and under great pressure, sometimes with little anxiety or acerbity, governments came to be elected through genuinely representative systems, and came to reflect the popular will, in so far as that phenomenon could be expressed in politics. Entrenched power and privilege was very greatly reduced, in some states completely eliminated between the 1790s and 1850s. Republican state government, with which the white populace became closely associated, was given real shape, if not by the enlightened statesmen of the Revolutionary age, then by the demagogic office-seekers and partisans of the Jacksonian era. With few exceptions, the Southern states of the 1850s were run by elected officials and legislators who made regular obeisance to popular approval, and who, though individually affluent, were not very sharply differentiated in social aspirations from their farming and land-owning constituents. Of course, differences of wealth and status continued to exist in the South and in places continued to enjoy some, if contracting, constitutional advantages. But the overwhelming impression gained from any examination of political rhetoric and state institutions, of the membership of state legislatures and of the content of petitions to them, is one of governments informal and responsive to popular pressures, and particularistic in their principal concerns.

In these various ways, therefore, the local and state governments of the antebellum South acted as essential social bonds to white society. If in safeguarding slavery they defended a minority interest, that defence was accomplished with few demands upon, and without much opposition from, the mass of whites. In turn, ordinary white opinion seemed to favour extremely limited government and maximum local initiative on such matters requiring state intervention as education. More concretely, by providing access to land and disentangling themselves from the blatant legal buttressing of privilege, the state governments developed their legitimacy and secured popular support. By the 1850s, party contests in the South had lost much of the edge they had possessed in earlier decades. While numerous political disputes remained in the years before the Civil War, one of the remarkable characteristics of those years was the absence of political discord threatening to disrupt white social harmony. However eagerly the Republicans hoped to win the electoral or moral backing of a disaffected Southern white lower class, this ambition remained a fond and unrealized one.

NOTES

1. Petition of Foster Cook *et al.* of Warren Co., 25 Dec. 1823: RG 47 Legisl., vol. 17; petition from Hinds Co., 20 Jan. 1829, petition from Board of Trustees of Township 6, Hinds Co., Jan. 1828: vol. 19; a Bill to establish office of Superintendant of Common Schools, Nov. 1858: vol. 23. MDAH.

2. Undated petition (early 1850s) from twenty-two citizens of Hinds Co.: RG 47 Legisl., vol. 27; memorial passed Dec, 1831: vol. 20; petition of 1826 from Natchez: vol. 18; undated petition (late 1820s) of seventy-seven memorialists: vol. 18; undated petition of forty-two Natchez merchants: vol. 17. MDAH.

3. Petition of Richard F. Floyd and John M. McMorrough 1831: RG 47 Legisl., vol. 20; petition concerning Joshua Reed undated (*c.* 1833): vol. 20; petition of David Ross, 21 Jan. 1833: vol. 20; petition of sixty-eight citizens of Monroe Co., 1831: vol. 20; a Bill to authorize Sec. of State to spend $175 p.a. 1830: vol. 19; undated petition of twenty-six citizens of Marshall Co.: vol. 27; undated petition of Maria C. Caperton: vol. 27; various petitions in 1825, vol. 18. MDAH.

Chapter eight

FAMILY

I

During the Civil War, one young Confederate soldier begged his father to write more often, and to overlook his earlier misdeeds:

> Wishing to hear from you I write you this, it being the fourth letter that I have written home and as yet have received only one from those I so dearly love. ... The time may come yet when you will be proud of your wild – reckless and disapated [*sic*] Son as I have been called, my mind is made up to be in the front rank if we ever get into a fight and there to make my mark.

Opinion at home, news of home and the emotional support from home were vital to the Confederates' morale and fighting determination (Wiley 1943: 192–4). That importance deeply affected the pre-war as well as the wartime South. The family in some accounts has emerged as more central to Southern whites' everyday lives and to their values than was the Northern family, vital to the preservation in the South of a traditional social order and a folk culture, and the focus of Southerners' hopes, ambitions and sense of honour (Wyatt-Brown 1975: 4–6, 28). Why this was so may be explained by reference to economic, structural, emotional and environmental factors.

The family was a business enterprise, savings bank, loan institution and insurance company, especially in rural areas. Family farms – and over half the adult males of the Deep South described themselves as farmers in 1860 – were economic units, using the labour (voluntary or not) of children to clear land and enhance production, increasing capital values through improvements and acting as reserves of realizable assets for the elderly (Wright 1978: 47). Families were sources of credit and employment. In much of the Deep South formal credit was difficult to come by; some states – Texas, Arkansas and Florida – positively prohibited note-issuing banks in the 1850s; while Mississippi was to all intents and purposes bankless from the mid-1840s, as was Alabama until the late 1850s (De Bow 1853: vol I, 107; Hammond 1957: 716). Yet these states flourished in the decade and a half before secession; their population increased and landownership spread. Clearly, credit was available, much of it flowing from New Orleans – the money market of the south-west – through factors, and through banking houses and insurance companies not issuing the offending paper currency. Planters and lawyers also acted as rural bankers. But a main source was probably familial assistance. Families were often too shiftless and transient to establish rooted and paternalistic relationships between planters and lesser farmers in given areas. Instead families often settled in kin-groups. In the initial development of Mount Holly, Arkansas, for example, seven households moved to that pioneer area in 1843–45, vetted and invited by the founder and drawn heavily from members of the McRae clan. Dog-trot cabins (with wide and open central passageways) were built by the whole community for neighbours, and the original Scottish Presbyterian character of the township was carefully retained as it expanded (Chester 1927: 10–11, 16, 21). Farming families were also able to provide job training (perhaps a euphemism on occasions) for their young, as well as deferred income and forced savings in the shape of assistance from parents for the offspring when they set up farms of their own. In the cotton-growing hinterlands of Augusta, Georgia, the vast majority of newly-weds moved into their own houses; often these were close by a parental farm and/or might well be family-owned (Harris 1981: 87, 103). Spreading landownership in this way was not difficult, for cheap land – in the public domain – was available somewhere in the South throughout the antebellum period. And building up family farms did not put wealth solely into the grateful and grasping hands of eldest sons. Partible inheritance was the norm. During the second half of the eighteenth century, for instance, only one-quarter of all wills left in Albemarle county, in a long settled part of Virginia, passed on all the landed estate to a single son (Smith 1980: 244–5). And where wills were not made, law and custom led to partible inheritance. In St Mary's County, Maryland, for example, as many as 43 per cent of even wealthy householders died intestate in the period 1790–1840; such estates were apportioned under Maryland law so that one-third went to any widow, and the rest was divided among all the children (Marks 1979: 368). The absence of primogeniture thus served to legitimate families' extraction of labour services from teenage children and young adults.

And the young were indeed expected to toil. A young woman teacher, privately tutoring planters' children in Georgia, recorded a local's adage, 'the school always closes when the cotton opens'. She added, 'The people here can not prize education very highly or they would not take their children from school to put them in the cotton field' (Dyer 1982: 61). These, it should be stressed, were parents who paid for their children's teaching. In 1836, the *Southern Agriculturalist* reported with enthusiasm that a nine-year-old girl had planted two acres in potatoes during the course of a single day. The *American Cotton Planter* in 1853 noted not only that a farmer's wife had for years been netting about $200 per annum by selling baskets which she made from swamp willow – all without interfering with her duties as the mother of five children – but also that her eldest daughter, aged eleven, had cleared $25 in her first year of following that worthy example (Hagler 1980: 415). For teenage boys and young men the expectation of work on the family farm was more predictable. But the period for such labours was also prolonged. In a three-county area of Georgia in the 1850s, 38 per cent of white males aged twenty to twenty-four years were unmarried and living with parents. Given the nature of the rural job market and of farmers' needs, such sons almost certainly formed a solid corps of farm labourers. Moreover, even those young, unmarried men who lived away from home probably tended to reside and work in a familial environment. In the same rural area, about 30 per cent of all households had other relatives than immediate kin, or boarders, resident in them (Harris 1981: 81, 100).

The family work ethic applied to all family members. One strand of Southern writing and rhetoric put women on pedestals where they were to be admired for their refinement, elegance and sexual purity. Such an idealization was not confined to the nineteenth-century South, but had its origins in a wider evangelical concern to improve sexual morality. Women, from being typically perceived as creatures of physical desires and even licentiousness in earlier centuries, were more commonly described in the nineteenth as, by nature, indifferent to or infrequently affected by sexual lust. This evangelical description had a number of ramifications, not all of them repugnant to women, who could turn the notion of 'passionlessness' into a defence against unwelcome male importunities (Cott 1978: 221–2, 233–6). But the idea of woman's moral superiority tended also to make women into moral exemplars rather than simply help-mates. And among the very affluent, women could often be rendered even more rarefied by their 'liberation' from mundane toil or managerial duties. Affluent girls and women were to a degree encouraged to flit gracefully into their gilded cages. Planters of reasonable means generally sought to endow their daughters with suitably lady-like accomplishments. Yet these aspirations in turn were much criticized in the mid nineteenth century. The agricultural press in the antebellum South argued for the traditional virtues of the farmer's wife as a partner in work; according to *The Southern Cultivator* of 1859, 'fashion-pampered women are almost worthless for all the great ends of human life. They have but little force of character; they have still less power of moral will, and quite as little physical energy' (Hagler 1980: 411). The last point was notably important, for even wealthy planters' wives, despite the images of ease so often projected, rolled up their sleeves to direct a multiplicity of grimy and unpleasant chores, from kitchen gardening to hog butchering, from care of the sick to drying vegetables for winter storage, from spinning and sewing to whipping recalcitrant house slaves (Scott 1970: 29–36; Mrs Lucilla McCorkle's Diary 4 Oct. 1858, McCorkle papers, SHC). The family farm was very much an exercise in partnership, involving numerous and vital housewifely tasks.

Ultimate responsibility for families' financial success fell upon men. On the whole, Southern males seem to have taken their responsibilities as household heads seriously enough; some would claim too seriously, for the overbearing patriarch was a not uncommon figure in the slave states. Men married later than women, perhaps to ensure that they could afford a family farm of their own on marrying. In the rural hinterlands of Augusta, Georgia, only 38 per cent of white males aged twenty to twenty-four were married; whereas 58 per cent of white females of that age were (Harris 1981: 81). Late marriage was typical of western Europe and North America in the early and mid nineteenth century; indeed it was even higher in Europe (Anderson 1980: 18). It may have been a form of birth control and/or inspired by the desire to postpone marriage until economic viability was assured. Whether intended for the latter purpose or not, marriages contracted by Southern men in their mid-twenties obviously held out better prospects for the newly wed couples' starting out on their own family farms than marriages entered into earlier in the male life-cycle. And the family farm offered the ideal to be striven for; if over half the Southern adult males in 1860 were farmers, some 70 per cent or thereabouts of farmers owned their farms. Men persistently translated the economic ideal into reality.

The extent of individuals' concern for the family's financial good fortunes is well, if over-dramatically, demonstrated by the case of Isham R. Howze. Howze was born in North Carolina in 1796 but started as a landowning farmer in Alabama in 1818. He moved on to Mississippi in 1839 where he continued, except for a brief sojourn in southern Tennessee, until his death in 1857. Although Howze owned a certain amount of land – at least 320 acres – and four, economically useless, female slaves, he suffered constantly in the 1850s from financial pressure. Crops fell short of expectations, medical bills for his family mounted. Partly because of these problems, partly because he suffered badly from a speech impediment, and partly because his religious faith did not square with that of any established denomination, he felt impelled to ease his sense of isolation by unburdening himself to a diary. In 1852 he noted,

> I feel great solicitude on account of my children – greater, and greater, and greater – every day, because every day brings me nearer and nearer my end; and when I am gone one of their best friends will be taken from them. It is because I feel my end approaching, that I mention my children so often in my books [diaries]. I would address them as from the grave and admonish them to attend to their eternal concerns.

He recorded also that he had no desire to dominate his wife, to whom he declared glowing affection, and seven children, all under twenty years old. Rather, he underwent great psychological pressure to provide materially, despite bad health, for his children: 'It is my duty to labor; but I cannot labor in the field or in the shop.' In 1853 he settled up some outstanding financial obligations – to be heavily in debt was to be 'like a slave' – and bought 320 acres in northern Mississippi. The move from southern Tennessee failed to raise his self-confidence as a planter or farmer; but he recorded repeatedly his devotion to his family as husband, companion, father, brother and ever-struggling Christian (Isham R. Howze's Book: 30 June, 10, 16 July, 3 Nov., 29 Dec. 1852, 4 Jan. 1853, vol. 8; 10 Oct., 15 Dec. 1853, vol. 9. Howze (Isham Robertson) and Family papers. MDAH).

Howze was exceptional – on other grounds than that he kept a revealing diary – as he himself unhappily knew. Why, then, should his testament interest us? For one thing, he well captured the ambivalent, but typically Victorian, mores of the rural South: a society of intensely religious sensibility and providential belief, yet one also materialistic to the point of rapacity. Howze, a slaveowner and farmer of but modest standing, was, if not rich, certainly among the affluent of the 1850s. Yet he felt the weight of debt and the business difficulties and social slights that attended the indebtedness of those commonly deemed to be poor. From this perception of his relative deprivation arose a persistent drive to do well by his wife and family, to provide materially, and spiritually, for their present and future needs. This is the second reason for his general significance. For what is often portrayed as the humbug patriarch trotting off to enjoy the challenges, profits and pleasures of the wider world was as often as not the conscientious, not uncaring husband and father winkling out a present competency, and future legacy, for his family's as well as his own benefit.

The strength of family ties was increased by the general character of nineteenth-century family structure. Although there were random variations in the precise details, the broad character of the family was similar in nineteenth-century North America and western Europe. The key differences between mid nineteenth-century and late twentieth-century families turned on the age of first marriage, child-bearing and life expectancy. These three factors gelling together greatly reinforced the family's importance in the nineteenth century. Marriage tended to occur in the mid-twenties for men, slightly earlier perhaps for women. In an age of limited educational provision for those aged fifteen to twenty-five years, and in a region of relatively limited job opportunities, such an age of marriage stretched out the period of dependence upon family and of residence at home. Once marriage was entered into, family obligations were, typically, shouldered for life. Women tended to bear children until they were in their late thirties or about forty. Life expectancy at forty was, roughly, another twenty years. Couples had little chance, therefore, of surviving beyond the child-caring or progeny-keeping age, since sons and daughters commonly lived at home into their twenties. The pattern of nuclear family living was thus radically different from that of our own day, when, again generalizing very broadly, child-bearing tends to be over by the age of thirty; at thirty, women can expect to live another fifty years, thus enjoying a long period free of immediate responsibilities for their offspring (Anderson 1980: 18–20).

This very general pattern appears to have obtained in the South; though it must be said that detailed research is still only at the primitive stage of accumulation. A fairly large sample of men and women from the, largely Virginian, planters' ranks and born after 1795 showed the following characteristics. While the vast majority of women were married by the age of twenty-five (65%), a more modest 47 per cent of men had married for the first time by that age. A sizeable number of women (29%) had married before they were twenty, whereas only 6 per cent of the men had done so. Although the membership of the average household in 1860 was only five and nearly one-third of households had a resident lodger or next of kin (Harris 1981: 95); and although the number of children borne was falling gently, marked variations in women's fecundity remained. Some 37 per cent of married women in the planter sample had more than six children, even if very nearly half (48%) had four or fewer children or no children (Clinton 1982: 238–42). And, of course, it has to be stressed that averages for household size are not necessarily very revealing about family membership; for many households consisted of younger couples who were only starting procreation, with the consequence that their small numbers of resident members depress the overall mean. Still, even allowing for an average decline of one in the number of children borne by American women in the period 1800–40, the population remained very youthful (Walters 1973: 229). In 1860, only 6–8 per cent of whites in six of the seven Deep South states were as old as fifty years or more; in New England, by way of contrast, 15 per cent of whites were of that age, though other parts of the North were well below that proportion. Even more dramatically, perhaps, only about 25 per cent of the white population in Alabama, Florida, Georgia, Mississippi and Texas were aged thirty or more (Potter 1965: 687).

Given this age profile, it is easy to see why ideas of patriarchy, and indeed patriarchal habits, flourished in the antebellum period. The middle-aged portion of the white population was relatively small and the structure of the family, as well as its essential economic duties, threw the responsibility for caring for children upon married couples effectively for the rest of their lives. The role of active family head almost had to be a fulfilling one, since it was about the only role available to the majority of adult white males.

Moreover, women had extremely few chances to live and work

outside their families. Only 3 per cent of white women aged twenty to twenty-four (against 24% of men) were both unmarried and not living with their parents in the rural region around Augusta during the 1850s. Some women – presumably widows – operated their own farms; varying from county to county, between 6 per cent and 14 per cent of farmers in that same four county area were women in 1860 (Harris 1981: 81, 91). Otherwise, the agricultural order left few openings for female employment. School-teaching was the obvious respectable possibility. But teaching jobs tended to be transient and insecure. One thirty-year-old single woman teacher in Georgia confided despairingly to her diary in 1857: 'It is indeed a hard lot for a penniless girl to go forth alone in this wide world to seek maintenance. I wish I was a man then I would not fear; but alas what can a poor timid woman do?' (Dyer 1982: 65). Towns offered more scope for women to pursue and possibly even to enjoy autonomous lives. In late eighteenth-century North Carolina, for example, about 10 per cent of households were headed by women, and these were mostly in towns. Tavern-keeping was one occupation in which women were quite well represented (Watson 1981: 18–19). In Mobile, Alabama, women furnished 10 per cent of the free work-force in 1860. Irish girls worked as servants; women provided three-quarters of the 150 workers in the Mobile and Dog River Manufacturing Company, a textile mill; women toiled in millinery and clothing production, and in confectionery shops; there were also four 'female lodging houses' run by women and looking ominously like brothels. More affluent women, however, objected to the general absence of opportunity and education open to them even in such a prospering commercial town as Mobile in the 1850s; their proper sphere seemed to be confined to benevolent associations and churches (Amos 1981: 4–5, 11–18). This lack of opportunity beyond the home partly resulted from the very facts of family structure. The whole pattern of family activity became self-sustaining. Women were tied into their families, as daughters or wives, for virtually their entire lives. Few alternative opportunities to this family milieu existed to broaden women's – certainly not 'respectable' women's – experiences when they were in their twenties. And, typically, there was very little or no life beyond the phase of nurturing and rearing the nuclear family.

II

Family was important not simply because people needed it and could not, demographically, get away from it. Southerners also found deep and lasting emotional reward in their family life and family ties.

The mid nineteenth century saw an outburst of literate interest in the family as an institution. As R. G. Walters (1973: 221) has observed, 'the pervasive metaphor of mid nineteenth-century America seems not to have been the individual but rather the family.' Religious evangelicals were anxious to promote moral restraint. Students of American society regarded family cohesion as essential to general stability. Moralists and medical men – and medical men might be moralists as well – both advocated sexual self-discipline within marriage. A Connecticut physician and publicist, William A. Alcott, argued in his widely read treatise, *The Moral Philosophy of Courtship and Marriage* (1857) that physical maturity for men did not occur until the mid-twenties, that early sexual activity impaired men's full development in other spheres and that intercourse once per month was sufficient for good health thereafter (Milden 1974: iii, 63–4, 130). Such moralizing or 'scientific' advising about personal sexual behaviour and marriage may have flowed readily from male pens, but it indicated very clearly the need for male restraint.

Despite this fact, there remains a pervasive belief that women, confined physically to the home and morally to faithful acquiescence in marriage, were the victims of a male double-standard, especially in the South. One feminist historian has asserted that 'antebellum patriarchs simultaneously emasculated male slaves, dehumanized female slaves, and desexualized their own wives'; and that 'The plantation mistress found herself trapped within a system over which she had no control, one from which she had no means of escape. Cotton was King, white men ruled, and both white women and slaves served the same master' (Clinton 1982: 222, 35). This is a contemporary and more forceful development of an old perspective. Not only did abolitionists at the time complain about the disruptive effects of slavery upon the white family. Early historians of the American family reiterated the view that morally wholesome family relationships could not survive the crushing weight of patriarchal authority or the opportunities available to slaveowning males to enjoy a sexual double-standard (Calhoun 1917: 159, 275). A false view of sexually 'pure' womanhood co-existed with rampant freedom of male sexual action.

This often repeated case for the prevalence of a double-standard has not been proven. One particularly lively diarist of the South Carolinian elite, Mary Chesnut, left a comment which historians have gratefully quoted whenever such matters are discussed: ' ... we live surrounded by prostitutes ... like the patriarchs of old our men live all in one house with their wives and their concubines ... every lady tells you who is the father of all the mulatto children in everybody's household, but those in her own she seems to think drop from clouds, or pretends so to think' (Woodward 1981: 29). In more resigned style, one slaveowner's wife informed her aunt that Jenny, a slave, had given birth to a child 'whiter than any of mine ... I am sorry he is so white' (Martha Battey to aunt, 1857: Battey Family Papers). Under such conditions, some Southern women naturally cursed their lot and viewed their own degradation as something akin to the slaves'. Yet Southern white males' transgressions of this kind have never been placed in any sort of comparative or quantitative context. It is quite possible that much sexual licence with slaves involved unmarried young men. It is possible also that small-town brothels and so on were patronized largely by unmarried men, transients, and the unchurched. It is equally possible that the broad mass of middle-class males accepted the teachings of morality and science and exercised considerable self-restraint. Sexual repression was not simply a male device for upholding the purity of their constrained wives (Walters 1976: 157–75).

Moreover, the language of complaint in which women compared their lot to the slaves' – and it was a private language almost uniformly – merely reflected common usage. To lend full weight to any grievance in the antebellum South, those complaining naturally used the analogy of slavery, as the worst, most graphic, and most immediately relevant measure of subordination. Isham Howze, when he deplored his financial indebtedness, confided to his diary that to be in debt was to be 'like a slave'. Southern politicians, especially in the 1850s, constantly described the South as being in imminent danger of enslavement to their opponents' pet measures, especially Republican plans for federal restrictions upon slavery's westward extension. Slavery served as a metaphor for degradation and defeat. So it served – very fleetingly and on occasion – in women's private writings, to convey a strong sense of personal rejection or private humiliation. To extrapolate from such frustrations an argument that Southern women believed their family life to be undermined or contaminated by slavery or viewed themselves as reduced by a patriarchal order and ethos to a level not far removed from enslavement simply inflates the rhetoric and metaphor of complaint.

Two further considerations arise concerning slavery's impact upon women's family feelings. First, no more than one in every four Southern families owned a slave in 1860; and no more than 35–50 per cent of households in the Deep South did so. Most of the slaveowning households were not grand plantations which could support pampered mistresses or domestic servants involved intimately with the white menfolk. Slavery's presence could not have directly affected the familial relationships of more than a minority of Southerners. The other is that late night private grumblings about slavery were never translated into public protests of the kind that women were fully capable of mounting in the 1850s against rabid intemperance. For example, no fewer than 124 ladies of the town of Pontotoc and its neighbourhood petitioned Mississippi's state legislature for a law to ban the sale of intoxicating liquors in both the town and an area three miles around it. These reformers well understood the general implications of their petition:

> The undersigned are conscious that females are rarely the immediate subject of intemperance. Yet its evil effects fall most heavily upon their

sex, and they feel well assured that any law calculated to remove the temptation to drink to excess will promote their happiness and secure the best interests of society (Undated petition, RG 47, Legisl., vol. 27, MDAH).

The evangelical impulse, in turning minds outwards to social purification, had the effect simultaneously of reinforcing familial obligations. No equivalent impulse – or any discernible impulse – was directed against slavery. As one slaveowner's wife recorded in her diary in 1860:

> I should myself feel a natural repugnance toward slavery if I did not find it existing and myself an owner lawfully and scripturally. As a class they are comparatively happy. No care and no concern for the future. And when really converted, having comparatively few temptations, they are most consistent (McCorkle Diary, 26 Aug. 1860. McCorkle papers, SHL).

Despite abolitionists' contention that the slaveowning family was corrupted by the possession of human chattels, and despite wives' occasional, lurid complaint against slaveowners' sexual immorality, the argument that the emotional underpinning to Southern family life was significantly weakened by a male double-standard is unproven and, very probably, much exaggerated.

Aspects of family life were, however, greatly affected by patriarchal attitudes. Women were repeatedly schooled by men in the proper deference to be accorded their spouses. The small-town *Aberdeen Whig* of Mississippi reprinted, from the *Richmond Enquirer,* this warning to newly married women:

> The first maxim which you should impress most deeply upon your mind, is never to attempt to control your husband, by opposition, by displeasure, or any other mark of anger. A man of sense, of prudence, of warm feeling, cannot, and will not bear an opposition of any kind, which is attended with an angry look or expression (*Aberdeen Whig* 21 May 1839).

Another small-town Mississippi newspaper similarly admonished potential scolds:

> When a woman seeks to guide her husband, it should not be like one who breaks a horse to her own purpose, using bit and spur, now checking, and now goading his career – but, like the mariner who steers the ship, and directs it by a single touch, while none can see the power that rules its actions (*Ripley Advertiser* 27 April 1844).

Yet another warned young wives that the transition from being wooed to being married was a difficult one, for the husband tended naturally to switch his attentions to other matters – even to prefer the nocturnal companionship of men friends to that of his wife – once he had 'won' his woman. Wives discovering this fact were best advised to avoid reproachful complaint and concentrate their efforts on making the home a 'sunny place' to the husband (Aberdeen, *The Weekly Independent*, 21 Dec. 1850). Such advice – and there was virtually nothing equivalent to it for the edification of husbands – was not merely printed; it was read. Lucilla McCorkle clipped a set of invocations from a newspaper in 1852 and pasted it in her diary. Mrs McCorkle, the reasonably intelligent, conscientious wife of an Alabama clergyman deeply involved in female education, clearly felt the need for some matrimonial guidance. She was reminded to conform to her husband's wishes, never publicly to criticize or joke about him, never to 'appear untidy or badly dressed' in his presence, never to let any consciousness of 'superiority of judgment or talent' show, and always to 'let your husband suppose you think him a good husband', for such conduct would be 'a strong stimulus to his being so'. Moreover, this 'Whisper to Wives' stressed, 'let home be the sole scene of your wishes, your plans, your exertions' (McCorkle Diary, 12 May 1852: McCorkle papers, SHC).

Invocations of this sort were nothing new. In the sixteenth century, for instance, Erasmus was saying similar things about marriage (Mount 1982: 206–7). But, in some ways, the emphasis upon the house and on ambitions constricted to it was more galling for women by the 1850s than it would have been centuries earlier. For men's sphere of action had greatly expanded, with education more widely available, with participation in politics open to men whose forebears would scarcely have dreamed of being admitted to public affairs, and with economic changes affording an increasing range of jobs and even careers. Women benefited far less than did men from these advances. Their education tended to concentrate on the decorative; entry into political life was blocked; respectable jobs available to women were extremely scanty. Even recourse against intolerable or intractable husbands was often difficult. Divorce was obtainable in the eighteenth century and well into the nineteenth only from the state legislatures. Their responses to divorce petitions varied. North Carolina, for example, granted a fairly high proportion of petitions submitted up to 1830; yet in South Carolina scarcely any divorce petitions were awarded before 1830 (Cott 1977: 5 6; Clinton 1982: 82).

And women's public image, devised and articulated largely by male writers, was of docility, acquiescence, domesticity and accomplishment. The South's most distinguished and successful antebellum novelist, William Gilmore Simms (1835: ch. XXIV), offered this detached and modest comment on womanhood:

> The affections of women are usually unselfish. They love the more
> profoundly, the more they serve. Their love grows with their
> labors – with their toil for the beloved – and, the idea of all injustice and

oppression excluded, their passion is proportionately increased by their cares. To be allowed to serve is, with them, to love the object of their devotion. It is for man to show himself grateful for the service; this, perhaps, in the warmth of their devoted homage, is the utmost that they ask. Yet even when this acknowledgment is withheld, the greater number of them will still continue the service. The service itself, to the dependent spirit, is a joy; and they will ask little more than the vine that only prays the privilege to be suffered to cling around the tree.

Even though the two leading ladies of the *Border Beagles. A Tale of Mississippi* (1835), from which this reflection came, were full-blooded and adventurous, their independent actions flowed from emotional attachments to male protagonists. More generally, women were portrayed, if not always by Simms, as largely decorous, and not sexually active or assertive. Even motherhood – their noblest avocation – was a declining role, given antebellum families' shrinking size.

In fact, the situation was far more fluid than the formal ideology maintained; and this fluidity, by making the family far less of a closed institution than some of the difficulties of family life might suggest, served to strengthen the family as a social bond. If women were excluded from politics, they enjoyed an important access to public matters through the churches. Evangelical congregations were especially active in policing their members' conduct, and women were prominent in the congregations. The leading offences brought before ten Baptist churches in Wake County, North Carolina, from 1850 to 1915 involved drunkenness and sexual immorality (Stroupe 1975: 169). These indicated both that the pattern of social behaviour was not quite as confined by the bounds of propriety as the outpouring of solemn advice claimed it should be, and that women actively maintained a moral code which is sometimes regarded as being merely the product of a patriarchal order and a male double-standard.

Women seem also to have possessed a good deal of freedom in their choice of spouses and an important role in laying down codes of family conduct. Freedom in selecting a marriage partner may have been inhibited by strict custom and financial calculation among the wealthy planters (Clinton 1982: 61–6); but more generally there seem to have been no oppressive constraints. From an admittedly very small sample in Georgia, some 62 per cent of marriages in the 1850s were between partners of similar economic standing (Harris 1981: 86). Individuals from this evidence apparently married across economic divides. A degree of free choice was also apparent in a small community in Spartanburg county, South Carolina, where two unusual marriages during a nine-month period were recorded in surviving correspondence. In one case, a young couple eloped; their marriage was formalized locally on the third attempt, after one clergyman and a justice had refused to perform that service. The girl's father pursued the couple, caught up with them at an inn and threatened dire consequences. The young people, however, gave him the slip and escaped into the stage, where 'They were rec^d [*sic*] with hearty cheers by the passengers.' In the other case, a colonel's widow 'fancied' a stage driver who arrived in the community shortly after her husband's death. She married the man; though, under pressure from her friends, she made a marriage contract to keep her own property beyond her new husband's reach, a device frequently employed by widows (William Summer to George Fike, 29 Sept. 1849, 14 May 1850: Summer Letters, MDAH).

Within their families, women exerted, or tried to exert, strong influence over the children. If formal ideology taught wives to obey, and laid down detailed instructions for them to do so, wives as mothers enjoyed much autonomy in their regulation of children's conduct. Mrs McCorkle took heed of printed advice on the proper conduct of housewives. But she also went to great and finely worked out lengths to educate and discipline her children, including the eldest son who had nearly reached manhood but had failed to find Godliness. At times she regretted her own admonishing of the children; but she took great pains to lay down rules for her eldest son's daily routine and conduct (McCorkle Diary, 23 and 24 Aug. 1859). Although men held the chief responsibility for decision-making and spread ideas of patriarchy, women retained significant measures of autonomy and authority within the family.

Moreover, close and fulfilling emotional relationships were not uncommon. Family interactions were as much the product of differences between 'roughs' and 'respectables' as were other relationships in the antebellum South. Some planters were authoritarian and scarcely got on with their wives and children; James H. Hammond was an excellent if perhaps exaggerated example of that 'type' (Faust 1982: 307–30). Yet others, the Jones family in Georgia spring to mind, enjoyed intensely pious, companionable and supportive relationships (Myers 1972). A merchant in Savannah, James Rhind, wrote to his fourteen-year-old daughter of the loss of his wife and her mother:

> The past year has been to me one of bitter and overwhelming sorrow and grief: the many trials to which I have been heretofore subjected have been light when compared to this dreadful affliction. I have lost my companion and friend, my counsellor and guide and life is now to me but a heavy burden.

If Rhind proceeded a shade heavy-handedly in his effusive description of his wife's virtues and character, and in urging her example of upright conduct upon the young girl, he was at least frank and open in his testimony to his late wife. And, a few years later, an aunt was equally direct in describing to this girl the feelings and responses of the girl's grandmother to a letter the teenager had written (James Rhind to daughter, 18 Feb. 1852; Aunt Mary to Maggie, 31 Dec. 1854: James Rhind Corresp., Rhinds–Stokes–Gardner Letters).

The family, then, acted as a social bond because it afforded an important, indeed in many cases probably sole, source of emotional comfort. Slavery's existence and the economic and social facts of nineteenth-century life undoubtedly isolated some women, notably those in wealthier planter households, and indeed virtually imprisoned some of them in gilded cages. Yet that aspect of Southern life was not universal and, as far as anyone can guess in such matters, probably not even typical. Dr Blake quotes one North Carolinian slaveowner contrasting the 'cold and selfish' world 'where persons usually act as though the chief object of existence was their own aggrandisement even if in so doing they trample on their nearest and dearest friends', and the ideal – not always attained – of 'unity and affection among relations'. He records a Georgian saying, during a family disagreement: 'I would let the *world* and everything in it go to the *Devil* before I would quarrel with my family' (Blake 1978: 54, 62). Despite shortcomings within and hypocrisy sometimes surrounding it, the affective family was a central element in Southern life. And it offered at times of political crisis a potent symbol, as the rallying cry for a 'hearth and home' party to unify Southerners and repel Northern encroachments went up.

III

The environment in which the family existed reinforced its effect as a social adhesive. In specific terms, we still know virtually nothing of the make-up of Southern families; it is probable that family size varied appreciably, that dependence upon the family varied also with differing economic conditions and with the character of the habitat. Town-dwellers, plantation families and the backwoods folk of the hill country may have experienced very different familial relationships. But if precise details of composition, attitudes towards pre-marital and extra-marital sex, and the extent of local kinship networks probably fluctuated widely, the family remained as the central institution common to all Southern communities and classes.

Slavery, as has already been noted, was often regarded as a major disruptive element at work upon the Southern family, and, naturally, peculiar to the South. The classic form, by repute, which this disruption took was in the realm of sexual relations. But, again, as has been stressed already, at least two facts countered this idea. First, not that many families owned many slaves and so not many existed in the state of incipient concubinage deplored by Mary Chesnut. Second, religious scruples operated among slaveowners and planters, as well as more generally, to bridle sexual excesses. Moreover, many whites regarded slaves as dehumanized beings. The first time Olmsted saw a woman (a slave) flogged, he remarked on 'the perfectly passionless but rather grim business-like face of the overseer' who inflicted the punishment. And on the same plantation, in the Deep South, he was told of the slave girls' sexual promiscuity (Rose 1976: 298, 300). Attitudes such as these – and they were common enough in the Deep South – suggest that the psychological dehumanization of slaves served, in effect, to trivialize physical relationships involving white men and slave women. A good deal of such interracial sex (and we do not know how much of it there really was) scarcely threatened, given its casual and unfeeling nature, the family's central position in Southern society.

But, in other ways, slavery strengthened family bonding. As an early historian of the family wrote, because 'plantations tended to isolation and self-support', the planter 'could turn only to his family for regular companionship' (Calhoun 1917: 229, 232). The plantations' isolation can be overplayed. In eighteenth-century Virginia, planters could lead extremely sociable lives, with frequent, virtually daily visits to and from neighbours and friends (Smith 1980: 199–225). And Mrs Chesnut's loathed country districts supported 'semi-village life', since 'though we live miles apart – everybody flying round on horses or in carriages – it amounts to a village community' (Woodward 1981: 176). But, although plantations were not entirely isolated, they clearly created a more insulated environment than did agriculture given over to farms. And the rural Deep South fostered more self-contained styles of living than prevailed in urban areas.

Far more important than the isolation of individual plantations or farms was the fact that the South was largely unpoliced, while its agriculture rested on labour extracted from a potentially rebellious populace often suspected indeed of being on the verge of rebellion. Upholding order in such circumstances fell squarely upon the male citizenry. In some heavily plantation areas, the whites were greatly outnumbered by blacks. And under half the white population, sometimes nearer 40 per cent than 50 per cent, was aged twenty years or more. In some parts of plantation belt South Carolina during the 1790s, white adult males constituted a mere fraction of the total population; in 1792, according to contemporary figures, St Paul's parish had only sixty-five free white males aged sixteen or more in a population of 3,433, while there were eighty-one such males in St Stephen's parish (2,733 people) and 145 among the 3,836 people of St Thomas's parish (Drayton 1802: 104). Throughout the South as a whole in 1850 the average slaveowner was forty-three years old; the majority of slaves were aged eighteen or less (Oakes 1982: 195). Averages can be as deceptive as individual examples, but the obvious point remains that white adult males were often in a distinct and vulnerable minority in a potentially hazardous environment.

Without going as far as to describe the South as an armed (white) camp, or to agree with Stanley Elkins's analogy between Southern plantation slavery and Nazi concentration camp conditions, one should stress that the maintenance of order was devolved very largely upon the citizenry (Elkins 1959). If we remember Lenin as well as Gramsci and note that 'power comes out of the barrel of a gun' as well as from the dissemination of an ideology, then clearly white power in the South, especially in heavily plantation areas, depended, if not solely on naked force, on the manifest capacity of the white civilian population to summon up and use daunting physical coercion. Since there was no army to call upon and but a feeble militia lurking in reserve, the force had to be supplied by the slaveowners themselves and their neighbours. In this respect, but informally, the South was indeed an armed camp. There were other ways of keeping order among the slaves; paternalism, often, perhaps even usually, sincere, was also important. Ultimately, however, the paternalist and the patriarch had to be capable of asserting his authority from the barrel of a gun. That necessity – far more pressing than any equivalent Northern requirement for vigilantism – bred a Southern type which sometimes became a self-parody. Yet the need to play a part, to sustain a public image of authoritativeness and force, may be accounted just as much a cost paid by many men to make their plantation rule effective, as it was a benefit that they undilutedly enjoyed. Just because so many planters were obliged to take on the patriarchal role as part of the dramatic ritual of Southern life, we need not conclude that the planter or slaveowner was immune to correction or contradiction from his spouse in the private, familial world where the masks of the public sphere were dropped.

Slaveowners were, to use the military phrase, at the sharp end of social interaction. It was not their wives or, for many planters, their surrogates the overseers, who ultimately bore responsibility for keeping the slaves down and for mobilizing white vigilantes to ensure racial control. This fact, and their consciousness of personal 'face' and of family achievement and even of family pride, led to the articulation of various codes of honour (Wyatt-Brown 1982). For many wealthier Southerners (those with most to defend) personal and family honour became a matter literally of life or death; though one suspects sheer frustration between rivals for land or office, and the bottle, frequently lay behind such duels. Whether this behaviour marked Southern planters down as aristocratic or quasi feudal hang-overs perilously adrift in the increasingly 'bourgeois' nineteenth century is irrelevant. Some grand planters may have believed they were keeping alive an 'aristocratic' notion of honour. But the reality was usually grubbier, and the need to accept the challenge more mundane. At root, the cult of patriarchal honour derived from the requirements of an unpoliced society in which white adults had to enforce public order and defend their families against both blacks and other potential challenges.

IV

The uncertainties and character of economic life, the growth of evangelical religion and whites' racial exclusivity all strengthened ideas of family obligation and loyalty. Southerners, indeed, saw themselves socially as members of families and races rather than as members of a class. It has even been argued that the intense evangelical revival of the late eighteenth century turned Virginians' sentiments and beliefs dramatically inwards, so that the affective family became in the early nineteenth century *the* central institution in their lives. Whether the undoubted increase in writing, publicly and privately, about family relationships should be interpreted as a sign of *withdrawal* from community affairs and as evidence for a decline in intellectual and individual attention given to notions of republican virtue is another matter (Lewis 1983). In the generation from the late 1820s, evangelical religion and devotion to family co-existed with an upsurge in popular politics, electioneering, participation in voting and public discussion of Southern whites' distinctiveness and defence of slavery. Southerners who faced the crisis of 1860–61 scarcely ignored public questions or relegated them to a strictly inferior role because of a preoccupation with the private sphere.

Slavery may have set up special tensions within slaveowning families; but these did not crack the essential foundations of family life. If some women complained that men enjoyed peculiar privileges resulting from the possession of slaves, slaveowners and their wives more generally struggled in the mid nineteenth century to pattern slavery after their image of a properly Christian family. Their regime was as much matriarchal as patriarchal and, while it could be heavy-handed, so it did much also to foster religious worship and familial values among the slaves themselves (Rose 1982: 18–31). If white men held the advantage of economic opportunity, travel and careers, their surviving testimony – in letters, diaries, wills, laws, habits, aspirations, religion, and invocations to good conduct – all points to the prime importance of familial ties, loyalties and connections in their calculations and world-view. The strength and continuing pervasiveness of this basic attachment helps explain the potency of Southerners' commitment to their larger, sectional cause.

Chapter nine

RITUALS

I

A discussion of ritual in society takes us back initially to a consideration of government's role. For government itself established rituals that helped provide social bonds. Partisan meetings and demagogic election campaigns intensified patriotism and, as the 1840s and 1850s unfolded, celebrated Southern identity. This is not to say that consensus reigned supreme in the antebellum South. Party and personal clashes obviously arose from and generated very real and obstinate disputes over issues and fuelled considerable differences of opinion within the South. But much consensus-building accompanied and resulted from election campaigns, for these served to laud both republicanism and the special and Providentially ordained Southern racial order. Just as Douglas Hay has cited the formal pomp and ritual of the English court system in the eighteenth century – the court processions and the imposing attire of the judges – in order to explain how a deferential order was sustained (Hay *et al.* 1975: 26–31), so it is worth noting that the rituals of representative and democratic government emphasized how 'informal' institutions were and how they depended totally upon the common citizens' approval. As Barbara Smith Bodichon, a British feminist and reformer, commented in 1857, on her first acquaintance with America:

> This is really a free country in the respect of having no privileged
> class – excepting the class of white over black. . . . One is so little used to
> freedom, real freedom, even in England that it takes time to understand
> freedom, to realize it. Nothing sent from upper powers to be worshipped
> or humbly listened to, no parsons sent by a class of born rulers to preach
> and lecture to another class born to submit and to pay. No race of men
> with honours they have not earned and power over others which the
> others have not consented them!

And this conclusion was penned at New Orleans; Mrs Bodichon did not distinguish between North and South over their attitudes to *white* social and political relationships (Bodichon 1972: 72, 117).

The fixed routine of election campaigns helped to focus attention on the institutions of popular government and to draw people together for the often raucous gatherings that punctuated those campaigns. If politics typically fed upon and expressed rival claims – regional jealousies were much played up, as were competing pressures for internal improvements – they also provided a necessarily indefinable sense of common purpose. White racial solidarity and distinctiveness were repeatedly prated about in election rhetoric. Moreover, the concentration of Southern politicians and newspapers upon national issues served to heighten sectional feelings and increase social unity. Other official events were less popularly supported, but, again, provided an element of ritual in Southern white society. Militia musters were customarily written of in semi-satirical vein; but the existence of some, however skeletal, militia organization added another focus for group activity. Finally, the quarterly meetings of county courts, for the ordering of local affairs from building bridges to imposing bastardy bonds upon fathers of illegitimate infants, afforded another regular occasion for community action.

These public events were, *qua* events, as much the occasion for a conflict of values between the roughs and the respectables and the quiescent and improving in society as festivals of fellowship and unity. State politics witnessed numerous disputes over internal improvements, over temperance reform, and over common schooling in the 1850s. Criticisms of the poorly equipped and casually drilled militia were also common. And county courts could be seen as occasions for giving respectability muscle, as petty offenders were dealt with and community improvement projects advanced. But, equally important, these events, so frequent and so regular, served to give shape to communities of farmers and cross-roads 'villages'. A sense of belonging to a county appears to have been widespread and deep. Petitions to Mississippi's legislature in the 1820s and 1830s especially were periodically concerned to have county boundaries modified in order to bring the county seats within comfortable travelling distance of all residents in the county (RG 47 Legisl. vol. 17, MDAH). This was a practical concern; but it illustrated the way businesslike attention was focused on county government. Given this context, a great deal of the emphasis of early twentieth-century state historians upon the laying down of county lines and the establishment of state and local government institutions is easy to understand. For it was something of an achievement – though one now treated as almost inevitable and unimpressive – to create a stable framework of judicial and administrative institutions and jurisdictions in the midst of rapid and often violent territorial expansion. W. J. Cash in 1941 emphasized how the antebellum South had to be seen in terms of its rolling frontiers (Cash 1954: 18). This frontier society faced not only the Indians, to add to its potential for both violence and instability, but also the internal threat posed by slaves. One antidote to the individualistic tendency to violence and lawlessness so much associated with the South was the swift planting of government institutions. And the regular rituals of government made their existence fully known, even if the actions of government were not often deeply felt.

While the rituals of government should be noted, these are not the rituals which much attract the attention of the latest generation of social historians. Borrowing heavily from social anthropology, historians of the antebellum South are increasingly seeking to understand popular culture from an analysis of such ritualized events as duels and charivari, and of such ritualized forms of expression as folk lore and folk 'architecture'. Even 'criminal' behaviour is scrutinized for the aperçus it offers upon the underlying social assumptions and relationships of the less articulate Southern whites.

From a traditional perspective, there are a number of qualifications to be made to the social anthropological craze. One is that the tools of social anthropology are developed to explore non-literate societies. Antebellum Southerners have left us an overflowing record of their anxieties, aspirations and beliefs. That no alternative idea of how Southern society should be ordered was advanced and actively promoted in the antebellum South suggests that the prevailing order commanded very considerable consent. Secondly, although the study of 'aberrant' behaviour may illuminate some social tensions, a close knowledge of murders, gang wars, vendettas, sexual abuses and so forth can hardly claim to reveal the fundamental dynamics of a society in which such phenomena were atypical, publicly and strenuously condemned, and, where possible, usually suppressed. These phenomena rather tend to beg the question of how the 'normal' pattern of individual conduct or social behaviour remained so prosaic and, apparently, conformist in the midst of deviant possibilities. Thirdly, there is a partial assumption in some recent writing that the 'middle classes' tightened social control and discredited a spontaneous and intricate folk culture as the nineteenth century proceeded. All this was manifested in the diffusion of scientific rationalism, in so far as it was diffused in the antebellum South; in the spread (penetration is the buzz word used, implying intentionality, purposefulness and even force) of market relationships; and in the steady displacement from the late eighteenth century to the mid nineteenth century of organic forms of building (log cabins and their naturalistic derivatives) by the more planned and stylized products of 'high' culture. Southern folk ways, in *some* accounts, join an already long list of victims to the inexorable march of capitalist economics and capitalist taste. Finally, if taken to its logical conclusion, the study of ritual ends up by becoming the study of every manner of personal behaviour. Erving Goffman's *The Presentation of*

Self in Every-day Life marks out the possibilities for the scrutiny of 'ritualized' conduct in ordinary personal transactions; life becomes, under his sharp eye, a series of dramaturgical happenings (Goffman 1971: 231–47).

Yet, despite considerable qualms about the extent to which social anthropology can transform our vision of the antebellum South, it is certainly worth examining social rituals. Our purpose in doing so is not to seek some novel psychological insight into the thought processes of Southern whites, but rather to understand how whites of different levels of wealth and education co-existed. There are two stages in such an examination: to stress that many rituals were socially divisive rather than integrative; and to balance against this description of rituals reflecting differences in education or social status those customs or happenings which drew people of various social groups closely together or served to weaken or dissolve distinctions of status.

II

In the first month of 1859 the affluent citizens of Natchez had at least two opportunities to revel at the Mansion House. One week they were reminded of their Scottish heritage by a Burns supper; another they commemorated the Natchez Indians with a Red Indian masked ball. Fancy dress or masked balls recurred throughout the year, to help raise money for charitable purposes, or for their own sakes, and their organizing themes remained as culturally polyglot as those of January. Yet such functions took place in a town which, despite its rampant prosperity, still had no theatre in 1859 to replace the one destroyed by a tornado nearly twenty years earlier (Natchez *Mississippi Free Trader,* 24, 31 Jan., 28 Feb., 14 March 1859). And they took place also in a town where social life was very dramatically segregated; for Natchez 'Under the Hill', on the river-front, had long possessed a reputation for gambling, prostitution and criminal receiving second to none in the Mississippi west (Matthias 1945: 215–16; Penick 1981: 57–9, 147–8). In 1858, community leaders were petitioning the state legislature to contribute substantially to the construction of a monument to General John A. Quitman, the first public monument, they avowed, to be erected to one of Mississippi's heroes; it was to dominate the Bluff, under which the hectic night-life of the river-front throbbed (Petition and newspaper clipping of 1858 in RG 47 Legisl. vol. 27, MDAH).

In some respects, the social life of Natchez was replicated across the South. Society entertainments went hand-in-hand with shadier social rituals. At one extreme, planters' houses were designed for public entertaining as well as mundane habitation. Entrance halls were usually large, taking up to a third of the internal space of large houses, not simply to reflect the householder's status, but also to furnish an area of easy social circulation for balls and parties (Crocker 1971: 34, 155; Crocker 1973: xi). Rooms were interconnected by sliding doors so that sizeable entertaining spaces could be created with ease. Yet juxtaposed beside this mode of recreation the rural South was dotted with cross-roads villages whose general stores and inns (often referred to as 'doggeries' or 'ordinaries') sold alcoholic beverages to a sometimes raucous clientele: 'those haunts of vicious depravity' (Baldwin 1853: 109). The hand-fights and gougings, the gun-fights and street deaths that were so much complained of in the antebellum South often originated in these informal gathering places. To counterbalance these disruptive tendencies communities erected county court-house after county court-house in ever more imposing and rarely uniform architectural style across the South. The ritual of the bar-room was set against the 'official' force of the county court-house.

It is right to stress the rural texture of Southern society, for towns were atypical. The big towns – and Natchez, for instance, was not very large – were few in number. They were far more ethnically variegated than the South as a whole; they held large numbers of free blacks and of foreign-born immigrants. In some overt ways they contrasted strongly with their rural settings. Among the most imposing and capacious buildings in the principal Southern cities, Roman Catholic cathedrals challenged for pride of place. At New Orleans, Baltimore and St Louis, Catholic cathedrals were consecrated in 1794, 1821 and 1834, well before the principal Episcopal or Presbyterian churches were built. Although Louisville's Catholic cathedral, completed in 1852, was beaten in point of time by the Episcopal church, it made up for that deficiency by announcing its presence with a spire 287 feet high. In Memphis and Mobile also, Catholic cathedrals, though not so prominently placed, were dedicated in 1843 and 1850 (American Guide series: vols. on Alabama, Kentucky, Louisiana, Maryland, Missouri, Tennessee). Other urban churches were also built; indeed the urban skyline was almost a thicket of spires. But the prominence of Catholic cathedrals in the very large Southern towns (particularly towns beyond the Appalachians) was incongruous to most Southerners, and added an element of urban ritual alien to Southern rural life. So, too, certain kinds of 'formal' culture were distinctly urban. In 1858, for instance, the New Orleans English Opera Company staged a tour which included Columbus (Georgia), Louisville (Kentucky) and Memphis (Tennessee); its programme at Columbus offered six operas in a week (Columbus, *The Daily Sun*: 3, 5, 8, 9, 10, 12, 14 April, 11 June 1858). Theatre companies also did the urban rounds. And towns boasted small colleges, lyceums for lectures, masonic lodges and even historical societies. In most cases, however, these cultural institutions were derivative – the 'best' taste in opera and in literature was, largely, to follow European fashion – and were patronized by affluent citizens.

There was some rural overspill for affluent urban leisure-seekers. America's best attended watering-places in the early nineteenth century were Saratoga Springs, New York, and White Sulphur, Virginia. But elsewhere efforts were made by enterprising hoteliers to develop springs as tourist attractions. By 1860 Georgia had eleven principal springs that lured tourists, and hotels blossomed to accommodate them. They became resorts patronized by professional people, sometimes with wives and children staying throughout the summer while husbands made periodic visits. At Indian Springs, Butts county, Georgia, up to 1,500 people could be found room in the hotels; and cabins, cottages and even tents were also enlisted for service. Grand entertainment centred on the ball-room, but billiards, bowling, card-playing, picnicking, reading and horse-riding were important. Madison Springs, Georgia even possessed a school offering a summer session (Norwood 1978: 3–15).

If the customers for these spas were probably town-dwelling professional people, there was also traffic from countryside to town. Charleston stood out in this respect as a summer resort for the planters of the coastal strip. The elegance of the Battery was supplemented by fine churches and a lively theatre. But even the South's premier resort was fairly small by international standards; Charleston's population was readily dwarfed by that of Bath, which was Britain's leading and most socially exclusive spa town. Moreover, Charleston, unlike Bath, was an important business centre, replete with banks and factors' offices and shipping houses. The *Charleston Daily Courier* in late 1857, for instance, reads like the business news section of any modern newspaper, except that modern newspapers appear frivolous in their reports on personalities and business policies by comparison. Political news was factual and unemotional and not much commented upon editorially. Column after column was devoted to market data. The summer ritual of socializing in the South's leading coastal or river ports was inspired as much by absorption in business as by attention to pleasure.

Quite clearly, a great deal of the most commonly described ritual of Southern white society was 'middle-class' in character. Balls and hotel visits, attendance at operas and plays, the erection of churches and of monuments were all diversions, or self-imposed duties, of the affluent. At the opposite social extreme, however, there is, apparently, little that can be said of the social rituals specific to the middling and poorer whites. Apart from their religious practices and involvements, and occasional social incidents arising from court cases, there is little contemporary testimony to go by. Two valuable sources do, however, exist in the shape of later oral evidence and folk-songs passed down from generation to generation.

An extensive examination of popular culture and popular mythology was carried out and written up by Vance Randolph in the Ozarks of Arkansas in the 1920s, 1930s and 1940s. There are some very severe drawbacks in taking the example of the Ozarks as a typical museum-piece specimen of earlier Southern culture. Although it was an exceptionally backward region in terms of physical isolation, cultural conservatism and ethnic homogeneity, it may still have absorbed ideas, attitudes or prejudices from the very long period after 1860; nor were the Ozarks, in being so isolated and insulated, necessarily typical of anything other than similarly mountain-bound and sparsely populated enclaves of Southern society. Only the foolhardy would claim to derive general truths for the mid nineteenth century from the oral history of early twentieth-century Arkansas. On the other hand, the source is an ample one, and the alternative sources are, so far as we know now at least, virtually non-existent. If the oral testimony cited consists of stories told by old people, usually referring to events or tales going back before 1900, then there is at least a plausible chance that what is being described obtained also in the antebellum period. Moreover, it may be possible to find corroboration of points deduced from this evidence in the ballads and folk-songs that have been passed down through the generations. Such folk-songs are not necessarily the most illuminating source, for much of what they contain is humdrum sentiment about love, lost innocence, labour, death and other eternal verities. Indeed, many such folk-songs originated in seventeenth-century Britain. While one may reasonably conclude that the feelings or views they expressed found sympathetic echo among their Southern listeners, these songs contained little that was peculiarly and notably Southern in content. But it may be worth suggesting at least that folk-lore illuminates some aspects of ordinary life in the antebellum South.

Oral testimony and folk-songs both reinforce the importance of family life and family ritual. If the findings of Vance Randolph may legitimately be applied backwards to the antebellum South, then they reveal that the apparently inert and acquiescent country people, customarily regarded as gnarled and silent stage-props by travellers to the section, were indeed immersed in an intricate ritual of daily happenings. The overall impression to be gained from these explorations of popular culture is not nearly as startling as some social historians might claim. For they serve merely to confirm the obvious deductions that the level of community development was low and that ideation was primitive. Communities were circumscribed agglomerations of families with few formal institutions and sparse education. But these facts did not mean that mountain people lacked a complicated, if intellectually parochial, world-view. What Randolph showed for the Ozarks of the early twentieth century was that folk memory and folk-lore supplied a rich store of explanations of daily events, prescribed a varied set of prophylactic remedies to ward off natural and supernatural distress or disaster, and laid down an intricate pattern of rituals that accompanied the rhythms of everyday life (Randolph 1947: 3–5).

Two central figures in the essential routines of the life-cycle were 'granny-women' and 'yarb doctors', the expositors of folk guidance and folk remedies on all medical matters stretching from pre-marital intercourse and child-birth to middle-age health and death. At the core of their practice was the ample use of herbal and other easily available concoctions, their use being related to the phases of the moon and the signs of the zodiac, and the maintenance of a core of prescriptions to guarantee propitious fortune. The 'granny-women' especially were the mid-wives, marriage guidance counsellors and agony-column advisers of the remote South. Unmarried girls who were no longer virgins went to these 'granny-women' in order to discover ways of deceiving husbands-to-be as to their true condition. If, in attracting male attention, women were not supposed to use artificial cosmetics, they were certainly meant to expunge basic blemishes. Facial blemishes, for instance, were supposedly removed by the touch of a dead man's hands; Randolph saw a three-year-old girl taken to a village funeral parlour to be thus touched. 'Granny-women' also egged on emotional courtship. A vast battery of charms and rituals was recommended for inducing boys and girls to fall in love with each other; such as placing specified objects in the lover's cabin, house or room. Girls, more generally, were warned not to comb their hair at night, lest they thereby reduce their sexual passions. They were also told never to bathe or even wash their hair while menstruating. Granny-women helped perpetuate an intricate folk-lore surrounding child-birth. A strong belief prevailed that pregnant women should be sheltered from adverse experiences; on the grounds that physical defects or deformities, notably bruises or markings, would result. Thus a husband after a bloody fist-fight should be kept from his pregnant wife, for otherwise the shock of her seeing him might result in a 'mirror' bruising upon the unborn child. Child-birth itself was the occasion for scrupulous attention to the omens. Placing a sharp axe under the mother's bed was supposed to ease child-birth; burning chicken feathers under the bed would forestall haemorrhaging. New-born babies, it was argued, should be carried around a cabin three times to protect the child against sore eyes or colic; and they should be separated from cats, who were supposed to suck babies' breath until the infants suffocated. The precise day and date of birth were significant, much anticipated and much discussed, for future character and career might well hinge on such matters. Following birth, many Ozark mothers did not wean their offspring until eighteen months or even up to two or three years after birth, in the belief that a woman nursing a child could not become pregnant and would develop immunities to various infectious diseases; a belief sustained in part by modern medical science (Randolph 1947: 103–16, 162–70, 192–209; Randolph 1976: 8–9).

These details of the behaviour and ritual laid down for pregnancy and child-birth serve merely to illustrate what folk wisdom ordained for one phase of the life-cycle. Similar rituals – involving charms, household ceremonies, due observation of the signs of the zodiac and deference to the injunctions of granny-women – punctuated the Ozark mountain people's existence. There was a mythology surrounding hunting; and animal behaviour was interpreted in rich detail, offering a steady and flowing stream of conversation and speculation to these largely non-literate people. Ghosts were firmly believed in. Late nineteenth-century pioneers in Arkansas invited friends and neighbours to their homes to exchange stories of supernatural events. Telling ghost stories reputedly provided an acceptable alternative to people who shunned dancing or card playing. From ghosts, it was an easy journey to witchcraft. Here the evidence is shakier, but Randolph avowed that he had interviewed two dozen women regarded as witches; virtually all of them were willing to acknowledge themselves only as 'witch masters', those, that is, who removed spells and curses. Yet, if these women refused to describe themselves as witches as such, powerful belief in the pervasiveness and strength of witchcraft remained among the rural populace. And this was given extra *frisson* by the heretical and sexually daring initiation rites supposed to be necessary for future witches. Sex and mystery were not, according to Randolph, the only ingredients of witchcraft: 'I am told, by women who claim to have experienced both, that the witch's initiation is a much more moving spiritual crisis than that which the Christians call conversion.' Widespread belief in witchcraft fed upon the difficulties facing an uneducated mountain people in explaining a multitude of natural and sometimes unusual phenomena. It was part of a larger quest to comprehend and give a regular shape to the rural world. But such belief also tended to condone a good deal of violence, not so much against witches but more because violence seemed to be an inevitable condition of such a mysteriously shaped universe (Randolph 1947: 211, 241–9, 264–8, 271, 300).

How far these rituals of the Ozarks in the early twentieth century may be projected backwards on to the antebellum South is difficult to say, even when, as here, care is taken to note only stories told by elderly people in the 1920s. Most travellers even to the mountain regions made no effort to understand the ordinary whites' folk lore; they simply left those whites as somewhat blank-faced and empty-headed spectators of the daily round. Very occasionally there was a fleeting reference to witchcraft in contemporary literature. For instance, the travelling widow of a slaveowner noted of a community in Alabama in 1821, 'the whole neighbourhood seemed to combine in a dangerous conspiracy, and the phrenzy of witchcraft at length alarmed the thinking part of the community', to a point where three or four 'gentlemen' solved a case in which the work of a witch was widely suspected (Royall 1969: 212–13). Again, *The Old Pine Farm* by 'A Southern Country Minister, S.C.' describes a neighbour telling a slaveowning minister's wife: 'there's no knowing how soap boiling will turn out. Sometimes it seems the thing is *witched* [*sic*], and you may boil and boil all to no purpose. Some people say it *is* witched' (A Southern Country Minister 1860: 43). It would be extremely difficult to build hypotheses upon such minor, infrequent references. Yet alternative sources of solid evidence for this submerged culture remain elusive. Court records yield sparse assistance. Spoken memories from the early twentieth century are somewhat timeless in quality and virtually never refer precisely to the years before the Civil War; there was no equivalent investigative impulse to that which encouraged oral historians to find and question blacks on their experience of slavery or of 'slavery times'.

Another collector of oral folk-lore, Arthur P. Hudson, argued that the stories and ballads he gathered in the mid-1920s testified to the social mores of rural Mississippi throughout the nineteenth century. His case for doing so was partly that the old people whose memories he recorded were describing rituals and customs already moribund by the 1910s. Among these were communal activities such as log-rollings, house-raisings, quilting parties and hog-killings, most of which have been associated by historians in the 1970s increasingly with slave culture. In addition to these working rituals, Hudson described pastimes which seem reasonably to have belonged to the nineteenth as well as to the early twentieth century. These rustic pastimes included after-dinner story-telling, dollar pitching and horseshoe-throwing, drinking in the barn away from disapproving women, wrestling matches, dog fights, usually spontaneous among farm dogs brought together, square dances and play parties. Hudson attested to the strength of very local attachments; gang vendettas were common and communities within counties were usually divided off by such natural boundaries as bluffs and creeks; a common reference, according to Hudson, was to 'Outlaws from across the creek' (Hudson 1928: i–iv, x–xv, 2).

What can be suggested, therefore, is that the mountain whites and probably poor whites elsewhere led lives which contained their own rigid and formally discussed and recognized structure; that the events of the life-cycle were closely commented upon and attended by well-established and earnestly regarded rituals; and that these rituals, perhaps infused with a good deal of witchcraft, stood apart from and unscathed by the culture of the educated and the affluent. At its point of sharpest contrast, therefore, white society was viable because it permitted the co-existence of two very different modes of social behaviour. The granny-mother with her herbs and poultices and the Southern belle with her piano-lessons and ball-room French were left to their own social devices.

III

One characteristic of the folk-lore gathered by Vance Randolph was its general lack of social or political criticism. The people of the Ozarks were simply distrustful of the outside world and sought to keep it at arms' length. From popular ballads and songs a little more, of a very generalized kind, can be gleaned.

The principal deficiency in the ballads and folk-songs recorded in the early twentieth century was their antiquity and provenance. Many were British in origin; many referred to events, such as western train robberies, which clearly occurred after the 1860s. Another obvious defect is that they are laundered; they contain no blue songs. This may not always have been the compiler's oversight; Randolph was unable to find a publisher in the early 1950s who would take his extremely full manuscript on the riper side of Ozark folk-lore (Randolph 1976: xii). But the process of selection amounts to a distortion of sorts. As research on life in the Confederate army shows, there was a full-blooded vein of strong language, hard drinking, gambling and whoring to Southern male life (Wiley 1943: 36–8, 48, 50–8).

Without going too far, one might argue that the balladry of the South reflected the values of respectable womanhood. A major lesson handed down concerned the dangers of consorting thoughtlessly with men. Numerous ballads recounted the sudden betrayal and murder of young women who had been persuaded to leave home by lovers usually promising marriage. These tales implied that family advice on affairs of the heart should never be spurned. And it may not be too fanciful to suggest that the violent deaths – often bloody ones – that befell impetuous and over-trusting young women were surrogates for sexual 'fall'. Ballads further warned girls against attachments to idle men or to their social superiors; the first would fail to supply their material needs, while the latter would exploit them without reward. Not all the advice was directed to female listeners. Young men, too, were urged to follow steady habits; the lot of outlaws and those embroiled in family feuds was not, according to the ballad-mongers, a happy one. In this respect the ballads afforded a celebration of respectable culture. They were also an endorsement of social conservatism (Cox 1925: 247–9, 494; Hudson 1928: 48–51, 57–60, 74–5).

Equally conservative were gatherings of country singers to give their renditions of white spirituals. Fasola singing was the term applied to the use of a very simplified musical notation system which took hold of the upland South in the early nineteenth century. Although the notation system itself and many of the songs were borrowed from Britain and imported via New England, the practice of fasola singing became a largely Southern upland phenomenon by the mid nineteenth century. In the years 1798–1855 thirty-eight different books of song in four-shape notation were published, twenty-one of them compiled by residents of Southern states. It was claimed that *Southern Harmony,* published in 1835 and in various subsequent editions to 1854, sold 600,000 copies, mostly before the Civil War. The other highly popular Southern song-book was the *Sacred Harp,* first published in 1844; about two-thirds of the composers of its words and tunes were from the South, overwhelmingly from Georgia and Alabama. Musical conventions were held in west-central Georgia from 1845 to 1867 devoted solely to singing from the *Sacred Harp;* fasola music was very much intended for singers, not listeners; it owed nothing to any heritage of choral music, and made no use of instruments. This musical sub-culture was Scotch-Irish in background, Methodist, Baptist and revivalist in religious orientation, and rural in appeal. The more sophisticated urban Baptists and Methodists ignored the fasola cult, which itself shrank increasingly in the early twentieth century. But the spirituals were clearly a vital part of rural white culture; they condemned finery and drinking, irreligion and such frolicsome activities as dancing and acting, and males' indifference to the proper rights of women. Above all else, however, they prefigured the welcome release that death and eternal salvation offered:

A few more struggles here,
A few more partings o'er,
A few more toils, a few more tears,
And we shall weep no more,
And we shall weep no more,
　　Happy thought to die no more,
No, never, never more.

Or:

Oh, that I had some secret place where I might hide from sorrow;
Where I might see my Savior's face, and thus be saved from terror.
O had I wings like Noah's dove, I'd leave this world and Satan;
And fly away to realms above, where angels stand inviting.

As did the ballads, these songs made almost no reference to any adverse social conditions impinging upon earth-dwellers (Jackson 1933: 3–4, 23–5, 63, 95–7, 100–1, 124–8, 155–9, 189–201, 229).

The telling of stories, the reciting of ballads and the singing of fasola hymns all provided cultural rituals for ordinary Southerners. While these rituals may have been socially differentiated – fasola singing was obviously not an activity indulged in by genteel planters – they did not raise many issues of class among Southern whites. Some class criticism was implied; humble girls should not be taken in by rich seducers' promises; true religious faith had to guard against the moral depravity engendered by wealth. But the central focus was upon moral duties and spiritual commitment. These twin concerns were further emphasized and promoted in rituals which did indeed draw all classes of Southern whites together, the religious camp-meetings.

Camp-meetings were characteristically, if not exclusively, Southern institutions. The first seems to have been held in July 1800 and organized by Presbyterians in Kentucky. The first large one, again set up by Presbyterians, was at Cane Ridge, Kentucky, in August 1801, and lasted six days; it was attended by between 10,000 and 25,000 people. As far as the originators went, these camp-meetings were part of that popularizing of Presbyterianism that led in 1810 to the Cumberland Presbyterians going independent, in order to provide more 'open preaching' and a more evangelical ministry. For most of the early and middle nineteenth century, however, camp-meetings probably drew greater inspiration from and resulted in more support for the Methodists and Baptists than the initiating sect. By 1860 only 7 per cent of Southern church members were Presbyterians; and that denomination was generally sceptical of the propriety and effectiveness of emotionally charged and perhaps doctrinally sloppy preach-ins. But this criticism – of the weak theology and shallow enthusiasm of the camp-meetings – did not prevent church elders and itinerant preachers from arranging them carefully and in a time-tabled way, throughout the antebellum period. It may have been that such gatherings were spurned by more socially exclusive churches (Bruce 1974: 3–10, 36–52; I am not sure that camp-meetings 'virtually disappeared' in the 1840s, p. 56). Daniel R. Hundley, an often prissy and snobbish commentator on the South, asserted in 1860:

> camp-meetings are rapidly falling into disrepute of late years, and we trust they will disappear altogether in time; for true religion consists much more in deeds of charity and works of love than in bodily shivers, or nervous shrieks, or sepulchral groans, or any kind of dreaming whatever, whether of devils, hell-flames, spirit-circles, broomsticks, or shovels and tongs (Hundley 1979: 93).

But it would probably be wrong to describe camp-meetings as the refuge of the rustic and the poor. Where they were held, they attracted widespread enthusiasm and support.

The camp-meetings aimed at conversion or the reconversion of the lapsed faithful. They occurred in the period July–October, but especially at harvest time, in late September. They thus took on the character of being celebrations at the conclusion of the agricultural year. If they adhered to a tight schedule of services, night and day, they also attracted people for the excitement and social relaxation offered (Bruce 1974: 64–7, 70, 75–83, 88–9). Critics regarded them as occasions for mountebank religion and social intercourse – especially between young men and women – of an impulsive and sometimes passionate nature. A serious-minded eighteen-year-old recorded in his diary that he spent the night at a camp-meeting organized by Mr Huffaker; 'the sociability, grace and cleverness of the three misses Huffaker *might possibly* have been the cause'. Yet the same young Tennessean noted a year later of another camp-meeting: 'O that a soul-stirring revival of religion might again break out in our village – my own much-loved home! And O that I could say or do something to further on the good work!' He became a Methodist minister and continued to look to these gatherings, small and large (one in 1860 reached, he believed, 3,000–4,000 people) for true and abiding conversions (Stringfield Diary: vol. 2, 6, 8 Sept. 1857, 19 Sept., 13 Oct. 1858; vol. 3, 16, 19 Aug. 1860. SHC). Whether many people were actually converted was disputed in the nineteenth century; it may have been that these meetings were most successful in securing reaffirmations of faith, and in providing popular mass rituals. Yet while camp-meetings appealed to men and women, boys and girls, from all social backgrounds, formal religion of itself remained a minority preoccupation in the antebellum South. Only about 20 per cent of Southerners were members of formally organized churches; although this figure ignores the population age profile and so misrepresents *adult* membership. If periodic camp-meetings were pronounced crowd-drawers, then regular church services did not hold the loyalties of those who so enthusiastically turned up for those religious extravaganzas.

Other rituals cutting across social divisions were either more or less carefully organized than such festivals of sermon and song. In the 1850s, at the formal end of the spectrum, there were state fairs. North Carolina's State Agricultural Society established the North Carolina State Fair in 1853 in the hope that regional rivalries within the state might be reduced and that state pride might be enhanced among ordinary people. Every effort was made to head off the growth of too many diversions; alcoholic drink was banned from the fair ground from the very beginning; gambling was prohibited in 1856. But nothing could stop state politicians from exploiting the opportunity offered by the fair to exhort the citizenry. And band-playing and the social activities afforded by Raleigh, where the fair was held, much diluted the effort to spur on agricultural improvements (McLaurin 1982: 213–16, 223–7). More informal in purpose – but no less well planned and certainly no less well patronized by all social classes of Southerner – were race meetings. Contemporaries noted, not always approvingly, that men and women, rich and poor, consorted at the race meetings which punctuated the calendar. In Georgia, the Columbus Jockey Club was flourishing by the mid-1830s (Johnson 1938: 415). Along the Mississippi, there were two-week-long meetings at the Pharsalia course of Natchez in December, especially well-attended meetings in April at the Metairie course in New Orleans, and a substantial meeting in Memphis in early May (Natchez, *Mississippi Free Trader,* 20, 27 Dec. 1858, 17 Jan., 11, 18 April 1859). Elsewhere, Charleston was notable for its meetings. These were grand social occasions, attracting throngs of visitors.

Hunting was not so formal a ritual or so neatly distinguished by class differences as it was in Britain. Robert Peel, the British Tory leader, complained in the late 1820s that most of his parliamentary supporters were quite unfit for government, as they so readily scurried from Westminster to the hunting field (Gash 1976: 94). Such a complaint was not voiced in Congress or in state legislatures. Although formally organized fox-hunting occurred throughout the South, it was, according to Daniel Hundley, engaged in by the sons of both the 'gentry' and the 'middle-class planters and farmers'. Hundley (1979: 35) added:

> At present, however, it is chiefly patronized by boys and young men, and in consequence, occupies much less of public attention than formerly, or than it does in England. Nor have we ever known an instance in the South of a lady's indulging in the sport, which is a common practice in the old fatherland.

The ritual of fox-hunting, then, was less widespread in one respect, but less formalized and less class-based in another. Deer- and game-hunting was generally indulged in by men of all ranks. Planters' and poor farmers' sons alike early learned to shoot game (Hundley 1979: 31–3, 95–6). Again, though, the ritual aspect was markedly informal. When a modestly affluent slaveowner – but not a planter – recorded his pleasure at participating in a rabbit-shoot, he was noting a casually contrived activity, and not a frequent or important ritual in his existence (Jeffreys Diary, 14 June 1844: William B. Williamson papers, SHC). There was a dramatic difference in attitude between planters joining an elaborately planned hunt in order to enjoy some sport and the poor farmers who hunted for survival; of one mountainous area, it was said that the number of dogs a farmer kept was in inverse ratio to his wealth, for the size of his pack distinguished the enterprising agrarian from the necessitous huntsman (Lanman 1849: 85). Yet, despite this very real difference, hunting – especially in the absence of socially differentiated rituals of killing game – provided a point of common interest to white males.

Related to hunting were more macabre rituals involving the capture and punishment of slaves. Charles Ball, in one of the most widely read of the slave narratives (his was published first in 1836), recounted a story of the pursuit of a slave malefactor. The escapee's absence was discovered one morning; messages were sent far across the neighbourhood to gather a party of planters and farmers for the hunt. A gentleman with a bloodhound who lived twelve miles away was summoned. By 10 a.m., fifty men and their horses were present at the aggrieved owner's house. And the chase soon after began and was brought to a successful (for the whites) conclusion. A cruel and fatal punishment was inflicted on the slave without any recourse to the proper judicial authorities. Ball told also of a slave hanging, to which vast crowds of whites went, bringing their slaves with them. The execution occurred on a Thursday; but the crowds did not fully leave the subsequent 'funereal carnival' until the following Monday. The elaborate execution had been capped by 'music, dancing, trading in horses, gambling, drinking, fighting, and every other species of amusement and excess to which the southern people are addicted' (Ball 1970: 251–6, 377–8). Ball's account provides some specific illustrations of generally observed phenomena. The summoning of posses was swift and effective in the antebellum South. The reasoning behind this responsiveness was explained in 1858 by a leading Georgian legal writer, T. R. R. Cobb: 'Reasons of policy and necessity ... require that so long as two races of men live together, the one as masters and the other as dependants and slaves, to a certain extent, *all* [*sic*] of the superior race shall exercise a controlling power over the inferior' (Quoted in Rose 1976: 206). The practical effect of this ideal was illustrated in Georgia by a Northern mechanic, Lewis W. Paine. Paine tried to help a runaway slave find freedom by posing as his owner. The two men were suspected on the road, however, by a party of five vulgar, abusive whites (including a Methodist preacher), and Paine was escorted by them back to the county which he had just fled; the slave made good his further escape (Paine 1852: 35–47). The pursuit and punishment of slave malefactors was a male ritual that reaffirmed, often in savage form, the twin ideals of white superiority and local self-rule. For the men who had recaptured a runaway or miscreant slave often decided on the spot how best to deal with their unfortunate captive; vigilante hanging, quite outside the canon of the law, was sometimes deemed an appropriate fate for a slave accused of raping a white woman (Columbus, Ga. *The Daily Sun,* 26 July, 6 Oct. 1858).

It is probably unlikely that a more general vigilantism obtained. A detailed study of law enforcement in four contrasting counties of Georgia in the period 1830–60 shows that justice was extremely loosely administered. Of 4,007 indictments recorded and concerning crimes allegedly committed by whites, only 27 per cent went to trial, and almost half simply disappeared from the local courts' dockets. Yet this informality was not accompanied, as far as can be ascertained, by widespread vigilantism. Few vigilante outbreaks were noted by contemporaries, and such as did occur drew the condemnation of the 'respectable' press (Bodenhamer 1982: 81–7). So, while the subject of vigilantism remains somewhat obscure, it is reasonable to conclude provisionally that whites, apparently of all social levels, enforced their racial control through informal and collective rituals, but tended to leave disputes among themselves to individual initiative or legal – and very frequent legal – action.

While it would be perverse to claim that such social rituals as ballad singing, camp-meetings, state fairs, horse-racing, hunting and vigilantism vitiated differences of manners, wealth or status, it should also be stressed that these various rituals were generally free of political content or criticism, and served a conservative purpose. Much popular religion concentrated on the after-life rather than worldly woes. Obviously secular ballads and white spirituals alike tried to promote a particular moral code and in that important sense were socially divisive; but, although there are occasional hints of class resentment in the ballads and white spirituals could be said to have represented a form of lower class puritanism and religious escapism, it was more typically the case that camp-meetings, horse-racing, hunting and vigilantism drew divergent ranks of Southern whites together irrespective of 'class'. Moreover, as will be argued more particularly in the following chapter, the pressure for moral reform tended to cut across the different ranks among whites. No one has yet shown that camp-meetings or campaigns against alcoholic drink or against gambling were class-based. And for most of the South geographically the essential social rituals of hunting and horse-racing and vigilantism were largely informal and often unstructured. Moreover, underpinning these social rituals were the frequent and regular political rituals, which themselves emphasized racial solidarity among whites, and which obliged the politically ambitious grandees to abase themselves before the ordinary citizens.

IV

Many antebellum Southerners were preoccupied by the so-called plantation ideal. Novelists, social theorists, even agricultural improvers wrote about it often and at length. They portrayed a rural society where whites' eyes focussed intently upon the plantation house and its occupants. John Pendleton Kennedy in 1832 wrote of one such Virginia potentate in the first classic plantation novel, *Swallow Barn*:

> There is a set of under-talkers about these large country establishments, who are very glad to pick up the crumbs of wisdom that fall from a rich man's table; second-hand philosophers, who trade upon other people's stock. Some of these have a natural bias to this venting of upper opinions by reason of certain dependencies in the way of trade and favor: others have it from affinity of blood, which works like a charm over a whole county.

The planter in question – Frank Meriwether – was related 'by some ties of marriage or mixture of kin, to an infinite train of connexions, spread over the state; and it is curious to learn what a decided hue this gives to the opinions of the district'. By speaking to his respectful inferiors on contemporary political and social issues – on which he becomes, through his family ties, well informed – Meriwether communicated his beliefs and prejudices widely and effectively throughout his neighbourhood (Kennedy 1832: vol. I, 25–9, 75, 78–81). Here, then, was a contemporary testimony to Genovese's planter paternalism. Yet this view was very much one from the top. Kennedy had little knowledge of or sympathy for the ordinary whites; in politics he was a Whig, having left the Jacksonian camp in 1830 and later complaining repeatedly about the excess of democracy (Evitts 1974: 20, 46–7). But democratic and demagogic politics advanced throughout the

South in the 1830s. Indeed, *Swallow Barn* was published after Virginia's constitution had been notably democratized by the convention of 1829–30. Moreover, even contemporary literary comment did not fully endorse Kennedy's paternalistic analysis. George Tucker's *The Valley of the Shenandoah* (1824) was deliberately set in a region where settlers of contrasting ethnic backgrounds and wealth had established themselves. A recurrent theme of the novel was the clash between declining gentility and unconscionable parvenus and assertive plain folk. One trivial incident, used by Tucker to document the frailty of deference, described the refusal of a surly waggoner to make way on a public road for a lady's carriage; though a young gentleman's response to such insolence was high-handed and vigorous, certainly the reaction of a gallant, the basic moral was that deference as such was moribund (Tucker 1970: 128–9).

If we are to pay anthropological attention to the treasure-house of such incidents available for study we could, of course, proceed for decades with such analysis. But although these incidents do reveal social antagonisms at work, they reveal also that a primary concern of social commentators of the 1820s and 1830s was the nature of social relationships in a democracy. Already, the preservation of privilege and a deferential order was a doomed, if not a lost, cause. The plantation ideal, in its fullest political and social sense, was increasingly an object almost of nostalgia by the 1830s, when the cotton kingdom was still spreading far and rapidly.

What stands out instead from this brief discussion of ritual is the dual character of Southern white social life. On one side, it tolerated and accommodated widely differing modes of discourse, from one rooted in folk-lore and possibly leavened by witchcraft, to one increasingly enlisting scientific rationalism in the defence of its racism and in the promotion of its economic interests. On the other, it supported a set of rituals, some of which were clearly defined by education and wealth, but some of which were markedly egalitarian in tone and content. It is this insistent, if not always successful, egalitarianism that leads us to a critical characteristic of nineteenth-century evangelical, reformist and 'middle-class' societies, the pursuit of respectability.

Chapter ten

RESPECTABILITY

I

Daniel Hundley noted in 1860:

> As in all other civilized communities, the middle classes of the South
> constitute the greater proportion of her citizens, and are likewise the
> most useful members of her society. In treating of these classes, however,
> we shall have to tread rather gingerly, for fear we squelch some
> neighbor's corns, owing to the false and ridiculous notions of
> respectability, which unfortunately prevail throughout the whole extent
> of the United States. In this country every man considers himself a
> gentleman, no matter what may be his social status (Hundley 1979: 77).

Hundley, however, found it difficult to define his middle classes
precisely, or to disentangle moral attributes and standards of public
behaviour from his depiction of 'class' more generally. Subsequent
historians of the antebellum South have never quite succeeded in
defining satisfactory social groupings. It has long been recognized that a
simple division between planters and poor whites was nonsensical. But
alternative categories have proved to be difficult to establish. Frank
Owsley described the bulk of Southern farmers as the plain folk forming
an essentially middle-class core to Southern life. Clement Eaton
separated the rural social order from his discussion of the middle class,
which was depicted in 'urban' terms as composed of lawyers, doctors,
businessmen, clergymen and teachers. Just as modern sociologists
equate the middle classes with white-collar workers, so Eaton tended to
equate urban expansion with the growth of the middle classes. In
contrast, Eugene Genovese followed Marx's journalistic commentaries
on the South by arguing that attention devoted to these essentially
peripheral elements in Southern society smoke-screened the central
relationship among whites, that between the slavocracy, the
monopolists of wealth, political power and social prestige, and the non-
slaveowning whites. In many respects, this was right; successful doctors,

lawyers and businessmen sought to become planters, partly to consolidate their social status, partly as a matter of sound investment policy. But the aura attached to planter status, and the supposedly distinguishing features of being a planter, have been much exaggerated.

There was a gradual shading of wealth and life-style from the very top of plantation society to the lower reaches of humble farmers struggling against real poverty. For this reason, social historians have divided white households into half a dozen or so ranks, taking into account slaveownership, landownership and personal property. Yet these categories, however useful they may be in giving us census-year snap-shots of the rows upon rows of white wealth-holders, provide little sense of the nature of status, the relationship between different groups of whites and the pressures, if any, for social and political change. Thus, for example, we are periodically told by social historians of 'bitter resentments' felt by the poor whites towards the planters. Yet, although class resentments somewhat affected voting behaviour and choice of party from the 1830s to the 1860s, and although some class rhetoric entered political debate in those decades, the overwhelming bulk of research into the link between 'class' (sometimes defined in very precise terms) and politics points only to the weakest of statistical correlations. If there were bitter resentments, they tended to be contained within, rather than articulated by, the party system. And when class rhetoric most vigorously exploded into political discussion, the discontent it reflected was customarily defused by modest reform.

This very elusiveness of class within Southern society has led historians to seek less tangible clues to the relationship among whites. One set of attitudes explored revolves around paternalism and patriarchy. Just as the South was a male-dominated, patriarchal society, so, it is argued, the most patriarchal males, the great planters, epitomized the highest cultural values of that society. By disseminating their ideas throughout the white order – a task made easy because they stood out as role models and they controlled political power – these planter patriarchs headed off class alignments and smothered class tensions. The trouble with this argument is that on questions of social policy (the debate over state common schooling is a good example), on questions of economic development (especially on regional transport interests and on the issue of whether the South should industrialize more), on questions of party (to be a Democrat or not?) and on questions of national policy (the timing of secession, often dismissed by historians as a tactical quibble, had vital repercussions) the 'messages' from the paternalistic elite were ambiguous if not contradictory. This is not to deny the social importance of wealth and planter status; it is to deny that 'planter power' was mobilized in a straightforward and coherent way for political ends.

For this reason, some historians have insisted that it is not simply intellectually sloppy but historically distorting to describe the South in terms other than its own ones. The argument over whether the South was modern or pre-modern, bourgeois or quasi-feudal, more akin to the nineteenth-century world of peasant Italy or of racist Southern Africa, appears ultimately inane. It was a unique amalgam of highly organized commercial enterprise, republican commitment, white egalitarian rhetoric, stern individualism, widespread property-owning, restless agrarianism and evangelical religion. If in commercial and intellectual respects it embraced British and European expertise, in some cultural and most political respects it rejected British and European practice. If Southerners built up typically American governing institutions, they also, according to Professor Wyatt-Brown, retained an anachronistic code of behaviour, rooted in ideas of personal and family honour and promoting a readiness among individuals to take direct charge of and responsibility for their fate (Wyatt-Brown, 1982). The good news was that this code stimulated family loyalty, self-reliance and self-respect; the bad news was that it encouraged arrogance, vigilantism, duelling, brawling and a general disinclination to abide by the canons of a formal and impersonal body of law. Moreover, the stress upon personal honour partially reinforces the emphasis placed upon patriarchy, for the defence of family reputation and position was a largely male duty.

There is nothing objectionable in trying to bring out the peculiarly traditional aspects of Southern society. The maintenance of personal honour and the assertion of what might now be called patriarchal values were indeed parts of Southern whites' public ideology. But these aspects should not be reified into the special and peculiarly symptomatic characteristics of Southern life. There were numerous ways in which the rule of law was called upon to counteract personal combativity and group vigilantism; there were numerous instances where the pulls of religious conscience counterbalanced the calls of family pride; and there were numerous points at which the spread of public morality in the South paralleled the extension of public morality – in terms of legal reform, temperance legislation and an evangelical desire to eradicate gambling and other depravities – both in Britain and in the Northern states of the USA. The collective voice of the religious congregation – often expressed in female accents – and the collective force of state and municipal laws were as important to Southerners' personal conduct as the dictates of patriarchy and personal honour. Moreover, the rulings of congregations and law courts did not simply parrot the prescriptions handed down from above by paternalistic planters. Instead, they reflected a very deeply felt drive for social improvement that emanated from individuals of conscience irrespective of 'class'.

The most direct word for describing the impulse to improvement is respectability. It avoids the ahistorical rigidity of phrases such as middle-class morality, values and so forth. The first reference given to respectability in the *Oxford English Dictionary* dates from 1785 and is entirely apposite: 'He is very sensible that there are in all classes of life, men of honour and respectability.' Precisely what is meant by respectability is rather more complicated; like equality, the word's meaning must of necessity alter with changing circumstances and perceptions. But in the following discussion it will be taken to mean a preference for increasingly formal taste in architectural styles and thus in housing – the choice of an individual's habitat being a primary decision – for the state's intervention to regulate personal behaviour, for religious activism, and for the laying down of legal guide-lines on owners' conduct towards their slaves. The first topic merely touches upon the outward 'image' Southerners wished to acquire, though it involved important attitudes about enlightened, as distinct from folk, culture. But the other three concerns challenged more traditional ideas of personal honour and informal vigilantism, linked Southerners, if tenuously, to non-Southern reform movements, and served to divide men and women across lines of social and economic status.

II

The major changes in house design which occurred over the long period from the seventeenth century to the mid nineteenth century were increased standardization and the edging out of vernacular styles (Glassie 1971: 236). Of course, a wide variety of styles remained in the 1840s and 1850s; indeed that period was renowned as one of rampant and romantic eclecticism. But the 'approved' styles were derived from pattern books and published architectural drawings, and newspapers also helped in defining good taste. Log cabins remained in the poorer regions. But even at the lower end of the housing market, supposedly cruder or vernacular materials and building designs became increasingly unfashionable as the nineteenth century progressed.

To a degree, a rolling frontier had always been at work in the adoption of architectural styles. Advanced fashions in frontier Kentucky of the 1790s had been commonplace ideas in tidewater Virginia forty or fifty years earlier. So, too, the piedmont planters of Georgia were just beginning to build themselves substantial houses in the 1840s and 1850s, although plantation great houses had sprung up in the coastal belt of states farther north over a century earlier (Nichols 1976: 2, 5, 53–5). But, even allowing for this natural time-lapse in the adoption of differing styles, there was a marked standardization, except for the very remotest and poorest pockets of the South, by the mid nineteenth century. That standardization discredited vernacular building, and meant that a more 'respectable' yardstick of architectural taste was applied.

During the seventeenth century in eastern Virginia, a vernacular style of cabin construction emerged, largely in response to the materials that were to hand. The simplest early cottage was of one chamber measuring about 20 feet by 16 feet; one wall was built around a brick chimney and was also of brick; the other walls were timber frame. This dwelling, often with a steep roof both for storage and to keep off the snow, was an American type. It had a long future ahead of it, as its successors were being put up in the Plains country during the nineteenth century. In early Virginia, however, the one-roomed cabin was soon superseded as the typical farmhouse by the 'hall-parlor' or 'Virginia' house of two basic rooms, one larger than the other, a brick chimney wall at each end of the habitation and a stair to a loft. This building offered increased, though still exceedingly modest, privacy and was modelled on English forerunners. By the mid eighteenth century, proper upper-storeys were being introduced into farmhouses, and by then also classical ideas of proportion were beginning to obtrude against the earlier dominance of practical concerns. But vernacular features still played a lively part in the planning of lay-out and in construction and decorative work (Herman and Orr 1975: 307–27). This process of increasing size and sophistication in design was then repeated as Southern frontier society moved west. For example, in Fayette county of Kentucky's bluegrass region, the log cabin began to acquire a weatherboard outer casing in the late eighteenth century, at about the same time that double-storey log cabins made their appearance. After the first few years of the nineteenth century, log cabins ceased to be built and existing log cabins were increasingly boarded over and painted. Boarding was feasible as saw-mills were introduced into the area; but it gained popularity from a desire for insulation and a concern for style. Large windows could scarcely be provided in pioneer days, since window-glass had to be imported into Kentucky until the 1790s. But as skilled craftsmen grew in number and as builders' manuals and architectural pattern books circulated more widely and freely, so the building materials employed and the standards of design adopted became more sophisticated (Lancaster 1961: 10–11, 19–28).

Greater space and greater style were not phenomena affecting just frontier Kentucky at the end of the eighteenth century. Farmhouses in the Albemarle Sound area of eastern North Carolina were gaining segregated central staircases, upper-storey rooms (not usually heated) and plans providing for two rooms in depth, both on the ground and on the upper floors. During the years 1800–40 a building boom swept the Albemarle area; full double-storey farmhouses, with far more symmetrical design overall and in detail, gained greatly in popularity and accessibility. No single style prevailed; and very modest houses remained the ordinary farmers' abodes for most of the nineteenth century. But, after the mid nineteenth century, vernacular styles died out. Balloon framing and the improved output of cut nails made house-building easier from the 1830s; staves introduced in the 1850s made the chimney-piece less important. Perhaps more critical, though, was the growing deference to approved taste as decreed in builders' handbooks.

The vernacular styles of the eighteenth century no longer commanded respect (Lounsbury 1977: 27, 41–8).

By different stages, therefore, the settled regions of the mid nineteenth century South came to accept common standards of architectural taste. Of course, there were areas where pattern books and builders' manuals, and their interpreters and copiers, did not penetrate. But they were few in number and usually poor. More generally, there were pervasive guidelines as to what constituted respectable standards of design and planning. Later judges have not universally applauded the teachings of these revered design books. Lewis Mumford in 1924 dismissed American architecture of the period 1820–60 as 'a collection of tags, thrown at random against a building' (Mumford 1924: 93). But the gains in space, in privacy, in light, and in orderliness of layout if not of decorative motifs, were considerable.

By the mid nineteenth century, the basic house design for substantial planters was a five-bay, two-storey building of one or two rooms in depth. This block provided the object upon which an assortment of decorative embellishments was grafted. A close study of house styles in a large region comprising parts of Tennessee, Mississippi and Alabama shows that the most popular, and practical, design was that of an English Georgian house and that the most commonly used decorative format was English Renaissance. But – inspired by the publication of design books – many other styles were adopted. Greek Revival, from the 1830s especially, was popular, probably more so in the eastern states of Maryland, Virginia and the Carolinas than elsewhere. Farther west the Georgian house, suitably enlivened in detail, won approval perhaps because it was reminiscent of the plantation houses of the eighteenth-century seaboard states. Prosperous settlers of the trans-Appalachian cotton belt harked back to the established style of their place of origin. Houses became larger during the affluent 1850s. But they also took on certain features in order to combat the Southern climate; rooms were high, windows numerous and doors opened between rooms in order to facilitate air-flow. Moreover, the typical plantation-house had a wide portico to afford maximum shade (Crocker 1971: 34–6, 95, 149–56). As building materials were readily available on the plantations, the costs of such houses were far from onerous. Even the extremely elaborate, octagonal Longwood House, which, with over twenty rooms, was one of Mississippi's largest, and which required workmen from Philadelphia for its construction, cost only about $28,000 to build in 1860–61. And that sum was about twice the cost of erecting a more run-of-the-mill but still very substantial country residence in the South (Crocker 1973).

The motives behind some of the more extravagant forms of house-buildings were widely commented upon. Individual pride and ostentation was one. Auburn at Natchez offered a good example. It was designed by Levi Weeks, an architect from Massachusetts who arrived at frontier Natchez in 1808. His early commissions were to smarten up existing houses, largely by appending classical porticoes; to add, in other words, a coating of refinement and respectability to what was still a frontier town. In 1812 came a greater opportunity and Auburn House turned out to be Weeks's masterpiece. His client, Lyman Harding, was a Massachusetts man by birth and education who had become a successful lawyer in Mississippi Territory and acquired a sugar plantation elsewhere. Weeks described the house to a friend in Massachusetts. Its proportions were 60 feet by 45 feet, inflated in their impact by the addition of a 31-feet broad portico projecting 12 feet out from the house itself. It 'is designed for the most magnificent building in the territory'. This objective was achieved in three ways; by its size, by its position of great 'romance' outside Natchez, and by the use of Ionic columns and Corinthian entablature to make it 'the first house in the territory on which was ever attempted any of the orders of architecture'. All this splendour was not solely for personal glorification; Weeks wanted to show that Yankees could do something grand, to counter South Carolinians' and Virginians' self-important boastings. Ironically, when Harding's son sold the house in 1827 – for $22,000 – the purchaser was yet another Northerner, Dr Stephen Duncan from Pennsylvania, who was to become one of the very richest of all slaveowners. Again, and somewhat later, when Frederick Stanton, an Irishman settled in Natchez, set out to erect the town's most palatial mansion, he chose to build in brick upon a hill, so accentuating Stanton Hall's height. He made the house three rooms, instead of two, deep, thus adding a library and music room to the usual complement of public rooms for entertainment; and he produced a more highly decorated façade as well as more lavish internal decoration than other houses in Natchez possessed (Crocker 1973: 19–21, 38–41).

Such emulative motives for building big and *à la mode* were not, of course, peculiarly Southern. What can be said is that the latest architectural styles were self-consciously introduced, if often adapted to local climatic and material circumstances, in order to lend an improved tone and respectability to the prospering planter pioneers of the expanding cotton belt. But it was rarely the case that Southerners built on a baronial scale or with lordly lavishness. They were warned in fact against doing so. Andrew Jackson Downing, the principal architectural publicist of the mid nineteenth century, argued in 1850 that the weakness of the hereditary principle in America militated against extravagant expressions of family status and fortune:

In our republic, there is no law of primogeniture, there are no hereditary rights. The man of large wealth dies to-morrow, and his million, divided among all his children, leaves them each but a few thousands. If he has been tempted to indulge in the luxury or pride of a great establishment, no one of his children is rich enough to hold it.

Laws and social customs rendered 'the whole theory' of creating large establishments 'a mistake'. Thus the laudable and intelligible desire to put down roots at a family home encouraged prosperous farmers or planters to build more modestly, with an eye to the future maintenance of a family dwelling. Downing urged that houses be built to suit individuals' characters (the flamboyant house, for example, for the man of soaring imagination), to meet regional climatic needs ('broad roofs, wide verandas, cool and airy apartments' in the South), to match owners' intellectual and cultural interests (in history, for instance), and to suit the republican temperament. Specifically referring to Southern requirements, Downing provided a detailed design for a utilitarian but comfortable country residence in his *The Architecture of Country Houses* (1850); a house with three principal rooms and a big entertaining hall on the ground floor and five bedrooms on the upper storey could be built, he estimated, for $2,500–3,000, depending on the locality and the local price of timber and labour (Downing 1969: 261–9, 312–17).

Downing's book was itself evidence of the spread of increasingly systematic ideas of approved taste. It was a work of major popularization, drawing heavily on British as well as American sources. First published in 1850, it sold over 16,000 copies by 1865 (Downing 1969: vii–ix). Throughout, it combined attention to practical matters of design and construction – providing careful plans and illustrations and precise costings – with a sustained contention that aesthetic and social considerations should be co-ordinated in the design of all manner of houses, from lowly cottages to Romanesque villas. It was also, and explicitly, a work of *national* interest and perspective, providing a reminder that the nineteenth-century country-house movement was a national and not merely a sectional one. Lying at the heart of the whole work was the assumption that a general improvement in architectural discernment and taste created a national demand for a mail-order selection of building designs (Crocker 1973: xii).

Ostentation and the desire to leave a personal mark were but supplementary reasons for the wave of architectural standardization and improvement in buildings. The importance of the country-house as a pacesetter in this trend must not be exaggerated. A majority of the substantial houses raised in antebellum Mississippi were village dwellings, not country-houses set in ornate parks. This was because many planters lived in the small 'towns' or marketing centres of the Deep South; it was also because the urban professionals built themselves spacious residences. Moreover, most houses were functional business headquarters, as well as living places (Crocker 1971: 36; Crocker 1973: 135–42, 145; Nichols 1976: 64–5). In general terms, they showed a conservative range of architectural tastes; the styles chosen were varied, but stereotyped. Ornamental detail offered scope for individual initiative. But only occasionally did owners build either very big or very idiosyncratically. Some of the richest Southerners continued in the

1850s to live in modest surroundings (Oakes 1982: 81–4). Otherwise, there was a pervasive conformity to rigorous planning, systematically laid down production procedures and accessible designs.

It would be difficult to draw hard conclusions about the values which guided the selection of house types. Greek Revival was popular. Gothic extravagances were sometimes found. But these types were very well known in the North as well as in the South, and do not normally inspire speculation about the psychological or philosophical rapport linking that section with the ideals of the slaveowning Greek republics or with the feudal barons of the middle ages (Hamlin 1944). One of the most imposing Gothic castles of mid nineteenth-century America was raised overlooking the New York town of Syracuse; its owner was the first American to ship ready-made suits to the west coast. Perhaps, following the spirit of Downing's invocations, C. T. Longstreet wished to match the boldness of his entrepreneurial endeavour with some striking statement of his architectural daring (Andrews 1960: 49). Yet his choice of style merely conformed to one of a number of available possibilities for a house in the grand manner.

If one should be cautious in extrapolating broad psychological and philosophical conclusions from the design and format of planters' houses, it can at least be said that Southerners generally were embracing more systematic and planned house designs from the late eighteenth century. Southern planters and farmers alike were subscribing to higher standards of respectable taste. If birth in a log cabin was an origin of which a politically ambitious Southerner might boast in the 1830s, life in log cabins or plain dog-trot farmsteads was increasingly by the 1850s a thing of the past, or of the receding frontier, for the respectable planter or farmer.

III

The intrusion of state and county courts into personal conduct was a second obvious aspect of the struggle between respectables and roughs. The brawl, the duel and the vendetta were not the only means of resolving personal disputes; nor did the courts invariably stand idly by while individuals meted out punishments in an individualistic and informal way. Moreover, the Southern states participated variously in general reform; penal reform and the erection of penitentiaries, temperance legislation and the regulation of gambling were all causes agitated and advanced in both Southern and Northern legislatures. Given the practical difficulties of enforcing laws upon so widely scattered a rural population, one of the more remarkable features of antebellum Southern life was the persistent effort to order personal behaviour and make it respectable according to evangelical and humane precepts.

The courts stepped in frequently to sort out personal disputes which had soured to violence. Of prosecutions brought in South Carolina between 1800 and 1860, 56 per cent were for assault. In a sample of North Carolina's county courts for the period 1801–55, 48 per cent of offences heard were for assault and battery. Many of these cases arose from personal squabbles and vendettas. In South Carolina, private prosecutions took up a great deal of the court's time; but many such prosecutions were terminated by the parties' mutual agreement, usually once the defendant agreed to pay the costs of proceedings to that date. Dockets swollen with such cases produced low conviction rates. Of cases going before South Carolina's grand or petty juries from 1800 to 1860, only 31 per cent ended in conviction. In North Carolina, a legislative investigation of prosecutions and convictions in sixty-four lower courts for the period 1811–15 revealed that under half the prosecutions ended in convictions. Whatever their other characteristics, Southern law courts could scarcely be described as imposingly regimented (Hindus 1980: 64, 97–8; Johnson 1937: 658, 666–7).

Nor was sentencing draconian. Under the seventeenth- and eighteenth-century penal codes, prescribed punishments could be savage. The introduction of more humane punishments accompanied the building of penitentiaries in the early and mid nineteenth century; the alternative of secure incarceration existed thereafter to the earlier infliction of mutilation. And secure was a notable emphasis, for many county gaols proved extremely 'leaky', with escapes being commonplace. Not all states made the necessary reforms. One reason, perhaps, for South Carolina's very low conviction rate was juries' reluctance to inflict the stringent punishments decreed by the existing codes (Hindus 1980: 90–4). But in Georgia, where penal reform and penitentiary building went hand in hand in 1817, the sentences imposed were light. From March 1817 to April 1828, there were 368 committals to Georgia's state penitentiary, including a handful of re-committals. Of those persons so consigned to the penitentiary, thirty made successful escapes and 136 were pardoned by the state governor; many pardons came late in the period of imprisonment and amounted to but modest remissions for good conduct or remissions on humanitarian grounds. But for whatever reason, nearly half the prisoners never served their full sentences. And sentences in themselves were far from onerous. Of the 102 prisoners sent to the penitentiary for the most serious crimes of manslaughter, horse stealing, slave stealing and rape, only eight received sentences longer than seven years. The two longest sentences – fourteen and twenty years – were both for rape (Central Register of Convicts. Inmate Administration Div. Georgia. Board of Corrections. GDAH). These Georgian figures omit sentences for murder, which was punished in the counties; executions fell to the sheriffs' charge. But as far as noncapital offences went, Georgia's laws and punishments by the 1820s bore little relationship to those of an age of 'ignorance and feudal barbarism, when the life of man was little estimated', which the Legislature had deplored in 1802 (J. of H. Ga. 1802: 56–8; Bonner 1971).

And capital punishment was not lightly imposed by the circuit or district courts. In 1838–39, a South Carolina politician, Benjamin F. Perry, made a survey of capital trials in his state and discovered that only three convictions resulted from fifty capital trials. In Chester District, South Carolina, only six convictions arose from fifty-one capital trials held between 1806 and 1835. In North Carolina, the rate of conviction in murder trials in the lower courts was 29 per cent during the period 1811–15 (Hindus 1980: 90–4; Johnson 1937: 666–7). If the courts did not always shrink from passing the death sentence, they were at least sparing in this grim duty.

Pardons often resulted from governors' susceptibility to pressure from the friends and neighbours of imprisoned criminals; and low conviction rates were sometimes the by-product of officials' laxness and inefficiency. Petitions for clemency tested governors' respect for local opinion and for humanitarian arguments. In 1799, for example, 126 inhabitants of Washington County, Georgia, asked that John Salter be relieved of part or the whole of a sentence for mayhem; they felt that the act against gouging was 'highly rigorous and penal'. In 1836, Elizabeth Foster appealed to the governor of Georgia to pardon her son Thomas, who had been in the penitentiary for four years. She was 'old' (nearly sixty), a widow of many years whose lot was getting harder with the years; she asked for Thomas's release in order to relieve herself of anxiety and suffering. In 1849, 113 citizens of Savannah asked that Terence Casey be released from the county gaol where he was imprisoned for two offences of assault and battery. Basically an 'honest, industrious, laboring man', Casey's difficulties had been brought on by 'temporary intoxication'. In 1853, a prominent local politician and lawyer, Junius Hillyer, urged Georgia's governor to pardon a slave, Nelson, for the murder of a black man. Hillyer had acted as Nelson's counsel, and had drawn up a petition which would soon be arriving from Habersham County. He pressed the governor:

> I write as a man actuated by the common principle of humanity to save the life of a human being who I am satisfied is not guilty. Judge Dougherty my associate counsel as well as Judge Jackson and every member of the bar not engaged in the case were astonished at the verdict.

An anxious mother, forgiving friends and neighbours, an outraged attorney: these were among the people who readily addressed the state governor in clemency petitions and sought to ensure that the law's provisions were suitably tempered by humanity. Of course, governors could be misled by such petitions. There was at least one instance in

Georgia of a spurious JP appearing on a petition. And in 1836 Governor William Schley was told that a petition for the release of a horse-thief had been got up by 'the last quality of characters in the county'; and that the few 'men of note' who also signed had done so in order to placate the miscreant's wife. But, on the whole, the petitions appear to have been legitimate expressions of humane concern for individuals' plight.[1]

In some instances, weak enforcement of the laws resulted from official laxness rather than from overwhelming humanitarianism. The solicitor general for the Southern Circuit of Georgia informed the state governor in 1833 that a murderer had escaped 'beyond the reach of ordinary process' and that the county could not bear the expense of bringing the suspected murderer to trial. Moreover, since, according to the solicitor general, the suspect was widely presumed to have been innocent, there was considerable 'public apathy' as to his capture. In 1860 it was, reportedly, the local officials who were apathetic. A citizen of Mitchell county complained to Governor Joseph E. Brown that a murderer had presented himself to the county officials, but the latter took no cognisance of the affair on the grounds that no one was prosecuting the case. And, even if suspects were properly pursued, they might not be held or brought finally to trial. One county gaoler in 1836 remarked to the governor that an escapee from his gaol was 'a noted villain and had broken a good many jails'. A deputy sheriff from Gwinnett county complained to the governor in 1831 that he could not cope with eleven convicted men because Gwinnett had no gaol and the neighbouring county's gaol was 'entirely unsafe' according to its sheriff.[2]

From the record of conviction rates, sentencing and pardons, it is clear that humanitarian efforts were being made to temper the enforcement of laws which were themselves much liberalized in the first three decades of the nineteenth century. Moreover, the idea of humane justice clearly ran deep; petitioning was frequent and petitioners presented strong pleas for individual circumstances to be considered. The quest for a respectable public order was not, then, carried forward without scrupulous attention to its human consequences, or with compulsive and ruthless force.

Upholding respectable values drew the courts' attention to a wide variety of personal misbehaviour. Repeated efforts were made to tame rowdy conduct; the noisy disruption of divine services was one complaint that reached state supreme courts. Organized gambling was often banned by laws applicable to specific municipalities. In 1839 a newspaper in Monticello, Mississippi argued that 'the moral and intelligent portion of this community, as well as the State at large' would welcome legislation to prevent gambling and betting on elections. While it grumbled that gambling had recently become so widespread as to require rebuke, it also complained that the officers entrusted with law enforcement lacked diligence in applying the existing laws (Monticello, *Pearl River Banner,* 16 Feb. 1839). On occasions, even the most minor cases were argued as far as the state supreme courts. Solomon Roper in 1835 appealed to North Carolina's Supreme Court against his conviction in a county court for indecent exposure on the public highway. He pleaded that the indictment against him did not specify that the offence was committed in the presence of any citizens. This got short shrift from the court; the offensive exposure did not have to be seen by the public, as long as it occurred at a place where it was likely to be seen (18 *North Carolina Reports,* 208). In 1840, the same supreme court decided that two laws of 1791 and 1837 to punish brawlers who bit off their opponents' ears applied as much to biting off a fifth of an ear as to the removal of the whole member (23 *North Carolina Reports,* 121). If the poor took to gouging eyes and biting off ears, the rich took to the duelling ground. State legislatures tried to stop both forms of violence. They had banned duelling by the 1850s. How effective legislative prohibition proved to be is open to dispute. Some of those who wrote about the more bloody brand of hand (and especially thumb) fighting gave the impression that it had largely died out by the 1830s and 1840s. But duelling certainly survived its legal interdict; public men continued to be involved in duels throughout the antebellum period in Mississippi, for instance; and the last formal duel there was not fought until the 1890s.

No one would suggest for a moment that the attempt to impose a set of 'respectable' values worked completely. There was a great deal of residual vigilantism and brawling left beyond the reach of the law. But the effort made was worth remarking upon. It provided an important bond that helped regulate and stabilize Southern society despite its widely dispersed and very rural population. Moreover, the establishment of legal procedures marked an important stage in the integration of state institutions and the raising of community identity. The dissemination of 'respectable' values, against the use of force in settling personal disputes, against gaming houses and excessive indulgence in alcohol, and in favour of formal methods of solving disputes, owed little to the power or ideology of the planter 'class'. It was successful, in so far as it was so, because men and women of all economic statuses sought an ordering of their social environment. And probably the strongest impulse creating that quest came from religious convictions rather than from any consciousness of 'class'.

IV

Religion was a central though not a controlling influence upon Southern white society. It provided an obvious and indeed, in many respects, sole institutional binding for many ordinary people. Although there have been disagreements over the extent of church membership and although there are no hard and fast statistics of that membership, the churches were the most popularly supported formal institutions, except for political parties, from the 1830s onwards; moreover, the number of church buildings and the number of ministers increased greatly in the early nineteenth century, Revivalist camp-meetings which gained strength from the one at Cane Ridge, Kentucky, in 1801, were occasions for intense relief, excitement and pleasure (Mathews 1977: 46–9). As Harold Laski wrote in 1949, 'The camp-meeting was as great an event to the scattered settlers as the visit of a famous actress to the troops in a distant theatre during the Second World War' (Laski 1949: 270).

On numbers, church membership often appears at first glance to have been somewhat thin. But, as Professor Mathews has pointed out, sheer numbers need to be adjusted for age, so excluding children who were not church members, and for the sex ratio, in that about two-thirds of members were women. By such reckoning, about 27 per cent of Southerners aged over sixteen belonged to churches in 1792; and the proportion of Southern families possessing at least one member of a church (more often than not a woman) was even higher (Mathews 1977: 47). Two generations later, in the wake of much proselytization and a great laying down of organizational infrastructure, the proportions were presumably greater. But how far evangelical sects' – and about 90 per cent of Southern churches were evangelical – influence stretched beyond invocation and preaching is another matter.

The very exuberance of the Southern, as of the American, churches weakened somewhat their impact. In rural areas, churches might be erected; but they were often small and primitive. Ministers were appointed, and were increasingly better educated; but they were either institutionally itinerant or obliged to serve a number of different churches, preaching only once or twice a month in each of them. Most ministers were obliged to be farmers, or take on other jobs. And while camp-meetings did much to stimulate interest in and recruitment to the evangelical churches, they clearly exploited the most raw emotionalism and tried to fill a void created by the loneliness and isolation of rural life. Young people welcomed them as meeting-places, not always as respectable as their elders desired, for youngsters of both sexes. An affluent Southerner travelling in Alabama recorded overhearing a conversation in which a man admitted to a preacher that he got a female member of the congregation pregnant. His explanation was that the woman and he met and 'talked about the things of God, till we got very happy' (Royall 1969: 105–7). For these various reasons, and perhaps because the denominations became wedded to more respectable ways of reaching wide audiences, revivalist camp-meetings, while continuing throughout the 1850s, were less depended upon to maintain church support (Bruce 1974: 6, 56–9). Yet even the drive for respectable behaviour could not suffocate, though it tried to stifle, evangelical fervour. A very young Methodist minister recorded how, at a camp-meeting in August 1860, a gentleman's younger daughter 'brought tears to many eyes' as she 'crammed her hankerchief [*sic*] into her mouth and used every possible effort to keep from shouting'. Once she left the congregation, however, 'she could control herself no longer, and gave vent to her pent-up feelings in a rapturous burst of rejoicing' (Stringfield Diary: vol. 3, 14 Aug. 1860. SHC).

Evangelicalism, however, stretched beyond invocation and recruitment. An important change attributed to their work – though disputed in some quarters – was the improved tone of social intercourse. In the late eighteenth century, the evangelical churches criticized the gambling, drinking, profanity and general irreligion of many members of the largely Anglican planter elite. This was especially true of Virginia, where many rich planters set themselves up as a self-conscious oligarchy. Methodists and Baptists, in abusing those planters, were partially advancing the cause and the case of plantation society's outsiders (Isaac 1982). By the mid nineteenth century, this situation had changed, perhaps even profoundly. Episcopalians remained as a tiny and rather self-consciously superior church. But they did not rule the religious roost. Methodists, Baptists and Presbyterians, in that order of size of membership, had become as respectable and as well supported by the wealthy, as they had appeared to be critics from beyond the governing pale eighty or so years earlier. To say that this process represented the triumph of 'middle-class' values begs the questions of causation and of the social basis of religious belief. By the mid nineteenth century, if not long before, all social groups spawned supporters of the evangelical churches. If differences of wealth distanced some leading Presbyterian churches from the most powerfully proselytizing Baptists, these differences were themselves subsumed under the general conviction that church members – the respectables – were at moral loggerheads if not at moral war with the irreligious, the gamblers and the drinkers of the South. This, after all, was the principal social message delivered week by week in sermon after sermon; the elect or the born-again or the faithful had to steel themselves against the secular world and to reaffirm repeatedly their faith in God's Kingdom (Mathews 1977).

To call this development the triumph of a middle-class or lower middle-class ethic is misleading. It affected all social groupings, but it also divided all social groupings; the irreligious were not confined to any one class. Furthermore, evangelical religion spread at the same time that representative and democratic ideas and institutions spread more widely. Tocqueville argued in the 1830s that the churches accommodated themselves to the democratizing spirit of the age and thereby maintained, indeed enlarged, their place in American society as a whole. Unkinder critics have asserted that the churches in adapting to the linguistic, cultural and social needs of an assertive democracy somewhat sold the pass. A vague religiosity, full of sentiment and generalized dogma, replaced theology; and a commitment to be 'good' within the world, rather than a rejection of the world and its trappings, displaced passionate moral purpose (Laski 1949: 316–17, 320–1). The truth of this latter criticism is quite impossible to ascertain; for compromises with the world have in all ages and places been difficult and extremely individual choices. But what may be said is that evangelical religion and political democracy grew together. A phenomenon viewed from one perspective as the triumph of evangelical moralism may appear from another angle to have been the product of both more representative government, and the elimination of the reserved political powers held by the conservative planters of the mid eighteenth century tidewater. Just as political evolution enhanced individual citizens' self-respect, so evangelical religion provided a pervasive moralism that quickened individuals' self-awareness and raised their consciousness of their own worth.

What practical results did this apparent – and there are some disputes over the change – long-term shift in the moral complexion of the South yield? An obvious topic of recent historical interest has been the impact of religion upon whites' treatment of slaves. The idea that evangelical churches were by their very nature inner directed and so largely oblivious to social issues has been thoroughly brought into question by the study of evangelicals' attitudes towards slavery. In the 1780s notably, but also until the 1830s, the evangelical churches at least criticized and often condemned slavery (Mathews 1977: ch. 2). Their stance, however, became increasingly pro-slavery from the 1830s. This shift was not an entirely dramatic one; for the anti-slavery conscience had, in truth, made little headway against the practical realities of the South's social system. Moreover, after the 1830s, the whites' religious position, *vis-à-vis* the slaves, was a complex one; for the Southern churches reached out into the slave quarters to convert and uplift, and the whites acknowledged both the spiritual side to slaves' existence and the intensity of slaves' religious faith. An unhappy double standard prevailed over slavery, with respect for slaves' humanity jostling with the contention that slaves were little more than chattels. Yet Christianity was not unaccustomed to trying to reconcile disparate moral imperatives and human moral dilemmas. Evangelical religion stimulated slaves' religious awareness and helped make some whites' treatment of slaves more 'respectable' (Mathews 1977: ch. 4). But, ultimately, economic interests and social and political acceptability dictated the surrender of anti-slavery conscience to the requirements of a Southern slave system.

Did this failure – though in some respects not a dishonourable failure – mean that piety led generally to social and political acquiescence? There are good grounds for contending that it did. Yet historians intent upon placing religion in its social context too readily overlook the nineteenth-century churches' absorption in matters of little or no fascination to the modern social historian. Nineteenth-century churches and congregations were, after all, much vexed by tangled disputations over liturgy, theology and organization. These debates fragmented evangelical effort, turned evangelicals in upon their churches, and served to divorce them further still from the world. When the undoubted pietism and introspection of many evangelicals is added to this, there is a solid case for concluding that social improvement was indeed overwhelmed by private piety in the evangelical order of things. Even where evangelical churches objected to slavery and tried to undermine it, they did so without as much vigour, commitment, and certainly without anything near as much success, as accompanied the task of conversion or of regulating their own congregations' internal affairs. While historians must necessarily do justice to Southerners' strivings of conscience over slavery, and should sympathize with the moral and emotional dilemmas experienced by evangelicals in the late eighteenth and early nineteenth centuries, they must also frankly admit that religious conscience neither overcame considerations of *Realpolitik* nor transcended worldly calculation. Sadly, such cannot be said to have been a peculiarly Southern failing.

While acknowledging these points, however, it must be said that evangelical churches exerted significant secular influence. Donald G. Mathews has described the evangelicals' ideal as 'the disciplined person within a disciplined community' (Mathews 1977: 224). If self-discipline were crucial, it was to be aided by discipline imposed by church congregations and reinforced by state laws or local regulations. Evangelicals played a leading part in the 1830s, 1840s and 1850s in founding colleges and spreading education, in pressing for controls over intemperance, and in stiffening the courts' resolve to curtail brawling, duelling, gambling and other forms of what they defined as misconduct. They gave a tone to Southern society, both white and, in important respects, black as well.

Their very buildings provided outward signs of respectability. This point – pompous in itself perhaps – was well made by a correspondent in the *Ripley Advertiser* in 1846:

> it is the duty of each and every good citizen to contribute his mite and
> influence to the propagation of a liberal share of religious, scientific and
> literary views and advantages in the town or neighborhood in which they
> reside. For it is a fact worthy of notice, that a community is oftener
> judged by the number and character of its churches and Seminaries, the
> cast of its inhabitants, for morals set down for good or evil ... than [by]
> any or all others.

A community's image depended particularly on the number of its churches and congregations and of its schools and scholars. Yet Ripley, in Mississippi, 'in the very centre of civilization and refinement, surrounded by all the advantages of civil and religious liberty', possessed a church that was half-finished and was used only in the summer, and a school that was 'one miserable smoky cabin' (*Ripley Advertiser,* 14 March 1846). This small town obviously needed a more respectable image; and the warning was implicit in this article that its continued growth, prestige and prosperity depended upon the projection of that positive image. The same emphasis emerged from traveller's account after traveller's account; a stress upon the respectable ensemble of market towns' squares or main thorough-fares, composed of bank, hotel, general stores and a collection of churches.

Equally important, the cult of respectability, much affected by evangelical sects, fashioned or qualified the treatment meted out to slaves.

It is a cliché in itself to state that there were acute contradictions in the formal, legally governed relationship between whites and slaves. The contest between material self-interest and humane concern agitated Southern legislators', lawyers' and judges' minds, and created some extraordinarily tangled court decisions. But, standing aside from the detail of the cases themselves, one may draw the general conclusion from them that many Southerners sought to improve the treatment of slaves, make it conform to respectable standards and bridle the excesses of punishment to which slaves were subjected. Throughout the period from the early 1830s to the Civil War, Southerners were swamped by a steady flow of printed advice and invocation on how to feed, minister to, care for, work and punish slaves. Behind all this propaganda were obvious economic considerations; a 'scientifically' managed and regulated labour force would also, it was claimed, be an efficient and productive one. But there was no unitary economic motive in this quest for a more regulated plantation order. Profit could be, and was, made without heeding this detailed advice. Rather, the decision to define ways of treating slaves emerged from those seeking a 'respectable' ordering of the slave community and of slavery. The more plantation relationships were codified and prescribed, the less they were left to individuals' whim and the violence of individuals' feelings. So, too, the attempt to set legal norms for the punishment of slaves was a reaction to uncontrolled vigilantism and its bloody, often repulsive, consequences. Evangelical religion and the drive for respectability thus combined almost to strengthen slavery, for they inspired notions of white stewardship and ideas about the proper treatment of slaves which legitimated the institution. Whites could grant that slaves possessed a spiritual equality but needed material guardianship in a world where they could not, of their own volition, cope with their inherently bestial urges or fulfil God's purpose to labour fruitfully on earth.

This respectable and evangelical quest for orderly race relations offered a model objective, not a description of reality. Southerners of powerful evangelical belief could be essentially indifferent to slavery and its resultant human suffering. In North Carolina, for instance, a slaveowning farmer, George W. Jeffreys, left an extraordinarily passionate diary recounting his struggle in the 1840s with fundamentalist belief. He seemed to assume that every material or personal reverse suffered was a Divine punishment for some lapse into the ways of the secular world. Thus, whenever his reading strayed from Richard Watson's sermons he attributed misadventures to that drift into the profane world of the ancient classics. On one occasion he recorded:

> As soon as I departed from Watsons Sermons and Hebrews sickness began and continued for seven or eight months and I had not only to pay about $100 to physicians but lost a valuable negro man and also in that unfortunate period a negro man ran away and was gone 15 months. See what I lost and what I suffered in my own body and feelings for my unfaithfulness.

But when things went smoothly, his first concern was his own spiritual happiness:

> It is going well with me and mine this morning – the servants are all enabled to go out to work – the weather is fine – but the best of all is I have peace and comfort in my soul and I feel that God is shining upon my path and I feel that all is encouraging (Jeffreys diary, 6, 18 April 1843: William B. Williamson papers, SHC).

Of course, any profuse diarist is unusual, perhaps even unrepresentative; Jeffreys certainly was an emotional roller-coaster. But his pre-occupation with his private spiritual world seems a highly predictable one; although Jeffreys was a lay preacher and so perhaps an extreme case.

Another diarist, Lucilla McCorkle, was the wife of a Presbyterian minister settled in Alabama. She exemplified the respectables' urge to order their relations with their slaves and with their Maker simultaneously. One entry of 1858 noted the events of a Sunday:

> O what a precious quiet sabbath! but it dawned rather unpropitiously. The severest whipping I ever gave my darling G——— I gave this morning before breakfast. Perhaps I was somewhat impatient with the tardiness of the servant, but whether previously chafed or not, I felt the satisfaction at the time that it was necessary and right.

A slave boy was whipped for impertinence and for the irreverent use of the name of the Holy Ghost. But the diarist then moved on to a discussion of the excellence of the Sunday sermon. Mrs McCorkle occasionally reflected upon, perhaps regretted, her harsh admonitions of the household slaves. But such chastisements were justified because of the slaves' 'tardiness and apparent absence of mind'. And slavery itself was necessary because of the slaves' indiscipline and fecklessness. Mrs McCorkle applied the same rigorous standards in laying out a programme of daily study and activity for her son, and expressed the same concern for orderly, serious and work-oriented conduct when discussing the girls who were pupils at her husband's college. In her diary entries for 1858–60, the subject which drew this sensitive, dutiful and scrupulous lady's ire was not slavery but dancing at a planters' picnic:

> No *evangelical church* in Christendom *sanctions* dancing any more than attending theatres – horse races – or chicken fighting – card playing or lotteries – wine drinking or dissipation in any shape. And so far as individual members transgress – in these respects they weaken their moral sense of rectitude, lower their standard of piety and when the fact becomes *notorious* – brings a scandal upon the church of Christ, a blemish upon their own good name.

A greater threat was posed to the respectable moral order by dancing than by the pattern of dominance established by slavery (Diary of Mrs Lucilla McCorkle, 4 Oct. 1858, 5 March, fourth sabbath in June, 24 Aug. 1859, 11 May 1860: McCorkle papers vol. 20 SHC).

In addition, the search for public security in a slave society did not permit the complete substitution of formal legal proceedings for vigilantism. An examination of a small-town newspaper in 1858 – *The Daily Sun* of Columbus, Georgia – leaves the reader with an oppressive impression of murders and shooting and summary justice. Revenge murders were approved of; the use of lynch law in dealing with slaves was condoned. When a black was dragged from a gaol in Enterprise, Mississippi, and hanged by the citizens, for raping a white teenage girl, the newspaper commented: 'Burning would have been the proper punishment if any punishment could be invented adequate to such a crime.' In Dallas county, Alabama, a group of citizens hanged a slave for raping a white girl aged twelve; the citizens collected $500 to compensate the owner for this sudden loss of a slave worth $1,000. And the *Selma Sentinel* was quoted as remarking of the initial crime: 'Perhaps a more diabolical deed was never before perpetrated in Dallas county.' Clearly, the creation of a respectable order confronted very serious challenge in a slave society that had to rely on vigilantism for public security (Columbus, Ga., *The Daily Sun* 1 April, 8 May, 17, 23, 26 July, 6 Oct. 1858).

Yet all this evidence of informal violence should not be taken too much at face value. The source itself is questionable. Newspapers cobbled together stories of mayhem and murder from far and wide, assembling a sort of collage of crime from across the South and indeed the nation. It was in their interests to excite, even to frighten, their readers. The cumulative image of Southern society was indeed a grimly violent one. But that was one side of a story which was rich also in efforts to govern, through churches and states, the relationship between slaves and whites and to bring respectable, if sometimes severe, standards of stewardship and formal justice to bear upon it.

V

The first sustained, book-length social analyses of the South appeared in the 1850s. Many of those were highly critical of their subject, but one notable defence was Daniel R. Hundley's *Social Relations in Our Southern States* (1860), a work published too late in the intellectual clash between North and South to secure much attention in its own day. Hundley rightly rejected contemporary Northern descriptions that cast Southerners into the crudely stereotyped roles of a ruling planter elite lording it over ordinary, non-planter whites. His alternative portrait ignored specifics of wealth, but outlined a set of social divisions which intermingled occupation, ethnicity and morality. The planters were subdivided into Southern gentlemen, cotton snobs (who were almost invariably parvenus) and Southern Yankees (who included the most ruthless slave-drivers in their number). The middle classes were mainly urban, while the yeoman farmers formed the independent and dependable backbone to Southern society. Below them were varieties of 'poor white trash'. Such groupings represented an advance on the prevailing simplicities. But Hundley, in trying to explain differences of personal and public morality in the antebellum South, fell into the fairly obvious error of linking social statuses with moral outlooks and attitudes. The Southern gentleman was a moral paragon; which characteristic he had presumably inherited from his aristocratic Virginian forebears. Planters falling below this level of moral excellence were the parvenus of the upper class, or were rapacious Yankee immigrants, or imitated Yankee materialism. After rebutting, to his own satisfaction at least, Northern charges that brutality and depravity were the inescapable consequences of the slave system, Hundley proceeded to refute also the suggestion that ordinary whites were subordinate to the planter elite by emphasizing the yeoman farmers' sterling qualities (Hundley 1979).

In his own way, Hundley fell into the modern sociologists' trap of creating a body of attitudes labelled 'middle-class values' and then plotting their rise and spread as those beliefs are discovered among other classes as defined by wealth and status. Although he advanced the analysis by bringing in values, he distorted it by tying those values to occupational and ethnic 'classes'. What he missed, therefore, was the important social bond provided across the different wealth-holding categories by religion and respectability. Those who sought to bring greater order to Southern life – in its architectural tastes, in its procedures for settling disputes, in its regulation of personal behaviour and in its justification and control of slavery – came from all wealth-holding categories. Inspired very often by evangelical religion, these respectables entertained secular as well as spiritual motives for their work of improvement. They were far from being united, single-minded or thoroughly successful. But they left an indelible imprint upon the South, both materially and in matters of culture, law and thought. It was their consciences, shared purposes and determined will that helped save the South from social fragmentation and far greater violence between persons than that which obtained in the 1850s. Respectability – as a vague aspiration and as a generalized moral code – was the last link, hastily fitted perhaps and seemingly liable to fracture, in the chain of social bonds that held the South together.

NOTES

1. Petition. Misc. Docs. 1799. Ga. Govrs.' papers. James Jackson. Box 44; Elizabeth Foster to Govr., 28 June 1836. Ga. Govrs.' papers. William Schley. Box 50; petition. 1849 file. Ga. Govrs.' papers. George W. Towns. Box 54; Junius Hillyer to Govr., 19 Oct. 1853. Ga. Govrs.' papers. Howell Cobb. Box 54; James Fulwood to Govr., 11 June 1836, Bartemus Reynolds to Govr., 2 Aug. 1836. Ga. Govrs.' papers. William Schley. Box 50. Telamon Cuyler Collection, University of Georgia.
2. Stephen E. Miller to Govr., 29 June, 11 May 1833. Ga. Govrs.' papers. Wilson Lumpkin. Box 49[a]. J. F. C. Settle to Govr., 22 Aug. 1860. Ga. Govrs.' papers. Joseph E. Brown. Box 55. Archibald S. Bryant to Govr., 10 Aug. 1836. Ga. Govrs.' papers. William Schley. Box 50. A. J. Clayton to Govr. 16 Sept. 1831. Ga. Govrs.' papers. George R. Gilmer, Box 49. Telamon Cuyler Collection, University of Georgia.

Chapter eleven

CONCLUSION: SOUTHERNISM

I

White Southerners differed individually in many respects: relative wealth, political attachments, material life-styles, relationships with slaves, gender, personal morality, intellectual proclivities, and educational attainments, to name but the most obvious ones. Such differences require and receive much analysis. But in the crisis of 1860–61 the Deep South and most of the Upper South identified and gave their tenacious support to a single cause: one with a near-universal appeal. This essay has suggested some reasons why the Confederate cause struck such a resonant chord. Social bonding, forged by a particular and successful historical experience, aggressive race pride, economic well-being, physical mobility, open yet unobtrusive government, common rituals, religion, and a strong regard for the ideals of family and respectability, gave substance to 'Southernism'. In defending their independence, the Confederates were defending more than a geographical region and the institution of slavery. Even though many of Southernism's distinguishing features may have applied equally to the North – such as mobility, family and respectability – by the 1850s these aspects of life, if not distinguishable in the abstract, were in practice endowed with a distinctive sectional character. Important developments in these social bonds occurred in the forty years before 1860. If one seeks to date the whites' breakthrough into the Indians' last lands east of the Mississippi, the consolidation of democracy and of the Cotton Kingdom, and the emergence of a Southern literature, a Southern historiography, and the first fully fledged defences of slavery, one is drawn repeatedly to the 1820s and 1830s. Southernism grew with increased literacy, improved communications and the spread of commercialization, just as community-consciousness expanded in those years and under those influences in the small-town North (Blumin 1976). But while the same general forces may have been in action, they produced divergent sectional loyalties in the period 1820–60.

The crucial sectional difference was over slavery; but a rural–urban contrast also arose from the South's retention of slavery. Not only did Southern publicists and politicians increasingly propound the 'positive good' defence of slavery on historical, sociological, religious and ethnological grounds; they asserted that the subordination of black by white advanced and secured white men's liberties, an argument stretching back well into the eighteenth century. They also depicted the twin products of contemporary industrial society in Europe – factory capitalism and its dialectical antithesis, socialism – as offering a model for the North's future, one, in imitation of European conditions, of economic exploitation and social strife. Fixing upon factory capitalism and socialism further enabled some Southern apologists to claim that slavery saved Southern whites from the indignities of wage slavery under one dispensation, and the religious heresies, materialistic pre-occupations and social turbulence engendered by the other. Slave society became a paradigm for orderliness; 'free' society became a synonym for hypocrisy and the capitalistic exploitation of white workers (Jenkins 1960: 285–308).

Moreover, the emergence of ever-expanding cities and industrial towns in the north-east during the decades up to 1860 inspired Southern attacks upon urban society and simultaneous defences of their rural world as more congenial to individualism, independence and Christian morality. Ordinary white Southerners consistently avoided urban life and resolutely sought their fortunes by migrating to new Western lands, not to growing ports or commercial centres. It would be absurd to suggest that large cities offered the only environments in which intellectual inquiry might flourish; Jefferson and his circle stood towering as very visible exceptions to that rule. Yet W. J. Cash, in his highly influential *The Mind of the South* (1941), had a worthwhile point to make when he asserted that antebellum whites knew insufficient complexity or discontent to experience vigorous dissent and rational discourse; 'the Southern world ... was basically an extremely uncomplex, unvaried, and unchanging one. Here economic and political organization was reduced to its simplest elements'. No controversial issues stirred this Arcadia's surfaces: 'satisfaction was the hallmark of Southern society; masters and masses alike were sunk in the deepest complacency; nowhere was there any palpable irritation, any discontent and conflict, and so nowhere was there any tendency to question' (Cash 1954: 106–8). Few modern historians would see the South as quite so devoid of internal contrasts, dynamism and friction as Cash maintained. But at least Cash's perspective provides a surer base for further analysis than, for example, do the contentions that the planter class 'was not a relaxed elite ... the potential for class unrest was always great', and that the 1850s witnessed an 'escalating conflict between white classes in the South' (Newby 1978: 151; Takaki 1980: 122–3).

As has already been stressed, the records of state governments do not indicate the existence of surging class resentments or potentially explosive clashes of social and political interest. State governments used their powers to open up new lands for settlement and, in the 1850s, to advance that economic diversification – through railway building and so the promotion of commercialization – which they allegedly ignored. Land remained cheap and available, even if short-run price shifts made slaves increasingly expensive during the late 1850s. While public life was hardly ignored, family connections remained of fundamental importance to Southerners, so absorbing energies and attentions that might, conceivably, have been channelled elsewhere. Where disputes broke into the open within the states, they concerned partisan contests for office, regional struggles for advantage in promoting railways or river improvements, or battles between 'roughs' and 'respectables' over the definition and regulation of personal conduct. Class rhetoric scarcely intruded into Southern political discourse during the 1850s, unless it was directed to sectional purposes. Thus the myth of the planters' cavalier origins had a larger polemical use, for it implied that Northerners took their forebears from the ranks of Puritan fanatics who grasped state power for their own narrowly conceived ends (Dawson 1978). John Pendleton Kennedy in his novel *Swallow Barn* described Virginia in these terms: 'In policy and government she is ... a republic: in temper and opinion, in the usages of life, and in the qualities of her moral nature, she is aristocratic' (Kennedy 1832: 75). Yet he was thus portraying a state that seemed *anachronistic,* not typical of the contemporary South; and Virginia was indeed at that very moment undergoing considerable constitutional reform. The conduct and language of Southern state politics overwhelmingly points to the existence of a *herrenvolk* democracy, in which civic freedom and equality of esteem and opportunity for whites was juxtaposed with elaborate and vigorous notions about the eternal ordering and subordination of 'inferior' races (Fredrickson 1981).

Southernism was characterized as much by a *herrenvolk* religion as by a *herrenvolk* democracy. Religious activity in the South was less diverse than it was in the North by the mid nineteenth century. Only about one Southern church-member in ten was not a Protestant; and about eight in ten church-members were Methodists and Baptists (McLoughlin 1978: 132). Episcopal and Presbyterian denominations, with their tendency to be more socially select than the Methodists and Baptists, formed distinct minorities, with very scattered congregations. The principal denominations evinced certain common characteristics. One was the informality of their organization and preaching. Even as late as 1860, rural camp-meetings were important to Methodists and Baptists alike. Entry into the ministry was relatively easy and did not, for the most popular denominations, depend heavily upon educational attainments. Rural preachers especially were often plain farmers doubling up in their ministrations to souls. While the denominations by the 1830s had sufficient money to build permanent churches and to found colleges in the Deep South, these outward and visible signs of religious commitment were, on the whole, modest in scale. With some exceptions, the churches' over-riding mission was to deliver a straightforward, if intense, message. Theologically rigorous Calvinism had long lost favour in the evangelizing and demotic South. Free will in effect (though with careful semantic safeguards) replaced predestination; and if a stern morality was essential to worldly good conduct, divine intercession was easily called forth and emotional, indeed passionate, prayer and singing of spirituals strongly encouraged (McLoughlin 1978: 114, 118–20).

The social consequences of evangelical Protestantism were various. Many committed white evangelicals reached out to convert and uplift the slaves; their actions virtually created a black alternative culture with emphases and a psychological importance for the slaves which did not necessarily correspond to the masters' intentions. Slavery as an institution was probably made more paternalistic in the sixty years or so before the Civil War by the quickening of religious enthusiasm among Southern whites, and the subsequent application of more humane values to the master–slave relationship (Rose 1982: 18–21, 31). But, however charitably disposed to white men and women of keen Christian conscience we may feel inclined to be, one cannot point to any effective sharpening of evangelicals' qualms about slavery as evangelical religion took hold. The reverse, if anything, happened; for a belief that slaves gained advantages from their condition – in conversion to Christianity, and in receiving decent, if paternalistic, treatment beyond the imaginings of their African forebears – became firmly implanted in Southern whites' consciousness. The full effect of this conviction was felt in the mid 1840s when the Methodist Episcopal church and Baptists divided nationally over slavery into Northern and Southern wings. If evangelical religion did not throw Southerners entirely into an other-worldly cast of mind, it failed in the South to spawn the anti-slavery fruits that it yielded in Britain and the North.

Perhaps the point may be made from the example of a North Carolinian slaveowner, George W. Jeffreys, who acted as a Baptist preacher, deriving intense emotional comfort from this religious work. Of a Sunday in 1844 he recorded:

> Had liberty, power and enlargement and comfort in P[reaching] –
> congregation serious and attentive – there was a quickening
> among the members and the Holy Spirit was acknowledged to be
> present – some sinners were serious – I got down on the floor and talked
> to them – Bro Garritt prayed a very warm and fervent prayer – I came
> home to dinner in a delightful frame of spirit and had remarkable peace
> and comfort of soul all the evening and up to this morning. Glory and
> praise to God.

A few weeks later he preached locally on two consecutive days: 'The Holy Spirit was evidently present – the congregation *were very attentive* – nay even a gay worldly young man remarked to me – that he never saw a *more serious congregation'* [*sic.*]. Such spiritual excellence had its earthly reward. A few days later Jeffreys recorded the return of a runaway slave, a sure and repeated sign to him of divine favour: 'Harrison who has been run away for upwards of three weeks came in this morning and seemed humbled and willing to make acknowledgements – so the overseer gave him but 40 lashes on his behind' (Jeffreys Diary: 17 June, fourth Sat. and Sun. in June, 29 June 1844. William B. Williamson papers, SHC). A good God for Jeffreys was one whose dispensation fostered his slaves' docility. Again, a Northerner working in Georgia during the 1840s, who fell foul of local whites because of his anti-slavery actions, had this to say:

> In the South there are men of the kindest heart, who regard their fellowmen with the liveliest emotions of sympathy, and who are noble, generous, and high-minded, yet who act and are governed by motives altogether different in relation to their slaves. They have been so educated as to regard these as another class (Paine 1852: 119).

Whites' conduct over the decades substantiated these views from inside and outside the body of slaveowners. Evangelical religion did nothing to loosen, it may indeed have tightened, slavery's shackles. Given their powerful certainties about slavery, the churches not surprisingly backed secession. For example, one young minister ascertained that, of the 118 travelling Methodist preachers known to him in Tennessee, no fewer than 44 were Southern Rights men and only 9 were Unionists in the secession crisis. Though he had not voted for the Southern Democrat in the presidential election of 1860, and indeed had tolerated an individual minister's expression of anti-slavery feelings in 1857, he too plumped for Southern Rights when the decisive moment arrived (Stringfield Diary: vol. 2, 5 March 1857; vol. 4, notes at back. Stringfield family papers, SHC).

Evangelicals helped to legitimate or minimize worldly suffering, and erode social distinctions. Individuals' spiritual destiny was, clearly, of overwhelming importance to evangelicals; but the twin principles of religious commitment – and occasional religious fervour – and restraint in worldly behaviour served to foster evangelicals' community-building work and their public activities as moral policemen, and, more important perhaps, policewomen. So, too, evangelicals' general indifference, if not outright hostility, to hierarchy reinforced a secular culture that rejected, from the 1820s, any relics of eighteenth-century interest representation, property qualifications and political deference that may have remained in the South. By the mid nineteenth century, evangelicalism was no longer, as it had been in the 1760s and 1770s, something of a social outsiders' protest movement against the alleged hedonism and secularism of a ruling gentry. Instead it offered the common language of discourse, with obvious differences in inflection, fluency and vocabulary, for all those 'respectable' Southerners who held themselves responsible for the welfare and future of their section (Mathews 1977: Isaac 1982; Lewis 1983).

And this similarity of sentiment and conviction was strengthened by a similarity of ethnic and geographical provenance. In 1860, much of the Deep South was a remarkably self-contained region. Of South Carolinians in that year, 92.7 per cent had been born in the Deep South, most of them in their own state. Of Georgians, 89.5 per cent shared that same background. In Alabama 86.3 per cent, Florida 84.7 per cent and Mississippi 79.9 per cent of the inhabitants had been born in the region. Only in Louisiana and Texas was the Deep South contingent more constricted. But in Louisiana, the 68.4 per cent of the people born in the Deep South still set the standard for American norms, since the bulk of the remaining population (21.5% of the total) were foreign-born, not native Americans. Only in Texas did those of Deep South birth fall to 60 per cent; even so they formed a firm majority of the whole (*Population*, 1864: 10, 56, 76, 196, 272, 453, 490). Southernism did not depend upon an ethnic, or a religious, uniformity; but it flourished amidst a uniformity in ethnic mix and in religious inclinations that was unusual by the standards of much of mid nineteenth-century America.

II

An historian of the South has recently commented upon the antebellum period: 'the democratic impulse was limited. It never threatened the unequal distribution of property, never concerned itself with the problems of the poor and dispossessed, and never addressed itself to racial, class, or sexual discrimination' (Newby 1978: 158). We must not expect too much of the mid nineteenth century. Democracy as then defined did not imply the redistribution of wealth, or the banishment of civil inequalities existing between blacks and whites and men and women. Universal white manhood suffrage and representative government together were objectives thought to be largely unattainable – as they were indeed unattained – in contemporary Britain and Europe. And democratic practice in America worked to advance the white male citizens' rights to property, to protection from government oppression and private molestation or assault, to 'liberty' generally conceived, and to such procedural guarantees as voting and jury trial. Government interference and imposition were viewed as the legacy of monarchical absolutism brought on by tax-gathering, war-mongering sovereigns and having the effect of constricting individuals' enterprise and endeavour (Temperley 1977). Nineteenth-century liberalism was founded upon the assumption that state power was tyrannous, always potentially, usually in practice. Even when Southerners exercised state power, they did so, therefore, in indirect ways. States urged the federal government to dispossess the Indians and pass on Indian lands; but the lands were quickly privatized. Governments' promotion of railway building was rarely done by direct ownership of companies, and often done through local (that is, very devolved) bond issuing and not by state investment. Educational provision was left, in most of the Deep South, to county or lower level initiative. And even such emergency safeguards of white supremacy as the state militias were poorly organized, scarcely trained and left largely in their infrequently mustered members' hands. The very localism and inactivity of state governments which would today be so deplored by liberal opinion provided evidence in the mid nineteenth century of the extent and strength of Southerners' independence and liberty.

The doctrine of governmental *laissez-faire,* as it was interpreted by Southerners, was vital in the secession crisis. First, as has been strongly urged by Professors Cooper and Thornton, the critical battle-cry of 1860–61 was the defence of Southern liberties, against Northern interference with slavery extension; that slogan echoed the clichés of political rhetoric during the explosion of party politics from the 1820s (Cooper 1978; Thornton 1978). But, more than that, governmental *laissez-faire* had long permitted Southerners to co-exist. Unobtrusive state and county administration allowed cultural differences to persist, communities to enjoy local rights and individualism (in a Tocquevillian not modern, exhibitionist sense) to flourish. State and county governments did not – despite much pressure to do so – enforce particular codes or modes of conduct; nor did they succour privileged, office-bearing elites. This very looseness of institutional bonding, with an extensive devolution of government initiative and administration as its corollary, served to reinforce Southern loyalty. What was one cause – the protection of slavery – was also many causes – the safeguarding of an unregimented white society that declined to impose uniform customs and culture. Diversity offered strength. The South of the commercial towns – Atlanta, Jackson, Richmond, Vicksburg – resisted the Yankees as doggedly as did the South of the plantation belt. Yeoman farmers and men from the mountains and the piney woods accepted, if they did not embrace, the Confederate cause.

To explain that phenomenon, though, we have to go beyond that point. What has been suggested here is that the social character of the antebellum South reveals additional reasons for the power and endurance of the Confederacy's appeal. A shared quest for cotton lands and a shared participation in the growing and marketing of cotton; a shared racial identity and pride in a heroic past; a shared materialism predicated upon physical mobility; a common reluctance to invoke state power for social or policing purposes; a shared round of social rituals and concentration on the family as a primary human institution; and a drive for respectability that cut across divisions created by wealth and birth: these were the social bonds that drew Southerners together despite their geographical separation and differences in wealth and habitat. When we add the moral certainties and energies which evangelical religion implanted in so many Southerners' hearts and minds, we may begin to understand more fully why Southernism and the Confederacy aroused such enthusiasm and commitment in the 1850s and early 1860s, even if we may neither like nor respect the 'Lost Cause'.

MAPS

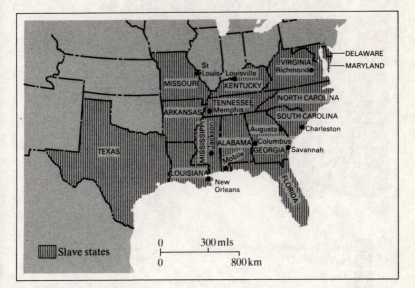

MAP 1. The South in 1860.

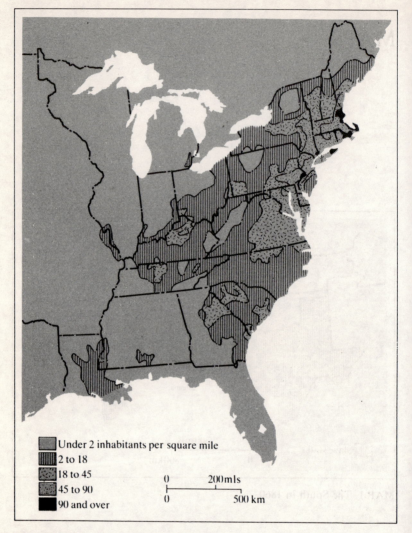

MAP 2(a). Density of population in 1810.

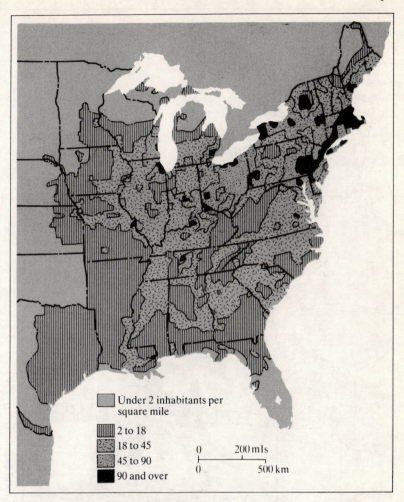

Legend:
- Under 2 inhabitants per square mile
- 2 to 18
- 18 to 45
- 45 to 90
- 90 and over

0   200 mls
0   500 km

MAP 2(b). Density of population in 1860.

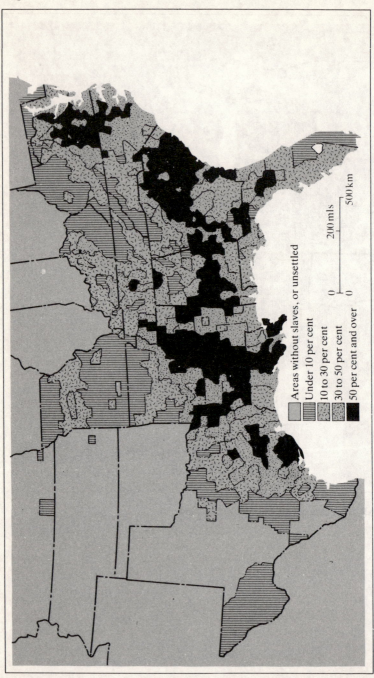

MAP 3. Slaves as a percentage of total population in 1860.

Areas without slaves, or unsettled

Under 10 per cent

10 to 30 per cent

30 to 50 per cent

50 per cent and over

200 mls

500 km

0

0

BIBLIOGRAPHY

The following is a guide to the references in the text. It is far from being a comprehensive bibliography for the study of the mid nineteenth-century South. The date of publication listed is that of the edition actually referred to.

MANUSCRIPT COLLECTIONS AND GOVERNMENT PUBLICATIONS

In writing a book of a general character, the research in original sources is necessarily selective. The following helped in shaping the arguments advanced in this book.

A. MISSISSIPPI

Law reports

Howard, Volney E., 1839, *Reports of Cases Argued and Determined in the High Court of Errors and Appeals of the State of Mississippi.* 3 vols, Philadelphia.

George, James Z., 1857, *Reports of Cases Argued and Determined in the High Court of Errors and Appeals for the State of Mississippi.* Vol. XXX, Philadelphia.

Mississippi State Cases: Being Criminal Cases Decided in the High Court of Errors and Appeals, 1818–1872. 2 vols, Jackson, Miss., 1872.

Government records

Petitions and resolutions in files R.G. 47 Legislature vols 17–23, 27 (1819–1860), Mississippi Department of Archives and History.

Newspapers

Aberdeen: *Aberdeen Whig; Mississippi Advertiser; Monroe Democrat; Weekly Independent.*

Monticello: *Pearl River Banner*
Natchez: *Mississippi Free Trader* (weekly edn)
Paulding: *True Democrat*
Ripley: *Ripley Advertiser; Ripley Transcript.*

Private papers in Mississippi Department of Archives and History
Fox (Tryphenia Holder) Collection.
Isham R. Howze's Book in Howze (Isham Robertson) and Family Papers.
Copies of Letters from William Summer of Pomaria

B. GEORGIA

Law codes and reports
Clark, R. H., Cobb, T. R. R., and Irwin, D., 1861, *The Code of the State of Georgia.* Atlanta, Ga.
Cobb, Howell, 1859, *A Compilation of the General and Public Statutes of the State of Georgia.* New York.
Reports of Cases in Law and Equity, Argued and Determined in the Supreme Court of the State of Georgia. Vols X–XII. Athens, Ga. 1853.

Government records
Journal of the House of Representatives of the State of Georgia, for the years 1799–1822, 1853–60.
Journal of the Senate of the State of Georgia, for the years 1799–1822, 1853–60.
Georgia. Board of Corrections, Inmate Administration Division. Central Register of Convicts (1817–28 examined). Georgia Department of Archives and History.
Georgia Governors' Papers. Boxes 44, 49, 49a, 50, 54, 55. Telamon Cuyler Collection. Special Collections Division, University of Georgia Libraries.

Newspaper
Columbus: *The Daily Sun.*

Private papers
Robert Battey Family Papers. Special Collections department, Robert W. Woodruff Library, Emory University.
Champion Family Papers. Special Collections Division, University of Georgia Libraries.
James Rhinds Correspondence, and Rhinds–Stokes–Gardner Letters in Rhinds–Stokes–Gardner Collection. Special Collections Division, University of Georgia Libraries.

C. MISCELLANEOUS

Law codes and reports
The Code of Virginia. Second Edition. Including Legislation to the Year 1860. Richmond, 1860.

North Carolina Reports, vols 18–26 (1834–44).
Johnston County North Carolina County Court Minutes 1827 thru 1830, Durham, N.C., 1981.

Newspaper:
Charleston: *Charleston Daily Courier.*

Private papers in Southern Historical Collection (University of North Carolina, Chapel Hill)
Diary of George W. Jeffreys. William B. Williamson papers.
Diary of Mrs Lucilla McCorkle. McCorkle papers.
Sermons (1847–1911). McCorkle papers.
Diary of James R. Stringfield. Stringfield family papers.
John W. M. Williams papers.

Population of the United States in 1860; Compiled from the Original Returns of the Eighth Census. Washington, D.C. 1864.
Statistics of the United States (Including Mortality, Property, etc.) in 1860; Compiled from the Original Returns and Being the Final Exhibit of the Eighth Census. Washington, D.C., 1866.

BOOKS, ARTICLES AND DISSERTATIONS

Abernethy, Thomas P., 1961. *The South in the New Nation, 1789–1819* n.p.
Affleck, Thomas, 1856. *Affleck's Southern Rural Almanac and Plantation and Garden Calendar, for 1856.* New Orleans.
Allman, John M., II, 1979. 'Yeoman regions in the antebellum Deep South: settlement and economy in Northern Alabama, 1815–1860' (unpublished Ph.D. dissertation, University of Maryland).
American Guide Series: 1939. *Tennessee.* New York; 1940. *Maryland.* New York; 1941. *Alabama.* New York; 1941. *Missouri.* New York; 1941. *Louisiana.* New York; 1954. *Kentucky.* New York.
Amos, Harriet E., 1981. ' "City Belles": Images and realities, of the lives of white women in antebellum Mobile', *The Alabama Review,* XXXIV, 3–19.
Anderson, Michael, 1980. *Approaches to the History of the Western Family 1500–1914.* London.
Andrews, Wayne, 1960. *Architecture in America. A Photographic History from the Colonial Period to the Present.* London.
Baldwin, Joseph G., 1853. *The Flush Times of Alabama and Mississippi.* New York.
Ball, Charles, 1970. *Fifty Years in Chains.* New York.
Barney, William L., 1974. *Secessionist Impulse. Alabama and Mississippi in 1860.* Princeton.
Barney, William L., 1981. 'The ambivalence of change: from Old South to New in the Alabama Black Belt, 1850–1870' in Walter J. Fraser, Jr. and Winifred B. Moore, Jr., *From the Old South to the New. Essays on the Transitional South.* Westport, Conn.

Barney, William L., 1982. 'Towards the Civil War: The Dynamics of Change in a Black Belt County' in Orville V. Burton and Robert C. McMath, Jr. (eds), *Class, Conflict, and Consensus.* Westport, Conn.

Bateman, Fred and Weiss, Thomas, 1981. *A Deplorable Scarcity. The Failure of Industrialization in the Slave Economy.* Chapel Hill.

Beeman, Richard R., and Isaac, Rhys, 1980. 'Cultural Conflict and Social Change in the Revolutionary South: Lunenburg County, Virginia', *Journal of Southern History,* XLVI, 525–50.

Belden, Henry M. and Hudson, Arthur P. (eds), 1952. *The Frank C. Brown Collection of North Carolina Folklore.* Durham, N.C.

Berkhofer, Robert F., Jr., 1978. *The White Man's Indian. Images of the American Indian from Columbus to the Present.* New York.

Berlin, Ira, 1974. *Slaves Without Masters. The Free Negro in the Antebellum South.* New York.

Berlin, Ira, 1980. 'The Structure of the Free Negro Caste in the Antebellum United States' in Edward Magdol and Jon L. Wakelyn (eds), *The Southern Common People. Studies in Nineteenth-Century Social History.* Westport, Conn.

Blake, Russell L., 1978. 'Ties of intimacy: social values and personal relationships of antebellum slaveholders' (unpublished Ph.D. dissertation, University of Michigan).

Blumin, Stuart M., 1976. *The Urban Threshold: Growth and Change in a Nineteenth Century Community.* Chicago.

Bodenhamer, David J., 1981. 'Law and Disorder in the Old South: The Situation in Georgia, 1830–1860' in Walter J. Fraser, Jr. and Winfred B. Moore, Jr. (eds), *From the Old South to the New. Essays on the Transitional South.* Westport, Conn.

Bodenhamer, David J., 1982. 'The Efficiency of Criminal Justice in the Antebellum South', *Criminal Justice History,* III, 81–95.

Bodichon, Barbara L. S., 1972. *An American Diary 1857–8,* Joseph W. Reed, Jr. (ed.). London.

Boman, Martha, 1953. 'A City of the Old South: Jackson, Mississippi, 1850–1860', *Journal of Mississippi History,* XV, 1–32.

Boney, F. N., 1974. 'Nathaniel Francis, Representative Antebellum Southerner', *Proceedings of the American Philosophical Society,* 118 (1974), 449–58.

Bonner, James C., 1971. 'The Georgia Penitentiary at Milledgeville, 1817–1874', *Georgia Historical Quarterly,* LV, 303–28.

Boorstin, Daniel J., 1965. *The Americans. The National Experience.* New York.

Botkin, B. A., 1935. 'Folk and Folklore' in W. T. Couch (ed.), *Culture in the South.* Chapel Hill.

Bowman, Shearer D., 1980. 'Antebellum Planters and Vormärz Junkers in Comparative Perspective', *American Historical Review,* **85,** 779–808.

Boyd, Julian P., 1934. 'State and Local Historical Societies in the United States', *American Historical Review,* XL, 10–37.

Breazeale, J. W. M., 1842. *Life As It Is: or Matters and Things in General.* Knoxville, Tenn.

Breen, T. H. (ed.), 1976. *Shaping Southern Society. The Colonial Experience.* New York.

Breen, T. H., 1980. *Puritans and Adventurers. Change and Persistence in Early America.* New York.

Brown, Robert E. and Katherine, B., 1964. *Virginia 1705–1786: Democracy or Aristocracy?* East Lancing, Mich.

Brown, Samuel R., 1817. *The Western Gazetteer; or Emigrant's Directory.* Auburn, N.Y.

Bruce, Dickson D., Jr., 1974. *And They All Sang Hallelujah. Plain-Folk Camp-Meeting Religion, 1800–1845.* Knoxville, Tenn.

Bruce, Dickson D., Jr., 1979. *Violence and culture in the Antebellum South.* Austin.

Brubacher, John S. and Rudy, Willis, 1958. *Higher Education in Transition. An American History: 1636–1956.* New York.

Bureau of the Census, 1960. *Historical Statistics of the United States. Colonial Times to 1957.* Washington, D.C.

A History of the Burns' Festival in Savannah, with the Speeches of all the Distinguished Men, made throughout the Union, on the same day. Savannah, 1859.

Cairnes, John E., 1863. *The Slave Power. Its Character, Career and Probable Designs.* London.

Calhoun, Arthur W., 1917. *A Social History of the American Family. From Colonial Times to the Present.* New York.

Callcott, George H., 1970. *History in the United States 1800–1860. Its Practice and Purpose.* Baltimore.

Campbell, Randolph B. and Lowe, Richard G., 1977. *Wealth and Power in Antebellum Texas.* College Station.

Carter, Samuel, III, 1976. *Cherokee Sunset. A Nation Betrayed. A Narrative of Travail and Triumph, Persecution and Exile.* New York.

Cash, W. J., 1954. *The Mind of the South.* New York.

Cassels, Samuel J., 1838. *Providence and Other Poems.* Macon, Ga.

Charlton, Robert M., 1845. *The Romance of Life, A Historical Lecture, Delivered before the Georgia Historical Society, on the 14th January, 1845.* Savannah.

Chester, Samuel H., 1927. *Pioneer Days in Arkansas.* Richmond, Va.

Claiborne, J. F. H., 1906. 'A Trip Through the Piney Woods', *Publications of the Mississippi Historical Society,* IX 487–538.

Clark, Blanche H., 1971. *The Tennessee Yeomen 1840–1860.* New York.

Clayton, T. R., 1982. 'The North Carolina Council, 1663–1753: The theory and practice of royal government in the colonial south' (unpublished Ph.D. dissertation, Cambridge University).

Clinton, Catherine, 1982. *The Plantation Mistress. Woman's World in the Old South.* New York.

Coleman, Kenneth, 1977. 'The Expanding Frontier Economy 1782–1820' in Kenneth Coleman (ed.), *A History of Georgia.* Athens, Ga.

Collins, Bruce, 1981. *The Origins of America's Civil War.* London.

Cooper, David, 1845. *First Published Annual Report of the Resident Physician of the Lunatic, Idiot and Epileptic Asylum of the State of Georgia.* Milledgeville, Ga.

Cooper, William J., 1978. *The South and the Politics of Slavery, 1828–1856.* Baton Rouge.

Cott, Nancy F., 1977. *The Bonds of Womanhood. 'Woman's Sphere' in New England, 1780–1835.* New Haven.

Cott, Nancy F., 1978. 'Passionlessness: An Interpretation of Victorian Sexual Ideology, 1790–1850', *Signs,* **4**, 219–36.

Coulter, E. Merton, 1925. 'A Georgia Educational Movement during the Eighteen Hundred and Fifties', *Georgia Historical Quarterly*, IX, 1–33.

Coulter, E. Merton, 1928. *College Life in the Old South*, New York.

Coulter, E. Merton, 1964. *Joseph Vallence Bevan, Georgia's First Official Historian*. Athens, Ga.

Cox, John H. (ed.), 1925. *Folk-Songs of the South*. Cambridge, Mass.

Craven, Avery O., 1953. *The Growth of Southern Nationalism, 1848–1861*. n.p.

Crocker, Leslie F., 1971. 'Domestic Architecture of the Middle South 1795–1865' (unpublished Ph.D. dissertation, University of Missouri, Columbia).

Crocker, Mary, 1973. *Historic Architecture in Mississippi*. Jackson.

Cunliffe, Marcus, 1969. *Soldiers and Civilians. The Martial Spirit in America 1775–1865*. London.

Davis, David B., 1975. *The Problem of Slavery in the Age of Revolution, 1770–1823*. Ithaca.

Davis, Kenneth P., 1979. 'Chaos in the Indian Country: The Cherokee Nation, 1828–35' in Duane H. King (ed.), *The Cherokee Nation. A Troubled History*. Knoxville, Tenn.

Dawson, Jan C., 1978. 'The Puritan and the Cavalier: The South's Perception of Contrasting Traditions', *Journal of Southern History*, XLIV, 597–614.

De Bow, J. D. B., 1853. *The Industrial Resources, etc., of the Southern and Western States*. New Orleans.

De Bow, J. D. B., 1854. *Statistical View of the United States*. Washington, D.C.

Degler, Carl N., 1974. *The Other South. Southern Dissenters in the Nineteenth Century*. New York.

Degler, Carl N., 1977. *Place Over Time. The Continuity of Southern Distinctiveness*. Baton Rouge.

Degler, Carl N., 1980. *At Odds. Women and the Family in America from the Revolution to the Present*. New York.

Downing, A. J., 1969. *The Architecture of Country Houses*. New York.

Drayton, John, 1802. *A View of South Carolina. As Respects Her Natural and Civil Concerns*. Charleston, S.C.

Dyer, Thomas (ed.), 1982. *To Raise Myself A Little. The Diaries and Letters of Jennie, A Georgia Teacher, 1851–1886*. Athens, Ga.

Eaton, Clement, 1961. *The Growth of Southern Civilization 1790–1860*. New York.

Eaton, Clement, 1977. *Jefferson Davis*. New York.

Elkins, Stanley, 1959. *Slavery. A Problem in American Institutional and Intellectual Life*. Chicago.

Elliott, Rt. Rev. Stephen, Jr., 1844. *A High Civilization. The Moral Duty of Georgians. A Discourse Delivered before the Georgia Historical Society, on the Occasion of its Fifth Anniversary, on Monday, 12th February, 1844*. Savannah.

Evitts, William J., 1974. *A Matter of Allegiances. Maryland From 1850 to 1861*. Baltimore.

Faust, Drew G., 1977. *A Sacred Circle. The Dilemma of the Intellectual in the Old South, 1840–1860*. Baltimore.

Faust, Drew G., 1979. 'The Rhetoric and Ritual of Agriculture in Antebellum South Carolina', *Journal of Southern History*, XLV, 541–68.

Faust, Drew G., 1982. *James Henry Hammond and the Old South. A Design for Mastery*. Baton Rouge.

Fehrenbach, T. B., 1968. *Lone Star. A History of Texas and the Texans.* New York.

Fitzhugh, George, 1960. *Cannibals All! or Slaves without Masters.* Cambridge, Mass.

Fleming, Robert (ed.), 1847. *The Georgia Pulpit: or Ministers' Yearly Offering. Containing Sermons and Essays from Georgia Baptist Ministers.* Richmond, Va.

Fogel, Robert W. and Engerman, Stanley L., 1974. *Time on the Cross.* London.

Folmsbee, Stanley J., Corlew, Robert E. and Mitchell, Enoch L., 1969. *Tennessee. A Short History.* Knoxville.

Foner, Eric, 1970. *Free Soil, Free Labor, Free Men. The Ideology of the Republican Party before the Civil War.* New York.

Formwalt, Lee W., 1981. 'Antebellum Planter Persistence: Southwest Georgia – A Case Study', *Plantation Society,* **1,** 410–19.

Fox-Genovese, Elizabeth and Genovese, Eugene D., 1983. *Fruits of Merchant Capital, Slavery and Bourgeois Property in the Rise and Expansion of Capitalism.* Oxford.

Fredrickson, George M., 1971. *The Black Image in the White Mind. The Debate on Afro-American Character and Destiny, 1817–1914.* New York.

Fredrickson, George M., 1981. *White Supremacy. A Comparative Study in American and South African History.* Oxford.

Freehling, Alison G., 1982. *Drift Toward Dissolution. The Virginia Slavery Debate of 1831–1832.* Baton Rouge.

Gash, Norman, 1976. *Peel.* London.

Genovese, Eugene D., 1965. *The Political Economy of Slavery.* New York.

Genovese, Eugene D., 1969. *The World the Slaveholders Made. Two Essays in Interpretation.* London.

Genovese, Eugene D., 1975. *Roll, Jordan, Roll. The World the Slaves Made.* London.

Glassie, Henry, 1971. *Pattern in the Material Folk Culture of the Eastern United States.* Philadelphia.

Goffman, Erving, 1971. *The Presentation of Self in Everyday Life.* Harmondsworth, Middx.

Goldfield, David R., 1982. *Cotton Fields and Skyscrapers. Southern City and Region, 1607–1980.* Baton Rouge.

Goodrich, Carter, 1960. *Government Promotion of American Canals and Railroads, 1800–1890.* New York.

Gray, Lewis C., 1933. *History of Agriculture in the Southern United States to 1860.* Washington, D.C.

Greven, Philip, Jr., 1972. 'The average size of families and households in the Province of Massachusetts in 1764 and in the United States in 1790: an overview' in Peter Laslett with Richard Wall, *Household and Family in past time.* Cambridge.

Hagler, D. Harland, 1980. 'The Ideal Woman in the Antebellum South: Lady or Farmwife?', *Journal of Southern History* XLVI, 405–18.

Hahn, Steven H., 1979. 'The roots of Southern Populism: yeomen farmers and the transformation of Georgia's Upper Piedmont, 1850–1890' (unpublished Ph.D. dissertation, Yale University).

Hahn, Steven H., 1982. 'The Yeomanry of the Nonplantation South: Upper Piedmont Georgia, 1850–1860' in Orville V. Burton and Robert C. McMath, Jr. (eds), *Class, Conflict, and Consensus.* Westport, Conn.

Hamlin, Talbot, 1944. *Greek Revival Architecture in America*. New York.

Hammond, Bray, 1957. *Banks and Politics in America from the Revolution to the Civil War*. Princeton.

Harris, J. William, 1981. 'A slaveholding republic: Augusta's hinterlands before the Civil War' (unpublished Ph.D. dissertation, Johns Hopkins University).

Haunton, Richard H., 1980. 'Law and Order in Savannah, 1850–1860' in Edward Magdol and Jon L. Wakelyn (eds), *The Southern Common People. Studies in Nineteenth-Century Social History*. Westport, Conn.

Hay, Douglas *et al.*, 1975. *Albion's Fatal Tree. Crime and Society in Eighteenth-Century England*. London.

Heath, Milton S., 1954. *Constructive Liberalism. The Role of the State in Economic Development in Georgia to 1860*. Cambridge, Mass.

Heller, Peter L., Quesach, Gustavo M., Harvey, David L. and Warner, Lyle G., 1981. 'Familism in Rural and Urban America: Critique and Reconceptualization of a Construct', *Rural Sociology,* **46,** 446–64.

Henretta, James A., 1973. *The Evolution of American Society, 1700–1815*. Lexington, Mass.

Herman, Bernard L. and Orr, David G., 1975. 'Pear Valley *et al.*: An Excursion into the Analysis of Southern Vernacular Architecture', *Southern Folklore Quarterly,* **39,** 307–27.

Herndon, G. Melvin, 1981. 'The Significance of the Forest to the Tobacco Plantation Economy in Antebellum Virginia', *Plantation Studies,* **1,** 430–9.

Hindus, Michael S., 1980. *Prison and Plantation: Crime, Justice, and Authority in Massachusetts and South Carolina, 1767–1878*. Chapel Hill.

Hollander, A. N. J., 1935. 'The Tradition of the "Poor Whites"' in W. T. Couch (ed.), *Culture in the South*. Chapel Hill.

Hudson, Arthur P., 1928. *Specimens of Mississippi Folk-Lore*. Ann Arbor, Mich.

Hudson, Arthur P., 1935. 'Folk Songs of the Southern Whites', in W. T. Couch (ed.), *Culture in the South*. Chapel Hill.

Huffman, Frank J., Jr., 1980. 'Town and Country in the South, 1850–1880: A Comparison of Urban and Rural Social Structures' in Edward Magdol and Jon L. Wakelyn (eds), *The Southern Common People. Studies in Nineteenth-Century Social History*. Westport, Conn.

Hundley, Daniel R., 1979. *Social Relations in our Southern States*. Baton Rouge.

Isaac, Rhys, 1982. *The Transformation of Virginia 1740–1790*. Chapel Hill.

Jackson, George P., 1933. *White Spirituals in the Southern Uplands*. Hatboro, Penn.

Jahoda, Gloria, 1975. *The Trail of Tears*. New York.

Jenkins, William S., 1960. *Pro-Slavery Thought in the Old South*. Chapel Hill.

Johnson, Amanda, 1938. *Georgia As Colony and State, 1733–1937*. Athens, Ga.

Johnson, Dudley S., 1969. 'William Harris Garland: Mechanic of the Old South', *Georgia Historical Quarterly,* LIII, 41–56.

Johnson, Guion G., 1937. *Ante-Bellum North Carolina. A Social History*. Chapel Hill.

Johnson, Michael P., 1977. *Toward A Patriarchal Republic: the Secession of Georgia*. Baton Rouge.

Johnson, Michael P., 1980. 'Planters and Patriarchy: Charleston, 1800–1860', *Journal of Southern History,* XLVI, 45–72.

Jones, Alice H., 1980. *Wealth of a Nation To Be. The American Colonies on the Eve of the Revolution*. New York.

Jordan, Terry G., 1979. 'The Imprint of the Upper and Lower South on Mid-Nineteenth-Century Texas' in David Ward (ed.), *Geographic Perspectives on America's Past*. New York.

Kennedy, John P., 1832. *Swallow Barn, or A Sojourn in the Old Dominion*. Philadelphia.

Kettell, Thomas P., 1860. *Southern Wealth and Northern Profits*. New York.

King, Hon. Mitchell, 1843. *A Discourse on the Qualifications and Duties of an Historian; Delivered Before the Georgia Historical Society, On the Occasion of its Fourth Anniversary, On Monday 13th February, 1843*. Savannah, Ga.

Klein, Rachel, 1979. 'The rise of the planters in the South Carolina backcountry, 1767–1808' (unpublished Ph.D. dissertation, Yale University).

Lancaster, Clay, 1961. *Ante Bellum Houses of the Bluegrass. The Development of Residential Architecture in Fayette County, Kentucky*. Lexington, Ky.

Land, Aubrey C., 1965. 'Economic Base and Social Structure: The Northern Chesapeake in the Eighteenth Century', *Journal of Economic History*, **25**, 639–54.

Lanman, Charles, 1849. *Letters from the Allegheny Mountains*. New York.

Laski, Harold J. 1949. *The American Democracy*. London.

Lee, Susan P. and Passell, Peter, 1979. *A New Economic View of American History*. New York.

Lewis, Jan, 1983. *The Pursuit of Happiness. Family and Values in Jefferson's Virginia*. Cambridge.

Livermore, Thomas L., 1900. *Numbers and Losses in the Civil War in America: 1861–65*. Boston.

Logan, John H., 1859. *A History of the Upper Country of South Carolina from the Earliest Periods to the Close of the War of Independence*. Vol. I. Columbia.

A Native Georgian (Augustus Baldwin Longstreet), 1835. *Georgia Scenes, Characters, Incidents, etc. in the First Half Century of the Republic*. Augusta, Ga.

Lord, Walter (ed.), 1954. *The Fremantle Diary. Being the Journal of Lieutenant Colonel Arthur James Lyon Fremantle, Coldstream Guards, on his Three Months in the Southern States*. Boston.

Lounsbury, Carl, 1977. 'The Development of Domestic Architecture in the Albemarle Region', *North Carolina Historical Review*, LIV, 17–48.

Lucas, Aubrey K., 1973. 'Education in Mississippi from Statehood to Civil War' in Richard A. McLemore (ed.), *A History of Mississippi*. Vol. I. Hattiesburg.

Luraghi, Raimondo, 1978. *The Rise and Fall of the Plantation South*. New York.

MacLeod, Duncan J., 1974. *Slavery, Race and the American Revolution*. Cambridge.

McCardell, John, 1979. *The Idea of a Southern Nation. Southern Nationalists and Southern Nationalism, 1830–1860*. New York.

McCoy, Drew R., 1980. *The Elusive Republic. Political Economy in Jeffersonian America*. Chapel Hill.

McDonald, Forrest and McWhiney, Grady, 1980. 'The South from Self-Sufficiency to Peonage: An Interpretation', *American Historical Review*, **85**, 1095–1118.

McLaurin, Melton A., 1982. 'The Nineteenth-Century North Carolina State Fair as a Social Institution', *North Carolina Historical Review*, LIX, 213–29.

McLoughlin, William G., 1978. *Revivals, Awakenings and Reform*. Chicago.

McPherson, James M., 1983. 'Antebellum Southern Exceptionalism: A New Look at an Old Question', *Civil War History,* **29** (1983), 230–44.

McWhiney, Grady, 1978. 'The Revolution in Nineteenth-Century Alabama Agriculture', *The Alabama Review,* XXXI, 3–32.

Mahon, John K., 1983. *History of the Militia and the National Guard.* New York.

Main, Jackson T., 1954. 'The One Hundred', *William and Mary Quarterly,* 3rd series, XIV, 354–84.

Main, Jackson T., 1965. *The Social Structure of Revolutionary America.* Princeton.

Manring, Randall C., 1978. 'Population and Agriculture in Nodaway County, Missouri, 1850 to 1860', *Missouri Historical Review,* LXXII, 388–411.

Marks, Bayly Ellen, 1979. 'Economics and society in a staple plantation system: St. Marys County, Maryland 1790–1840' (unpublished Ph.D. dissertation, University of Maryland).

Marx, Karl and Engels, Frederick, 1961, *The Civil War in the United States,* New York.

Mathews, Donald G., 1977. *Religion in the Old South.* Chicago.

Matthias, Virginia P., 1945. 'Natchez-Under-the-Hill', *Journal of Mississippi History,* VII, 201–21.

May, Henry F. 1976. *The Enlightenment in America.* New York.

Menn, Joseph K., 1964. 'The large slaveholders of the Deep South, 1860' (unpublished Ph.D. dissertation, University of Texas).

Merrington, John, 1975. 'Town and Country in the Transition to Capitalism', *New Left Review.* **93,** 71–92.

Milden, James W., 1974. 'The sacred sanctuary: family life in nineteenth-century America' (unpublished Ph.D. dissertation, University of Maryland).

Mills, Robert, 1826. *Statistics of South Carolina, Including A View of its Natural, Civil, and Military History, General and Particular.* Charleston, S.C.

Mingay, G. E., 1976. *The Gentry. The Rise and Fall of a Ruling Class.* London.

Moneyhon, Carl H., 1981. 'Economic Democracy in Antebellum Arkansas, Phillips County, 1850–1860', *Arkansas Historical Quarterly,* XL, 154–72.

Moore, Barrington, Jr., 1966. *Social Origins of Dictatorship and Democracy. Lord and Peasant in the Making of the Modern World.* Boston.

Moore, John H., 1958. *Agriculture in Ante-Bellum Mississippi.* New York.

Moore, John H., 1982. 'Local and State Governments of Antebellum Mississippi', *Journal of Mississippi History,* XLIV, 104–34.

Morison, Samuel E., Commager, Henry S. and Leuchtenburg, William E., 1977. *A Concise History of the American Republic.* New York.

Mount, Ferdinand, 1982. *The Subversive Family. An Alternative History of Love and Marriage.* London.

Mumford, Lewis, 1924. *Sticks and Stones. A Study of American Architecture and Civilization.* New York.

Myers, Robert M. (ed.), 1972. *The Children of Pride: A True Story of Georgia and the Civil War.* New Haven.

Newby, I. A., 1978. *The South. A History.* n.p.

'Ebenezer Newton's 1818 Diary' in *Georgia Historical Quarterly,* LIII (1969), 205–19.

Nichols, Frederick D., 1976. *The Architecture of Georgia.* Savannah.

North, Douglass C., 1966. *The Economic Growth of the United States 1790–1860.* New York.

Norwood, Martha F., 1978. *The Indian Springs Hotel as a Nineteenth-Century Watering Place.* Atlanta, Ga.

Nossiter, T. J., 1975. *Influence, Opinion and Political Idioms in Reformed England.* Hassocks, Sussex.

Nye, Russel B., 1974. *Society and Culture in America, 1830–1860.* New York.

Oakes, James, 1982. *The Ruling Race. A History of American Slaveholders.* New York.

O'Brien, Gail W., 1977. 'Power and Influence in Mecklenburg County, 1850–1860', *North Carolina Historical Review,* LIV, 120–44.

Olmsted, Frederick L., 1971. *The Cotton Kingdom* (ed. David F. Hawke). Indianapolis.

Olsen, Otto H., 1972. 'Historians and the Extent of Slave Ownership in the Southern United States'. *Civil War History,* XVIII, 101–16.

Osterweis, Rollin G., 1949. *Romanticism and Nationalism in the Old South.* New Haven.

Otto, John S., 1980. 'Slavery in the Mountains: Yell County, Arkansas 1840–1860', *Arkansas Historical Quarterly,* XXXIX, 35–52.

Otto, John S. and Bank, Ben W., 1982. 'The Banks Family of Yell County, Arkansas: A "Plain Folk" Family of the Highland South', *Arkansas Historical Quarterly,* XLI, 146–67.

Owsley, Frank L., 1949. *Plain Folk of the Old South.* Baton Rouge.

Paine, Lewis W., 1852. *Six Years in a Georgia Prison.* Boston.

Parish, Peter J., 1979. *Slavery: the many faces of a Southern institution.* British Association for American Studies.

Pearce, Roy H., 1965. *Savagism and Civilization. A Study of the Indian and the American Mind.* Baltimore.

Penick, James L., Jr., 1981. *The Great Western Land Pirate. John A. Murrell in Legend and History.* Columbia, Mo.

Perdue, Theda, 1979. 'Cherokee Planters: the Development of Plantation Slavery before Removal', in Duane H. King (ed.), *The Cherokee Nation. A Troubled History.* Knoxville, Tenn.

Perkins, Edwin J., 1980. *The Economy of Colonial America.* New York.

Persico, V. Richard, Jr., 1979. 'Early Nineteenth-Century Cherokee Political Organization', in Duane H. King, *The Cherokee Nation. A Troubled History.* Knoxville, Tenn.

Pessen, Edward, 1980. 'How Different from Each Other were the Antebellum North and South?', *American Historical Review,* **85,** 1119–49.

Peterson, Merrill D., 1977. *The Portable Thomas Jefferson.* Harmondsworth.

Phifer, Edward W., Jr., 1979. *Burke County. A History.* Raleigh, N.C.

Phillips, Ulrich B., 1913. 'The Correspondence of Robert Toombs, Alexander H. Stephens, and Howell Cobb', *Annual Report of the American Historical Association for the Year 1911,* vol. II.

Pickett, Albert James, 1851. *History of Alabama, and Incidentally of Georgia and Mississippi, From the Earliest Period.* 2 vols. Charleston, S.C.

Pillar, James J., 1973. 'Religious and Cultural Life 1817–1860', in Richard A. McLemore (ed.), *A History of Mississippi.* Vol. I. Hattiesburg.

Potter, J., 1965. 'The Growth of Population in America, 1700–1860' in D. V. Glass and D. E. C. Eversley, *Population in History; Essays in Historical Demography.* London.

Potter, David M., 1954. *People of Plenty. Economic Abundance and the American Character*. Chicago.

A Late Staff Officer (Woodburne Potter), 1836. *The War in Florida: Being an Exposition of Its Causes, and an Accurate History of the Campaigns of Generals Clinch, Gaines and Scott*. Baltimore.

Ramsey, J. G. M., 1853. *The Annals of Tennessee to the End of the Eighteenth Century*. Charleston, S.C.

Randolph, Vance, 1947. *Ozark Superstitions*. New York.

Randolph, Vance, 1976. *Pissing in the Snow and Other Ozark Folktales*. Urbana, Ill.

Reese, Trevor R. (introduction by), 1972. *The Most Delightful Country in the Universe. Promotional Literature of The Colony of Georgia, 1717–1734*. Savannah, Ga.

Reid, John Phillip, 1979. 'A Perilous Rule: the Law of International Homicide', in Duane H. King (ed.), *The Cherokee Indian Nation. A Troubled History*. Knoxville, Tenn.

Remini, Robert, 1981. *Andrew Jackson and the Course of American Freedom, 1822–1832*. New York.

Ridgway, Whitman H., 1979. *Community Leadership in Maryland, 1790–1840. A Comparative Analysis of Power in Society*. Chapel Hill.

Rogin, Michael P., 1976. *Fathers and Children. Andrew Jackson and the Subjugation of the American Indian*. New York.

Rose, Willie Lee, 1976. *A Documentary History of Slavery in North America*. New York.

Rose, Willie Lee, 1982. *Slavery and Freedom*. New York.

Royall, Anne Newport, 1969. *Letters From Alabama 1817–1822*. Intro. by Lucille Griffith. University, Ala.

Russell, John H., 1913. *The Free Negro in Virginia, 1619–1865*. Baltimore.

Scarborough, William K., 1966. *The Overseer. Plantation Management in the Old South*. Baton Rouge.

Scarborough, William K., 1973. 'Heartland of the Cotton Kingdom', in Richard A. McLemore (ed.), *A History of Mississippi*. Vol. I. Hattiesburg.

Schoolcraft, Henry R., 1851. *The American Indians. Their History, Condition and Prospects, from Original Notes and Manuscripts*. Buffalo.

Schultz, Christian, Jr., 1810. *Travels on An Inland Voyage . . . performed in the Years 1807 and 1808; Including a Tour of Nearly Six Thousand Miles*. New York.

Scott, Anne Firor, 1970. *The Southern Lady. From Pedestal to Politics, 1830–1930*. Chicago.

Sellers, Charles, 1966. *James K. Polk. Continentalist 1843–1846*. Princeton.

Sharp, James R., 1970. *The Jacksonians versus the Banks. Politics in the States after the Panic of 1837*. New York.

Sheehan, Bernard W., 1973. *Seeds of Extinction. Jeffersonian Philanthropy and the American Indian*. Chapel Hill.

Shils, Edward, 1981. *Tradition*. Chicago.

Shortridge, James R., 1980. 'The Expansion of the Settlement Frontier in Missouri', *Missouri Historical Review*, LXXV, 64–90.

Shugg, Roger W., 1939. *Origins of Class Struggle in Louisiana*. Baton Rouge.

Simmons, R.C., 1976. *The American Colonies From Settlement to Independence*. Harlow, Essex.

Simms, William Gilmore, 1835. *Border Beagles. A Tale of Mississippi.*

Simms, William G., 1840. *The History of South Carolina. From Its First European Discovery to its Erection into a Republic.* Charleston, S.C.

Simms, William Gilmore, 1964. *The Yemassee. A Romance of Carolina.* New Haven.

Skates, John R., Jr., 1981. 'In Defense of Owsley's Yeomen', in Frank A. Dennis (ed.), *Southern Miscellany: Essays in History in Honor of Glover Moore.* Jackson, Miss.

Slotkin, Richard, 1973. *Regeneration Through Violence. The Mythology of the American Frontier, 1600–1860.* Middleton, Conn.

Smith, Daniel B., 1980. *Inside the Great House. Planter Family Life in Eighteenth-Century Chesapeake Society.* Ithaca.

Smith, Julia F., 1973. *Slavery and Plantation Growth in Ante-bellum Florida 1821–1860.* Gainesville, Fla.

Soltow, Lee, 1975. *Men and Wealth in the United States 1850–1870.* New Haven.

Soltow, Lee, 1980. 'Socioeconomic Classes in South Carolina and Massachusetts in the 1790s and the Observations of John Drayton', *South Carolina Historical Magazine,* **81,** 283–305.

Soltow, Lee, 1981. 'Land Inequality on the Frontier. The Distribution of Land in East Tennessee at the Beginning of the Nineteenth Century', *Social Science History,* **5,** 275–91.

A Southern Country Minister, S.C., 1860. *The Old Pine Farm: or, the Southern Side.* Nashville.

Stampp, Kenneth M., 1964. *The Peculiar Institution. Negro Slavery in the American South.* London.

Stiles, William H., 1856. *An Address, Delivered Before the Georgia Democratic State Convention.* Atlanta.

Stroupe, Henry S., 1975. '"Cite Them Both To Attend the Next Church Conference": Social Control by North Carolina Baptist Churches, 1772–1908', *North Carolina Historical Review,* LII, 156–170.

Sydnor, Charles S., 1948. *The Development of Southern Sectionalism 1819–1848.* n.p.

Takaki, Ronald T., 1971. *A Pro-Slavery Crusade. The Agitation to Reopen the African Slave Trade.* New York.

Takaki, Ronald T., 1980. *Iron Cages. Race and Culture in Nineteenth-Century America.* London.

Taylor, William R., 1961. *Cavalier and Yankee. The Old South and American National Character.* New York.

Temperley, Howard, 1977. 'Capitalism, Slavery and Ideology', *Past and Present.* **75,** 94–118.

Thomas, Emory M., 1979. *The Confederate Nation: 1861–1865.* New York.

Thomas, William, 1966. 'Ante-bellum Macon and Bibb County, Georgia' (unpublished Ph.D. dissertation, University of Georgia).

Thompson, Alan S., 1979. 'Mobile, Alabama, 1850–1861: economic, political, physical, and population characteristics' (unpublished Ph.D. dissertation, University of Alabama).

Thompson, E. Bruce, 1945. 'Reforms in the Penal System of Mississippi, 1820–1850', *Journal of Mississippi History,* VII, 51–74.

Thompson, E. P., 1965. 'Peculiarities of the English' in R. Miliband and J. Saville (eds.), *The Socialist Register.* London.

Thompson, E. P., 1968. *The Making of the English Working Class.* Harmondsworth, Mddx.

Thornton, J. Mills, III, 1978. *Politics and Power in a Slave Society. Alabama, 1800–1860.* Baton Rouge.

Tise, Larry E., 1979. 'The Interregional Appeal of Proslavery Thought: An Ideological Profile of the Antebellum American Clergy', *Plantation Society in the Americas,* **1,** 58–72.

Tucker, George, 1970. *The Valley of the Shenandoah.* Chapel Hill.

Tushnet, Mark, 1981. *The American Law of Slavery 1810–1860. Considerations of Humanity and Interest.* Princeton.

Van Tassel, David D., 1960 *Recording America's Past. An Interpretation of the Development of Historical Studies in America 1607–1884.* Chicago.

Wailes, B. L. C., 1854. *Report on the Agriculture and Geology of Mississippi, Embracing a Sketch of the Social and Natural History of the State.* (Published by Order of the Legislature, Mississippi.)

Walters, Ronald G., 1973. 'The Family and Ante-bellum Reform: An Interpretation', *Societas,* III, 221–32.

Walters, Ronald G., 1976. 'Sexual matters as historical problems: a framework of analysis'. *Societas* VI, 157–75.

Walters, Ronald G., 1980. 'Signs of the Times: Clifford Geertz and Historians', *Social Research,* **47,** 537–56.

Watson, Alan D., 1981. 'Women in Colonial North Carolina: overlooked and underestimated', *North Carolina Historical Review,* LVIII, 1–22.

Watson, Harry L., 1981. *Jacksonian Politics and Community Conflict. The Emergence of the Second American Party System in Cumberland County, North Carolina.* Baton Rouge.

Weaver, Herbert, 1945. *Mississippi Farmers 1850–1860.* Nashville.

Weir, Robert M., 1983. *Colonial South Carolina. A History.* Millwood, N.Y.

Welter, Rush, 1962. *Popular Education and Democratic Thought in America.* New York.

Wiener, Jonathan W., 1978. *Social Origins of the New South. Alabama. 1860–1885.* Baton Rouge.

Wiley, Bell I., 1943. *The Life of Johnny Reb. The Common Soldier of the Confederacy.* Baton Rouge.

Williams, John L., 1837. *The Territory of Florida; or Sketches of the Topography, Civil and Natural History, of the Country, the Climate, and the Indian Tribes, From the First Discovery to the Present Time.* New York.

Williams, T. Harry, 1981. *The History of American Wars From 1745 to 1918.* New York.

Wish, Harvey, 1960. *The American Historian. A Social-Intellectual History of the Writing of the American Past.* New York.

Wooster, Ralph A., 1965. *Politicians, Planters and Plain Folk. Courthouse and Statehouse in the Upper South, 1850–1860.* Knoxville, Tenn.

Woodward, C. Vann (ed.), 1981. *Mary Chestnut's Civil War.* New Haven.

Wooster, Ralph A., 1969. *The People in Power. Courthouse and Statehouse in the Lower South, 1850–1860.* Knoxville, Tenn.

Wright, Gavin, 1978. *The Political Economy of the Cotton South.* New York.

Wyatt-Brown, Bertram, 1972. 'Religion and the Formation of Folk Culture: Poor Whites of the Old South', in Lucius F. Ellsworth (ed.), *The Americanization of the Old South, 1803–1850.*

Wyatt-Brown, Bertram, 1975. 'The Ideal Typology and Ante-Bellum Southern History: A Testing of a New Approach', *Societas,* V, 1–29.

Wyatt-Brown, Bertram, 1982. *Southern Honor. Ethics and Behaviour in the Old South.* New York.

Young, Mary F., 1961. *Redskins, Ruffleshirts and Rednecks. Indian Allotments in Alabama and Mississippi 1830–1860.* Norman, Oklahoma.

Young, Mary F., 1980. 'Women, Civilization, and the Indian Question', in Mabel E. Dentrich and Virginia C. Purdy, *Clio Was a Woman. Studies in the History of American Women.* Washington, D.C.

INDEX